BECOMING WORLD CLASS

Becoming World Class

Clive Morton
OBE PhD CEng BSc MICE
FIPM FInst Mgt FRSA

Foreword by Sir John Harvey-Jones

MACMILLAN
Business

0005414789 0010

First published 1994 by
MACMILLAN PRESS LTD
Houndmills, Basingstoke, Hampshire RG21 2XS
and London
Companies and representatives
throughout the world

ISBN 0–333–62560–9

A catalogue record for this book is available
from the British Library.

10   9   8   7   6   5
03   02   01   00   99   98   97   96

Copy-edited and typeset by Povey–Edmondson
Okehampton and Rochdale, England

Printed and bound in Great Britain by
Antony Rowe Ltd, Chippenham, Wiltshire

To Pamela

List of Tables

List of Figures

Contents

Acknowledgements

I could not have produced this book in my spare time as a full-time practitioner without a great deal of understanding, patience and co-operation from my family, who have had to live with my preoccupation with the subject matter at weekends, during holidays and even over dinner. Similarly, I could not have completed this project without the active encouragement of a great range of people, and I am sad that the late Professor Keith Thurley cannot see the fruits of his support for me over the years. Latterly, Karl Watkin, Chairman of Crabtree of Gateshead, and leader of the Manufacturing Challenge in the North East, galvanised the concept into action by using a phrase in common with Keith Thurley: 'For evil to triumph it is only necessary that good men (and women) do nothing' (Edmund Burke).

The seed found fertile soil in my deeply held faith and belief in our responsibility to realise the potential in those we work with for their benefit and that of the economy. The place of manufacturing in the economy is another crusade that I wish to give my weight to.

I wish to thank many others who have encouraged and given open ended support, in particular Tetsuya Katada, President of Komatsu Ltd, and his colleagues in Tokyo and Europe; Sir John Harvey-Jones MBE for his generous comments and encouragement. Tony Hadfield, Chief Executive of Northern Electric PLC; Peter Carr CBE, Chairman of Northern Region Health Authority; Dr Adrian Wilkinson of UMIST and Professor Greg Bamber of Queensland University of Technology. Lastly, my thanks to Carol Featherstone for ploughing through my complex drafts and producing a readable result.

CLIVE MORTON

Foreword

Sir John Harvey-Jones

I have long believed that when British skills and national characteristics are linked with those of the Japanese, the resulting combination can produce a highly successful mixture which could help our country reverse its apparently inexorable economic decline. There has never been any possibility that Japanese ideas could be implanted in their entirety into a British or continental setting, but curiously – despite the immense cultural gap that exists between our two countries – many of our skills are in fact complementary. The best of both worlds' approaches really do offer advantages to both countries, although the greatest single benefit to us lies in the possibility of reversing the trends which we have accepted for so long. Clive Morton has been in a unique position to learn the differences and difficulties, but also the glittering prizes which can be achieved by learning from the Japanese and working together with them, in order to produce a unique Anglo-Japanese admixture which progresses the whole concept a step further. Rather than reading book after book detailing exactly how Japanese do it, or why it is impossible to compete with the Japanese industrial machine, I would commend my fellow manufacturers to read this book. As well as giving us the benefit of his hard-won personal experience, Clive also has a number of pertinent observations and comments on our national failure – and that of our government – to fully appreciate the opportunities which this inward investment has given us.

This book is all the more relevant because, much though I love and admire my friends in the North East, no one would describe the area as being one in which it is easy to introduce change. Generations of bitter experiences at the hands of industrialists have made the inhabitants of the North East extremely suspicious of new ideas and revolutionary concepts. They have been understandably reluctant to take the enormous risk and degrees of training necessary to enable them to contend in the sort of world-competitive business which involves a continuous and mind-boggling rate of change if it is to succeed. It says a lot for the approach of the British managers who work with the Japanese in the North East that the whole experience has been a success. The sad thing is that most of us who supported so strongly the inward investment by the Japanese believed that the trickle-down effect on the suppliers and the regional infrastructure would be faster and even more effective than it has been. It is still not too late. The 'tricks' that have been employed by Japanese manufacturers are not some weird black magic, and do not require British people to abandon their hallowed way of life. They do demand, that we look at every aspect of the way in which we work together in order to try to achieve world-competitive success in a different way, and that we continue to embrace new thinking and change.

Even though the field is one which I thought I knew a fair amount about, I have learnt a great deal from Clive's book, and would be very surprised if there is any manufacturer, supplier – or indeed anybody who wants to do business with the Japanese, or to succeed in world-competitive terms – who could not find something worthwhile in *Becoming World Class*. There is only one alternative to becoming world class – and that is that we go out of business. As the business of Britain seems to continue inexorably to fold up, the choices that we as a country have for our people become fewer and fewer. I hope very much that this valuable book enjoys the readership and attention that I believe it deserves.

Introduction

Yet another book on Japan and Japanese management techniques? So what does this one offer that has not already been said? In order to answer the latter question, it will be useful to examine the categories that the literature on Japanese management falls into:

1 Popular sociology books (as per Ouchi,[1] Pascale and Athos[2]) advocating Japanese industrial superiority.
2 Critiques of the above thesis – e.g. Katama – *Japan in the Passing Lane*.[3]
3 The Japanisation debate examining the influence of ideas and techniques, e.g. Oliver and Wilkinson, *The Japanisation of British Industry*,[4] and I. Gow, *Raiders, Invaders or Simply Good Traders?*[5]
4 Japanese companies operating abroad – research by K.E. Thurley,[6] Jonathan Harris,[7] and Stephanie Jones, *Working for the Japanese*.[8]
5 Adaptation and adoption of Japanese management techniques in the UK, e.g. Peter Wickens, *The Road to Nissan*,[9] and M. White and M. Trevor, *Under Japanese Management*.[10]
6 Critiques of Japan's future as an industrial nation and international player, e.g. *Sun at Noon* by Dick Wilson,[11] *The Trojan Horse* by Barrie James,[12] and *Japan, the Coming Collapse* by Brian Reading.[13]

Despite all this information, though, what is lacking is research and findings based on *lengthy experience* of the new relationship of Japanese inward investment. What this book offers is the benefit of six years' experience and analysis of chosen techniques in practice in the West, as opposed to prospective policies and theories. It is therefore possible to close in on the nub questions: 'Are Japanese management techniques transferable to the UK? How much does their success depend on the non-transferable culture and framework of Japanese society? Can we compete and become world class using our own culture and these developed techniques?'

Dick Wilson, in *The Sun at Noon*, has written:

Managers have gone crazy in the past decades trying to follow the Japanese model, in the hope of emulating Japan's industrial success. The way the Japanese manage their factories has two distinct ingredients, one spilling out of the native tradition which western societies cannot hope to replicate, the other judiciously imported from America and Europe at an earlier stage. . . . What is missing from all the prescriptions is the formula for reconciling individualistic western workers to the self effacing patterns of Japanese style cooperation. If those vital family-style relationships . . . do not exist on the shopfloor, how can any Japanese style edifice be built on top of them?

Peter Wickens, in *The Road to Nissan*, builds on this thought: 'We have concluded that much that is good about Japanese management practices is transferable, with modifications to a Western environment. Indeed, those elements which are transferable can almost be regarded as "international" rather than "Japanese".'

How is it, then, with every conceivable management consultant offering prescriptions to British business on everything from Total Quality to Just in Time that so many companies fail to enter the world-class arena even when the medicine is taken?

The Japanese have long understood the West's inability to change radically in order to make the breakthrough. In the 1980s, Japanese factory management was asked by curious Western executives: 'Why are you so open about your processes, techniques and commercial decisions when we could go away and copy this formula in competition with you?'

The response was at once both realistic and depressing: 'Because we know you won't do it anyway. You will not change.'

The evidence produced in this book is based on the unique opportunity I had in setting up a successful UK manufacturing subsidiary of a Japanese multinational in my role as Personnel Director for Komatsu UK; and then operating the policies chosen with care for the following six years to give the 'best of both worlds' approach. The account of this period is set in the context of the history of the company and its steady progress towards 'internationalisation'. This context gives the opportunity for exploring and concluding on such issues as:

- Understanding and dealing with the Japanese
- The future for the Japanese multinational
- Can joint ventures and share ownership work between Japanese and Western companies, or are the cultures too far apart?

The second relevant context is the growth of this Japanese subsidiary in the North East of England and therefore within the UK and Europe. What effect has this and other examples of Japanese inward investment had on local and national economies and with companies that supply them, and on competition with other European manufacturers?

A related question is also whether these best practices can be applied in other sectors of the economy, such as the service sector, utilities and public service. Here, my recent experience as Director of Personnel for Northern Electric plc (a newly privatised utility) and also as non-executive Chairman of Gateshead Hospitals NHS Trust has been relevant.

Have the techniques used been infectious and has the language of change become universal? Has the reality of change followed?

Lastly, is there a manufacturing future for the North East, the UK and Europe in the face of competition from the Pacific Basin?

NOTES

1. W. Ouchi, *Theory Z – How American Business can meet the Japanese challenge*, Addison Wesley, 1981.
2. R. Pascale and A. Athos, *The Art of Japanese Management*, Penguin Business, 1986.
3. S. Katama, *Japan in the Passing Lane*, Allen & Unwin, 1983.
4. N. Oliver and B. Wilkinson, *The Japanization of British Industry*, Basil Blackwell, 1992.
5. I. Gow, 'Raiders, Invaders or Simply Good Traders?', *Accountancy*, March 1986, pp. 66–73.
6. K. E. Thurley, unpublished papers.
7. Jonathan Harris, unpublished papers.
8. S. Jones, *Working for the Japanese*, Macmillan, 1991.
9. P. D. Wickens, *The Road to Nissan*, Macmillan, 1987.
10. M. White and M. Trevor, *Under Japanese Management. The experience of British Workers*, Heinemann, 1983.
11. Dick Wilson, *The Sun at Noon*, Hamish Mamilton, 1986.
12. B. James, *The Trojan Horse*, Mercury, 1989.
13. B. Reading, *Japan, The Coming Collapse*, Orion, 1992.

1 The Best of Both Worlds

It was late 1985, and the price of oil had plummeted from $40 a barrel to $10. I had spent the previous three years building up the resources of Wimpey Offshore and Wimpey Engineering to cope with the second wave of North Sea exploration that had dissipated before it became a reality. I found myself with the task that I disliked the most: telling valuable people that they were no longer valuable – in fact, they were dispensable. We mounted a voluntary severance programme, which I suggested should be aimed at all levels to avoid the inevitable concentration at the lower end of the organisation.

Like most people, I wondered about the future and what I would do. Luckily, my skills seemed to be in demand, and a job was offered to me through a search consultant. I had suggested the principle of severance at all levels, including director level. I offered my resignation, it was accepted – and the next day my prospective new employer withdrew his job offer.

By January 1986 I was facing unemployment. Out of the blue, a head-hunter rang me with the suggestion of a strange-sounding Japanese company, Komatsu. This company wanted to set up a new factory in the North East. As a Southerner with roots in the Home Counties, the prospect was not what I had in mind. However, I then had the tangential thought that my first degree from Leeds and my marriage to a Mancunian would give me some credibility in the North. Not so. To a Geordie, Manchester and Leeds are the deep south.

I met Torio Komiya, the first Managing Director of Komatsu UK, in early February and we hit it off immediately. He is a very experienced Japanese businessman, but with a very gentle and open attitude. My last day with Wimpey, after ten years with them, was 27 February; I started with Komatsu on 1 March. I was technically unemployed for only one day.

Now was the time for rapid action. Komatsu moved into Birtley in February 1986 and were aiming to produce their first hydraulic excavators by October of that year. Within two weeks of starting with the company, I was in Japan learning the background of

Komatsu, and in particular what had made the company so success-ful. My agenda was to find out what plans had already been made for personnel at the UK plant, how much scope I would have, and especially how we could achieve 'the best of both worlds'.

There was little doubt in 1986 – and it has become even clearer since then – that the Japanese are the most successful manufacturing nation of the world. I had worked in industry for over twenty years and was convinced that British people could equal the productivity and innovation of any country in the world given the opportunity. I was persuaded that the reasons we had declined as a manufacturing nation were self-inflicted. Whereas I do not doubt that many aspects of the business environment – such as investment policy and practice, government and City versus industry and so on – have acted as a dragging anchor, the critical brake on progress has been the attitudes of those in industry. My experience told me we were not short of talent, but that we were short in developing and using the talent that was there. I did not subscribe to the 1980s philosophy that this was all the fault of the trade unions – generally, management inherit the trade unions they deserve. Change in attitude, the release of talent and contribution comes down to management. The 1980s brought an environment for change, and the process of learning from Japan during the last part of the decade has revolutionised attitudes where contact with the demonstration of success has been greatest.

My search was based on a faith and optimism that change could happen and success would result. The next six years turned out to be a vindication of these beliefs. However, translating Japanese success into British business was another thing entirely.

I can now be clear about the method that lies between two extremes. There is the Japanophile school, which subscribes to the belief that nothing short of complete replication of techniques and cultural style will do. At the other extreme is the systems approach; this is piecemeal, adopting solutions within the existing corporate culture and structure.

The former takes too little account of the host culture, does not give credit to the pluralism that can result from a marriage of cultures, and, if it survives, will give an inadequate role to indigenous staff employed by the organisation.

The latter approach has been practised by many and various companies for over twenty years, often as a result of a benchmarking approach promoted by a management consultant on the basis that this or that was the secret of success in Japan. Even where the system has taken root, success in a general sense is rarely apparent. Usually the reason is that it has no chance of changing attitudes or behaviour. It is not fundamental or universal, and does not address the necessary change in culture.

My conclusion is that nothing short of a 'best of both worlds' approach will work, based on cultural change with a continuous benchmark to ensure 'world class' results. The object of the exercise is not to create the perfect company, but to succeed competitively and on the basis of people contribution. There is no simple formula; solutions must be tailored to the organisation and marketplace.

WHAT THIS BOOK IS ABOUT

This book is the story of creating success where failure was endemic and demonstrating that so-called Japanese management techniques can be applied in the UK; and that this approach can be replicated by other Western companies to obtain market supremacy. It is a story of personal experience, but related to theory – not based on it. Being experiential, it is both total and real, but because it relates to theory and frameworks it is of use to others anxious to change where they work for the better – both for the organisation, for themselves, and (without being grandiose) for the economy as a whole.

It has been a cause of sadness to me that Western politicians have often given up on industry as the wealth creator of the economy. At best in recent decades, it has received lip service for its potential role. At worst, our leaders in the 1980s declared that manufacturing was dead and that overseas earnings could in the future be gained by the service industries. This calculation was flawed, and the result was clear by the end of the decade as service industry suffered most in the deepest European recession since the 1930s.

The contrast in attitudes to industry between UK and Japanese administrations since the war could not be more marked. To the Japanese, it was 'export or die' in perpetuity. In the UK, this slogan died with the Attlee years, and we relied on prop after prop – from Commonwealth through to 'whitehot technological revolutions', to North Sea oil and service industries.

Financial commentators now cast doubt on whether the UK industrial sector is large or diverse enough to lead the economy out of recession and whether we are now too dependent on component imports to create sufficient GDP to affect the balance of payments;

they question whether we will ever reach the magic level of 30 per cent of GDP coming from manufacturing, which is said to be the key to a positive balance of payments for the future.

Achievement is possible, but requires a sea change in attitudes from industry and government. What I have seen in practice can accelerate UK manufacturing to world-class competitiveness, but we need universal adoption of the world-class approach and expansion of effective capacity. Moreover, it is necessary to have a clear focus from government on industry as the wealth creator as being central, not fringe, in a long-term strategy that takes responsibility for growth. It should be neither wholly market-forces led nor interventionist, but have its problems 'owned' by government, not left to sink or swim. My motivation is to share and replicate success in order to provide an opportunity for a viable future.

AIMS

The aims of this book are to tell the story in such a way as to be helpful to those wanting to implement similar change and to answer a number of questions:

- The West has its success stories, but the Japanese are *consistently* successful – why?
- Can we compete and become world class using our culture *and* Japanese management techniques?
- Are techniques enough?
- Are they valid for sectors other than manufacturing?
- How do we understand and deal with the Japanese?
- What is the future for the Japanese multinational?
- Are joint ventures with the Japanese viable?
- Is there a manufacturing future for the UK and Europe in the face of competition from the Pacific Basin?
- How do we achieve world-class competitiveness? How do you start this in your business?

Understanding what the Japanese are up to may seem to be obvious to many British managers. A nation that in the space of forty years has accelerated from an image of poor-quality, copy-cat products and cheap labour to the premier manufacturing nation of the world, can now claim to be producing goods of the highest-quality, which it designs and develops itself. In Western terms, surely the Japanese cannot be playing according to the rules – it must be because of unfair practices, trade barriers, inscrutability, robots or exploitation of labour, we argue. We refuse to accept that this is real, above-board competition. In fact, we have pretended for decades that this was a passing threat, largely irrelevant to our situation, blithely averting our eyes as large sectors of industry disappeared, starting with motor cycles and ships, and ending with practically everything else that is made.

Without accepting and learning from Japanese examples, we have taken refuge in depicting a 'new role' for Britain. Gone is the 'premier workshop of the world', and enter the UK as 'premier retailer in the world' – our future, we argue, is in tourism and services. In short, we have lost confidence in the possibilities of industrial success – certainly up until this decade. Now, recognising that North Sea Oil revenue is declining and that we cannot live on the back of services (only 20 per cent of which can be exported), we have been forced to rediscover that we have talent – human resources – under our noses, and not just brilliant inventors and Nobel prize winners.

Strangely, some new reasons for confidence in British talent are starting to come from Japanese firms in the UK. For a variety of reasons, Japanese inward investment in the UK has accelerated in recent years and the approach they use to 'people management' has given the opportunity to British management and labour to demonstrate that poor quality and labour relations are not necessarily synonymous with the UK.

BECOMING WORLD CLASS

Within this context of new-found confidence in a potential industrial future, I set out to explore what can be achieved with indigenous talent and how companies can become 'world class'. Essentially, the issue is one of competitiveness and survival. The solutions are inevitably multi-faceted. For instance, to achieve world-class quality at competitive cost is not the end solution – often, it is only the entry ticket to highly competitive markets.

Quality is a term that is often misunderstood. In a traditional context it means measurement of output quality against a standard: quality assurance by inspection, either by inspectors or self-inspection and analysis.

Quality improvement usually encapsulates the involvement of people in enhancing quality standards, and embraces the concept of people seeing that they have two jobs – one to do their specified task and the other to think how to improve the way they and others tackle the job, a process-related approach rather than exclusivity of results. (See Fig. 1.1 for a contrast between the technical or systems approach and improvement components.)

Quality Assurance is a systems approach and has been developed in manufacturing and service sectors to the nth degree and is festooned with standards and measurements such as BS 5750 and ISO 9000. Quality Improvement is the stuff of total quality control, Total Quality Management and Kaizen, and regards the systems approach as essential support on the rungs of the ladder of improvement, not as an end in itself. This distinction is important, since many companies have adopted the systems approach, seeing it as the accolade of world-class quality, whereas (in spite of the benefits) it is merely an important step along the way.

The theme explored in Chapter 6 is that of interpretation of quality into the long-term strategy of companies, and essentially changing the role of management and those who work for them. The dimensions to quality improvement are pursued. The first is the conventional area of quality improvement at the 'sharp' end, typically applied to production situations embracing Total Quality for individuals, teams, groups, Quality Circles and so on.

The second dimension is to do with creating horizontal teams across functional boundaries to break down the 'silo factor' endemic in corporations and to integrate planning, design and manufacturing specialisms.

The third aspect concentrates on the integration of quality into the business planning cycles of the company. It addresses the essential need for a culture that creates the environment for quality growth and demonstrates the integration of business policies and plans from board level to team, and individual plans and objectives.

CONTINUOUS IMPROVEMENT OR 'STEP CHANGE'

Kaizen is unmistakably Japanese, but is now the most commonly adopted 'quality' term in the West. It appears so easy in the Japanese context to achieve continuous improvement as a real theme, but it is often elusive in the West; yet the Japanese are envious of the West's ability to achieve 'Step Change' in organisations and technological improvement (see Fig. 1.2).

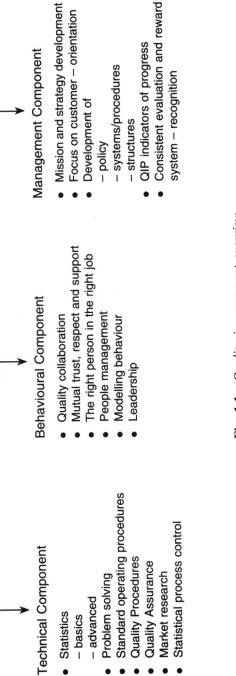

Technical Component

- Statistics
  – basics
  – advanced
- Problem solving
- Standard operating procedures
- Quality Procedures
- Quality Assurance
- Market research
- Statistical process control

Behavioural Component

- Quality collaboration
- Mutual trust, respect and support
- The right person in the right job
- People management
- Modelling behaviour
- Leadership

Management Component

- Mission and strategy development
- Focus on customer – orientation
- Development of
  – policy
  – systems/procedures
  – structures
- QIP indicators of progress
- Consistent evaluation and reward system – recognition

QIP

Fig. 1.1 *Quality improvement overview*

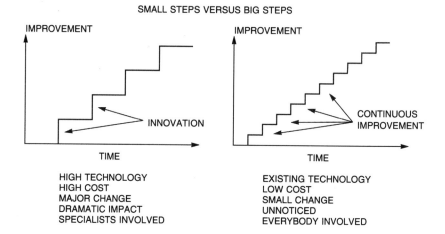

SMALL STEPS VERSUS BIG STEPS

HIGH TECHNOLOGY
HIGH COST
MAJOR CHANGE
DRAMATIC IMPACT
SPECIALISTS INVOLVED

EXISTING TECHNOLOGY
LOW COST
SMALL CHANGE
UNNOTICED
EVERYBODY INVOLVED

Fig. 1.2 *Improvement concept*

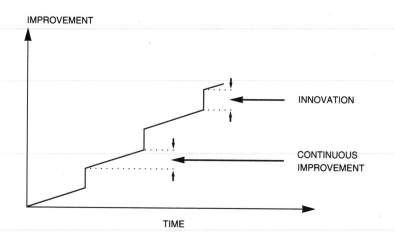

Fig. 1.3 *Best results*

The world-class standard has to include an ability to achieve both on an integrated basis. The challenge is then to cut the Gordian Knot harnessing group or team-based momentum in continuous improvement, and at the same time encourage individuals to 'think outside the box' and produce Step Change ideas (see Fig. 1.3).

The Japanese education system, as we will see in Chapter 2, has been able to produce a general quality of education for the vast majority of the population to a higher standard than anywhere else in the world. However, the inhibition against individualism is so powerful that students will not question information and are bereft of ideas and original thought.

In 1992 I gave a lecture to final-year students at Hitotsubashi University, and was amazed at the contrast with Western undergraduates. In the West you meet continuous questioning, perhaps even in excess of healthy cynicism, but the students generally end up owning the ideas after testing them out. In Japan, facts and knowledge are just soaked up like ink on blotting paper. Yet collectively, the Japanese are the most educated, industrious and innovative people in the world.

Thus we return to the central question – how do we compete? I hope this book offers some of the answers.

WHICH PANACEA?

Apart from the products of 'quality' gurus, other competing management theories abound. Consultants and academics have made a good living by developing, adapting and applying management systems towards the Holy Grail. Much has had the hallmark of fad and fashion, but a few systems have been longer lasting. The theme today has shifted from techniques and skills to more fundamental approaches to running the business. In Chapter 6, I examine the three mainstream revolutionary theories:

- Total Quality
- Lean Production
- Business Process Re-engineering

to see whether they compete with one another or complement one another other.

An early conclusion is that for success all three depend on cultural change in organisations where they are applied.

WHAT CULTURE?

It is becoming clear that, whatever star is being followed, the days of the macho-manager in world-class companies are in the past. Whatever philosophy or combination of systems is followed, the key to success is people contribution within the organisation. My experience both as a line manager and personnel professional indicates that the role of motivation and performance lies with line management and not the personnel specialist.

Management style is all important. The days of 'correcting and directing' as a manager have rightly given way to greater ownership in a people-oriented style that 'listens and learns' along with the team.

To use Professor Charles Handy's classification as developed by Dr Roger Harrison (see Appendix II for definitions), the cultural style has to change from 'power' and 'role' to 'achievement' and 'support' in order for employees to participate effectively and believe that management really do want their ideas and *will* implement change. In other words, as we will explore in Chapter 3 onwards, in order to achieve 'bottom up' contribution, top management must demonstrate the devolving of real responsibility to teams and individuals.

WEST AND EAST
The trick is to marry individualism and initiative from the West to 'group-think' from the East.

In the West, we are competing with a culture whose bottom line is 'I must not let the group down'. In contrast our knee jerk response as individuals is 'Have *I* got real responsibility?' If the answer is no, the result is usually minimal contribution.

Kazao Murata, Managing Director of Yuasa Battery in South Wales during the 1980s, concluded that in the UK there were three basic attitude problems to deal with:

- Work for the money: 'I will produce a given amount and no more'
- There are company rules, but they are not followed and the enforcement of them is not strict
- Improvement in working practices and productivity is not my business, but should be left to the experts[1]

I begin Chapter 4 with a quote from Konosuke Matsushita, who founded Matsushita Electric:

We will win and you will lose. You cannot do anything about it because your failure is an internal disease. You firmly believe that sound management means executives on one side and workers on the other, on one side men who think and on the other men who can only work. For you, management is the art of smoothly transferring the executives' ideas into the workers' hands.

To reinforce this picture of Western decline, I quote from Sir Peter Parker's Dimbleby Lecture some years ago:

'We [in the UK] are the world's original, originating industrial power; we are the world's oldest parliamentary democracy; and we have failed to make the right connections between them. That, alas, is our glorious heritage' (Sir Peter Parker).

I do not take a deterministic approach. The whole point of this book is that I have helped to demonstrate that this decline is reversible. Matsushita may be right about an 'internal disease', but it is not incurable. My conclusion is that much of the effort to improve has been only skin deep and has treated symptoms not causes: applying systems, not fundamental cultural change.

The West has actually an advantage in team building when it is applied correctly. Because of Japanese homogeneity and the submersion of the individual, team selection by personality type is not seen as relevant in Japanese companies; in contrast, it is now viewed as critical for success in the West. Where management embrace the right cultural change and where team selection and team building takes proper account of personality type, then industrial and commercial supremacy can follow.

GREEN FIELD–BROWN FIELD, SERVICE SECTOR, PUBLIC SECTOR

This account, with its blend of theory and practice, is firmly rooted in a green field site experience, even though the factory building was second or third hand.

Most managements do not have the luxury of starting afresh with employees, many of whom had been previously unemployed, and with the opportunity to commence with a clean sheet of paper in terms of policies and precedents. However, this was the experience I had. So is this example relevant and helpful?

My later experience in the service and public sectors has been useful. Chapters 4 and 5 describe the application of some of the measures common to manufacturing and service sectors. It is without doubt easier to establish world-class criteria in manufacturing and easier to start 'as you mean to carry on' on the green field site. However, there are many examples of success both in terms of brown field in manufacturing and service and public sectors. It takes great determination from the top to change and to demonstrate that this determination is backed by real change from the top down. I believe the lessons from this experience are not just valid, but vital for competitiveness in other sectors.

WHAT THIS BOOK IS NOT ABOUT

Such a study as this cannot hope to cover everything. Its scope is large, but it is focused on using an example of successful improvement in both the context of the origins of developed systems in Japan and the context of the West, where the seeds were planted and were to grow and seen to transplant into other related species. Some day, I hope, we can talk in terms of harvest.

This volume is not intended to be an in-depth academic study, but is instead designed for the practitioner. Therefore, there are limitations. The book does not address issues of international harmony, trade wars, the place of modern Japan in world order, or issues of domestic politics within Japan. It does not concern itself with the effect of internationalism within Japan, Japan's changing culture, or speculate whether internal instability in Japan will undermine industrial superiority.

It does not spend time demolishing myths about Japan, for there are parallel works that do that effectively. The study of Japan is confined to 'Understanding the Japanese' and 'the Future of the Japanese Multinational', since this is where Western management impinges on Japanese thought and practice.

The argument herein does not encompass a devastating critique on 'Japanese management systems', nor is it Japanophile or uncritical in accepting lock, stock and barrel all that these encompass. Rather, it confines itself to those systems and lessons where effective transferability to the West is demonstrated to advantage. It also recognises

that achieving world class is a complex business and simplistic solutions involving quality and cost are foundations, but not the ultimate.

First, though, we need to understand the context, and this means understanding the Japanese people.

NOTE

1. K. Murata and A. Harrison, *How to Make Japanese Management Methods Work in the West*, Gower, 1991.

2 Understanding the Japanese

A mediaeval head of the Mouri family summoned his three sons to his death bed. Taking an arrow out of a quiver, he broke it in half before them. Then he had three arrows bound together and invited each son in turn to break them. They could not do it. The message of family unity did not need to be spoken. Every Japanese knows the story and has its lesson imprinted in his heart (Dick Wilson, *The Sun at Noon*, p. 18).

The West has attempted to understand the Japanese for centuries. Depending on the context, the Japanese have been seen in dismissive or racist terms as insular, little people, with no individual character, totally conformist, bent on imitating the world or even dominating it.

Like most inaccurate mythology, grains of truth can be found, and can, in context, explain behavioural characteristics. The West has come reluctantly to terms with post-war Japan, explaining its success away in terms that do not apply to the Western way of life or threaten it.

We may grant that the Japanese are successful, but when until recently did they *invent* anything? Look at the disparity between the UK and Japan in terms of Nobel prize winners – surely a factor of forty times in Britain's favour demonstrates an inventive ability? Yes, but what happened to those ideas – are they now in profitable production? The UK undoubtedly has its business success stories: those men and women (often from relatively uneducated backgrounds) who became the Thatcherite entrepreneurs of the 1980s. However, Japan has been *consistently* successful. Not all Japanese businesses are the same, but together they have consistently produced the world's highest GDP per capita, outstripping the most successful Western economies. Why?

It is simply because the Japanese have found a formula that works. It works for the vast majority of their society, not just an elite group. It is consistent with and builds on their culture and is relatively timeless. It does not depend on particular leaders, personal characteristics, or theories of organisations. It is fundamentally rooted in human behaviour – the behaviour of all humans involved in the process, not just a minority. It does depend on philosophy: philosophies that

all, with education, can sign up to, and which can demonstrate outcomes for the individual, the team and the organisation.

To understand how this formula has taken root, we need to understand the culture and constraints of Japanese society.

JAPANESE CULTURE

1 Attitudes

The Japanese have enormous respect for their history, traditions and culture. Although homogenous today, they are very conscious of the multi-faceted origins of the Japanese people – islands populated by nomadic water-borne settlers bringing vastly different religions and philosophies. These strains are preserved – no single one has dominated the rest. The Japanese are proud to be able to adhere to preserved elements of at least four religions or philosophies: Shinto-ism, Buddhism, Confucianism and Taoism. It is often reported that 80 per cent of the Japanese consider themselves Shintoist and 80 per cent Buddhist, since these religions have complementary benefits – Shinto is about renewal, life and nature, whereas Buddhism offers an afterlife. A simple explanation, but it illustrates the origin of the expression that the Japanese are the world's greatest pragmatists. The ability to avoid dogmatism can be seen as a definite advantage in a business world that demands rapid response dependent on today's circumstances rather than yesterday's.

The most significant cultural difference between Japan and the West relates to their group approach. The Japanese life rotates around teams and groups. These groups occur in all aspects of society and at all stages of life, whether social, educational, or leisure – but above all at work. From the first steps to kindergarten to the funeral at the Buddhist temple, the Japanese life is never independent of 'the group'. In fact, it can be said that if you don't belong to a group you do not exist in Japan. Group norms and peer group pressure are probably the most powerful motivators that exist in Japanese society. This is in such contrast to Western society, and is so fundamental to Japanese organisations, that any comparison of systems and techniques *must* take this into account.

The group norm is not a new phenomenon devised to support industrial regeneration since the war. It originated thousands of years ago in the rice-growing economy of Japan, where extended family groups, deliberately isolated by their feudal Shogunates, saw their priority as working together to harvest the rice crop between the typhoons:

> From their forbidding land base the Japanese people derive a tendency towards intuitiveness, naturalness of emotion. The land's habit of frequently breaking up and burying everything inspires a certain fatalism and the challenge of growing large amounts of food on tiny or difficult plots of ground has conditioned the people to cooperativeness and group consciousness rather than individualism. That is the contribution of the Japanese earth.[1]

Successive feudal governments saw this as an effective method of satisfying two aims – achieving a submissive population with a constrained local focus on production. The Japanese, on the other hand, see Western society rooted in individualistic hunting traditions with an emphasis on independence, self-reliance and a relative freedom to travel – too simplistic perhaps, because it skips over the development of our feudal regimes. However, our society tasted relative individual freedoms from the fifteenth century, whereas Japan reverted to isolationism and a frozen feudal society from the sixteenth to the nineteenth centuries.

When forced into the bright light of international trade by US Commodore Perry's black ships in 1853, Japan's innate pragmatism reasserted itself. The biggest 'U' turn in history took place when, with the Meiji Restoration, Japan's priorities reversed from isolation to catching up with the Western world as quickly as possible. Hence the Japanese became the world's most astute shoppers – carefully sifting systems, methods and technologies to build an educated, cultured and industrial democracy in the most accelerated development of modern times.

2 Conformity

'A nail that sticks up gets hammered down.'

One of the most quoted Japanese sayings is that 'a nail that sticks up gets hammered down'. Inconspicuousness is a virtue: self-confidence is not encouraged. Japanese abroad are often taken aback by the self-confidence displayed by individuals in the West. 'We are the opposite', they will say, 'we are very unconfident as individuals, but confident in a group'.

> 'We (Japanese) are very unconfident as individuals, but confident in a group.'

Western individualism is often seen as destructive. If you openly challenge others and lose, you are asking for humiliation: Why not close your eyes to the incompetence of other people and give them the benefit of the doubt and preserve the fiction that they are all the same? It has been argued that Japan has developed a 'maternal' society as opposed to the father-ruled West. Mother loves all the children equally, regardless of ability. Father wants to know who is the brightest. Mummy has become the saviour of the modern Japanese family, taking over Daddy's role, since he is out at work all day and every evening and too tired at weekends.

Any competition that the children may experience is with their peers where determination is encouraged. The ancient symbol for boys, in particular, is the fresh water carp, because of its persistent struggle to swim upstream against the odds. On 5 May – 'boys' day' – Japanese homes will have carp-shaped wind socks flying at their small mastheads to demonstrate identity with this national symbol.

Conformity is not without its admirers in the West. One of the first four Komatsu UK supervisors trained in Japan was interviewed at Newcastle Airport on his return.

'What have we to learn from the Japanese?' he was asked.

'I like the way the women bow and leave the room backwards – I am going to ask my wife to do that tonight when I get home!'

'And what can they learn from us?'

'They are all going to drink sake out of *big* Geordie glasses from now on!'

With the inevitable strains between cultures, it was just as well to keep a sense of humour.

3 Education

The remarkable thing to outside observers in the last one hundred years is that Japan has been able to achieve change at the same time

as holding on to its cultural heritage from feudal days. The foundation has been in the education system that absorbed Western
objectives of education within Japan's cultural framework. Hence
the 'group think' is a core value in education – witness Japanese
children on the move along city streets and station platforms. All
rigidly uniformed, and shepherded and chaperoned by elders or
'monitors' with safety and unity as prime objectives.

The downside of overbearing academic pressure on children, from
mothers in particular, is a major negative in Japanese society.
Children are expected to attend crammers and burn the midnight
oil with homework from a very early age. The Japanese meritocratic
education system has casualties through stress and pressure to a
degree unknown in the Western world. On the other hand, of course,
it has produced a better general level of education than anywhere
else, a numerate and literate population with a clear vision that
education is the foundation stone for a successful economy that has
surpassed all the competition:

> Japan's competitive success is firmly rooted in high-quality school-
> ing and advanced vocational training. Numerous studies in the US
> and Europe attest to the fact that Japanese schoolchildren attain
> substantially higher skills in mathematics and science than their
> Western counterparts and more emphasis is placed on the devel-
> opment of technical skills.[2]

By establishing clear national standards open to continuous
improvement, providing adequate and evenly distributed resources,
according a high status to the teaching profession and fostering a
highly competitive system, Japan has been able to make significant
progress in developing the quality of its education system. To the
outside it looks conformist and suppressive, from the inside it is the
entrance ticket to the best job. Blue chip companies select graduates
from the best universities, creating a section of young people called
'Ronin', who try year after year to gain entry to Tokyo University as
a means of potential access to the top jobs. (Ronin were leaderless
Samurai who wandered the country without identity.)

4 The group

For the sake of the group, conformity and subjection of the
individual to the group extends to individual self-control. The
Japanese are often regarded with great suspicion because they are

noticeably the most guarded of people. 'I think of my community or family, parents, company or group,' a Japanese businessman explains, 'before speaking to outsiders, and I will stop speaking out if it may harm my group even if I know that it is true.'[3]

This is not so much suppression, but recognition that this is a better way of achieving what you want: a sense of belonging, and also the fear of alienation at the other extreme. Being excluded from the group is the most appalling thing any Japanese can imagine.

Having surrendered individual autonomy to achieve your goals, it is difficult to retreat. The group becomes addictive and the Japanese spends his life transferring this allegiance to the group with which he identifies.

5 The sixth sense – Tatemae and Honne

It is a short step from self-control to perception. The Japanese admire the man who senses what others are thinking and wishing, without uttering a word himself; who avoids hurting others' feelings; who remains ambiguous if he cannot say 'yes', in the hope that the recipient will understand without forcing him to use the blunt and hurtful Western 'no'.

'Tatemae' – the face – is what the Japanese are prepared to present publicly. Whereas 'Honne' – the truth – is reserved for very close friends.

'Tatemae' – the face – is what the Japanese are prepared to present publicly as an argument or reply, whereas 'Honne' – the truth – is reserved for very close friends. To the West, 'yes' which in fact means 'no' merely seems dishonest.

The reticence that stems from protecting the group and the first duty in not offending the listener links directly to the 'double speak' of Tatemae and Honne. The intention is in Japanese terms totally honourable, and to be fair, the practice is hardly unknown in the West – often termed, 'diplomatic language'. However, to Westerners who are in close working relationships with Japanese, it appears at the least as undue secrecy, and at the worst as something amoral or duplicitous. Japanese who become more international become more open, and learn to use 'Honne' to build trust.

6 The long-term view

When British and Japanese staff work together in Japanese companies abroad, cultural differences quickly come to the fore. Japanese
reserve can be seen to be deceptive, and evidence of inscrutability not
what it was intended to be – a question of good manners, a method of
sparing a person's feelings. The elite British graduate looks for
accelerated development and will change jobs if it doesn't happen.
Generally, the Japanese graduate, even from Tokyo University,
accepts that he will have to wait until age 35 or thereabouts before
reaching managerial status. At every point, Western short-termism is
confronted with the long-term context of Japanese society. Japan is
changing rapidly, however, and international Japanese are adopting
Western aspirations. The Japanese manager abroad with a family will
often reach a point of no return when it is more advantageous for his
children to be educated in British or American universities rather
than face the disadvantage of trying to catch up in the Japanese
system.

There is deep disquiet with the education system in Japan. Right-
wing politicians regard teachers as inherently left-wing and anti-
discipline, and some industrialists would rather see their children
educated in the West: Akio Morita, Chairman of Sony, said, 'People
and teachers have mixed up freedom and democracy with the result
that discipline has been lost in family life. That is why I sent my two
boys to school in England.'

The products of universities are not seen by managers to have the
mettle of yesterday's graduates (perhaps a familiar feeling in the
West). Not surprisingly, today's Japanese graduates do not follow
slavishly in their forebear's footsteps, and even Japanese manufacturers now report the difficulty in recruiting engineering graduates
because of the migration to the financial and other service sectors.

SHARED CULTURE

We both have blind spots

The Japanese in the UK cannot understand the contrast between the
obsessional tidiness of English gardens and the litter in the public
thoroughfare outside. I came across an example in Japan that
provides the contrast. Workers leaving a smoke-filled train on the

way to work stubbed out their cigarettes before walking through a housing estate in order not to spoil the environment. On the other hand, of course, the Japanese corporately have a poor record at protecting the environment.

CULTURE-BASED PERCEPTION: PERCEPTION AND REALITY

In attempting to understand the Japanese it is important to recognise our own cultural traits, because they often seem very strange to the Japanese and at odds with what we say about ourselves. We are individualists, encourage freedom to act without restraint, but turn a blind eye to those who abuse these freedoms or get caught.

Recently the Chief Constable of the Metropolitan Police in London complained about the hypocrisy of the middle classes who expect police protection of property and person, while seeking to flout the law in 'middle-class' ways – such as being 'economical with the truth' over tax returns and expenses – because they were unlikely to get caught.

Fundamentally, the Japanese are a far more law-abiding society, constrained by rules and self-discipline, who are shocked at the contrast they find in the West between our outward pretence and the reality. They too have their contradictions, though. You are most unlikely to be burgled, mugged or raped in Tokyo, where the crime rate is only 30 per cent of the UK average, but corruption is rife in high places – as successive revelations have shown.

Understanding the Japanese is fraught with difficulties over stereotyping. It is easier to picture the Japanese nation in terms of stereotypes than almost any other country – after all, they are so homogenous, or are they? To the untrained eye, they all look the same, act the same, and travel in groups, photographing the same things, wearing similar clothes. Variations from the norm, though, are increasing in Japan, and so are the elements of unpredictability. The West always see career patterns in Japan as that of the 'salary-man' who typically commences work for his company on leaving college, never to consider changing employment until retirement age. This only really applies to about one-third of Japanese workers – those employed by the large corporations, with inferior conditions often being operated by smaller companies. The Japanese themselves also encourage the stereotype, since it shows them in a good light.

PRODUCTS OF CULTURE

1 Lifetime employment

The pattern of the 'salaryman', although only applying to less than one-third of the Japanese workforce, has become a symbol inside and outside Japan. It is the embodiment of lifetime employment and the seniority system. It means an unwritten but deeply held mutual obligation between employer and worker, giving the Japanese salaryman an unshakeable faith in the employer always finding work for the individual, no matter what the circumstances, until he (I have never met a female salaryman!) retires. International Japanese working alongside Westerners always cause amazement when they discuss this. Their Western counterparts cannot understand such simple faith – it just does not accord with their experience. This too is changing, with lay-offs also happening in Japan, but only after an extraordinary effort is made to find other solutions.

Together with the 'group' philosophy, this pattern of employment forms the basis for compliance and contribution to company objectives. Innate loyalty and compliance is of course deep in Japanese society – witness the suicidal behaviour (to Western eyes) of Japanese troops during the Second World War. Even today Western staff, working for Japanese companies, are wide-eyed over the willingness of individual Japanese to focus so completely on company needs and to put their families a very firm second.

The difference, of course, is one of perspective. To the career-oriented salaryman, the company is everything – it even provides identity. The wife of the salaryman will introduce herself, for example, as 'Mrs Hirano of Komatsu', which must be the true definition of the corporate wife. The question of identity is immensely important to the Japanese. As we saw earlier, they regard themselves as very unconfident as individuals, but confident in a group – the complete opposite of the West, where we are taught to be individually confident, or at least to appear so, and not so sure about being part of a group.

Few practitioners would insist on the transferability of lifetime employment systems to the West. It is so inextricably linked to Japan's past, and examples of lifetime employment in the West are generally, often falsely, associated with low productivity or a 'civil service' mentality, that it rates low on the hierarchy of needs. The issue is really one of mutuality – how can the West replicate the system of reciprocal obligation that lifetime employment has fundamentally contributed to in Japan?

2 Decision-making and control

To Japanese working with Westerners abroad, decision-making is a problem because they are expected to react in traditional Western ways as managers and directors of overseas subsidiaries. Western staff expect direction and decisions from top management whatever their origins. Japanese managers operate by consensus, which typically involves much reference back to Tokyo. This looks weak to Westerners, although the strength is in shared and prepared decisions based on facts not feelings.

When I first encountered this, I found it difficult to understand. Early on in the life of the Komatsu UK plant it emerged that a British manager and his Japanese counterpart were at loggerheads. It was clear that I could not solve this problem on my own, since neither reported to me. I spoke to Torio Komiya, the Managing Director, about this: he was sympathetic, but merely kept repeating 'we must have teamwork'. I retorted that yes, I agreed, but I recommended that he as the Managing Director should see both in an effort to achieve common purpose. His reaction took me aback. No, he said, *they* must solve their problem and we should all take responsibility. He would raise the matter at our managers' meeting when all would be present including the combatants. I was horrified. It went against every instinct, for I saw it as a potentially uncontrollable situation. To deflect this outcome, I offered to mediate to ensure peace. That was probably what he wanted, and in the short term oil was added to troubled waters. In the long term it didn't work, and at separate junctures both individuals left the company. Today, with hindsight, I would probably use conflict counselling or team building techniques (see Chapter 5) to attempt to resolve the situation.

THE BLEND OF CULTURE

Learning to live together

Over the years in Komatsu UK we learned the best way of managing with a cosmopolitan team, and elements of both cultures were adopted. The problem often is that both Westerners and Japanese see benefits in their diverse systems and individually shift to the confusion of everybody. The non-macho Western manager is tempted to become rather too democratic by mimicking consensus, and the macho-minded Japanese manager is attracted to 'fire from the hip' decision-making methods, which apparently save time and avoid frustration. Just as it is a mistake to view Japanese as all the same, so it is a mistake to think that all Japanese are happy with their traditional ways of working. Most see the systems of nemawashi[4] (consensus) and ringi (management approval) as laborious, time-consuming and inflexible. The Western alternative often appears attractive. The reverse is often true in that Western managers, despite all the exposure to the benefits of consensus, rarely adopt consensus on a day-to-day basis, since it seems to call into question their individual management ability, and possibly even their virility.

International Japanese are attracted to rapid decision-making – 'firing from the hip' as in the West.

In turn, Western managers are often attracted to their consensus (nemawashi) approach.

Broadly, the result is far from clear-cut and the pattern of decision-making, even the culture in Japanese overseas subsidiaries, will depend on the personalities and distribution of indigenous/Japanese managers at the top.

Culture depends on the degree of indigenisation

Where Japanese dominate the directorate, the company will operate as an outpost of Tokyo with top management rotating on a two- or three-year secondment basis, often with day-to-day decisions being shared with Tokyo. Indigenous staff provide support and liaison at lower levels. Two cultures will live alongside each other, but, like oil and water, will not mix, and few indigenous top managers emerge. Typical examples are in trading houses, sales and distribution, insurance, banking and other service sectors.

In manufacturing there is a greater perceived need to indigenise operations and local top managers are appointed and developed.

Again Japanese expatriates are only in a post for relatively short periods and there is a desire to 'do as the Romans do' and let local management manage in typical ways. The boundaries of performance are defined of course, but inside this there is often confusion and fuzziness that will depend on interaction between such cosmopolitan management.

Oddly, British staff sometimes regret the return of Japanese to the home base because the increasing dominance of British managers can bring a return to old class-ridden values of distance and macho management, and rejection of consensus.

VALUE SYSTEMS

In a survey by Lewis Austin[5] entitled *Saints and Samurai* for Yale University, 42 Americans and 42 Japanese 'elite' were studied to determine differences. The results showed striking contrasts, i.e.:

American	*Japanese*
Equality	Hierarchical
Individual	Group
Competition	Harmony
Universal Law	Particular Cases (Pragmatism)
Reason	Truth Beyond Reason
Progress	The Past
Liberal	Profoundly Conservative

In short the study concludes the American emphasis is on performance traits, the Japanese is on personality traits.

CHARACTERISTICS – A CONTRAST IN ENVIRONMENTS

Fig. 2.1 illustrates the polarised differences that create a cultural divide.

UK general environment

Increasing number of races, becoming multi-racial	Single language (minority group languages)	Not densely populated (by Japanese standards)
Western philosophy and religions	Welfare state	Conscious of class
Individualism	Tolerant of behaviour differences	Variety of educational backgrounds
Critical constantly seeking improvement	Age not a prerequisite of success	Business relations based upon competition

Japanese general environment

Homogeneous race	Single language	Densely populated country
Oriental philosophy Buddhism Shintoism	No welfare state	Middle-class consciousness
Group orientation	Expected behaviour and performance in group	Similar educational background
Conformance with accepted practice and traditions reluctant to criticise	Respectful of age and seniority	Business relations based upon trust and human relations

UK individuals

Mobility of employment – staying with one company is not seen as broadening the work experience	Limited job security	Strong identity with the skill or profession
Promotion linked to ability	Group and team working not seen as important	Company not seen as playing a social role in the working environment

Japanese individuals

Expectation of lifetime employment in major companies. Very little opportunity to change employer	High job security	Strong identity with the company
Promotion linked to age, length of service and seniority	Respect for teamwork and commitment of the team. Puts the interest of the group above the interest of the individual	Prepared to conform by wearing company uniform, participating in company organised events

Fig. 2.1 *UK and Japanese environments. Key differences between the general environment, companies and individuals in UK and Japan are shown in this figure to illustrate the very different culture that helps shape Japanese industry.*

Will we ever understand each other?

Westerners will always be at a disadvantage in a society that is so separate, conditioned, and whose roots owe nothing to Western traditions. In fact, there is said to be a 'logic gap' between Western and Japanese culture. Paul Norbury, in *Business in Japan*,[6] says that this is 'a communication barrier resulting not so much from language as from a set of values and thought processes that, if one can generalise, run parallel with the West's and never meet'.

All is not lost, though. If Western companies are adopting Japanese systems and modifying their culture, then we are also seeing evidence of Japanese management adopting Western priorities and practices:

> ' "Japanese-style management" and US and European-style management are moving closer together'.

'Japanese managers are discovering the importance of managing people, rather than factories, in their efforts to cope with worsening economic conditions. . . . One contributing factor has been the westernising of the Japanese economy: the service sector has grown, capital costs more, working hours are shorter and consumer desires have become more diverse. . . . The result, according to Takeshi Murakami of Nomura Research Institute's consumer and services industries department, is that 'Japanese-style management' and US and European-style management are moving closer together.[7]

NOTES

1. Dick Wilson, *The Sun at Noon*, Hamish Hamilton, 1986, p. xxi.
2. *Financial Times*, 28 February 1993.

3. Wilson, *The Sun at Noon*, p. xx.
4. Nemawashi: literally means preparing the roots of a tree from transplantation with extreme care – the parallel is to transplant ideas with infinite patience.
5. L. Austin, *Saints and Samurai*, Yale University Press, 1975.
6. P. Norbury and G. Bownes, *Business in Japan*, 2nd edn, Macmillan, 1980.
7. D. Green, 'Japan Adapts to Western Practices', *Financial Times*, 11 December 1992.

3 How We Made It Happen – The Best of Both Worlds at Komatsu UK

KOMATSU AND CATERPILLAR – THE COMPETITION

It is 1 March 1986 – my first day at the new Komatsu plant at Birtley, Tyne and Wear, in the North East of England. By a strange quirk of circumstance, this was the site of a failed plant belonging to Komatsu's eldest and most prominent rival, Caterpillar, the US giant in plant manufacture.

The competition went back a long way. Komatsu had built an enormous reputation within Japan after the Second World War, outperforming rivals by achieving a 60 per cent market share. In the 1960s, the Japanese government lowered a trade barrier and allowed Caterpillar to enter the Japanese market for the first time. It established a joint venture with Mitsubishi Heavy Industries to manufacture and market Cat-designed products in Japan. Caterpillar entered Japan with a well-deserved worldwide reputation for effective products, tried and tested in every continent.

Komatsu in these terms was a minnow, with a turnover of $168m p.a., and was regarded by the Japanese government as a potential sacrifice to enable trade barriers to remain to protect their fledgling automotive and electronics industries. It is now clear that Komatsu was made of sterner stuff. It took a hard look at what the competition had to offer. Machine for machine, Caterpillar offered better quality than Komatsu. Thus Komatsu looked around for ways in which to catch up.

The first move was to persuade the Japanese government to oppose or delay the start of the Mitsubishi–Caterpillar joint venture. The Japanese Ministry of International Trade and Investment (MITI) believed that Japan did not possess a long-run competitive advantage in this industry. Komatsu managed to achieve a stay of execution, and hence a breathing space of two years. The President of Komatsu, Yoshinari Kawai, focused on two particular aims:

- Upgrading of technology by joint ventures with other manufacturers
- A major leap in product quality

TOTAL QUALITY

The next move was to follow what so many of Japan's industries were doing in the 1950s and 1960s – listening to the American gurus on quality: Deming and Juran. The evolution and adoption of their philosophies in Japan is detailed in Chapter 6.

The President's son Ryoichi Kawai, then a senior manager, spoke with Professor Ishikawa of Tokyo University, the 'father' of the Japanese Quality Circle Movement. Ishikawa reputedly took on the task of introducing Total Quality into Komatsu on the simple condition that the President, Mr Kawai, escorted him around the factories in person. It seemed easy; however, it turned out to be an object lesson. On these terms, Ishikawa repeatedly asked detailed questions on the operations to make the point that, in order to gain success, senior management has to know what is going on and be personally involved and committed to quality as an essential philosophy. This lesson was well learned. The President's son, Ryoichi Kawai (today Chairman of the company), allocated ninety new bulldozers on special terms to regular customers in Japan on the understanding that they would collect operating data every day, report on performance – and in particular any problems. This cut the feedback loop and accelerated quality improvement. The Total Quality Control (TQC) programme was launched, and Ishikawa's three-pronged formula was used:

- Mass education
- Simple tools for quality measurement
- Teamworking

Within three years, from a position of great disadvantage, Komatsu had won the Deming prize for dramatic improvement through the promotion of company-wide quality activities.

TOTAL QUALITY AND GROWTH

The policy on Total Quality Control has been the cornerstone for Komatsu's success and has transformed the company from being domestic to Japan to the world's largest integrated manufacturer of construction plant and industrial machinery. TQC ensured the product was what the market required, was of the right quality, at a competitive price, and available at the right time.

The now famous Harvard Business School Study published in 1985 on the Komatsu versus Caterpillar story (U385-277) quotes the company philosophy of TQC at the time: 'The TQC umbrella spreads over all our activities. Virtually everything necessary to develop, to produce, and to service our products – and to keep customers around the world satisfied with those products' high performance, reliability and durability – is incorporated into our scheme of Total Quality Control.'[1]

All personnel, from top management to every worker on the assembly line, were expected to strive for TQC. Quality was seen in 1964 as such a high priority that the President told staff to ignore costs and instead produce world-class products.

The new Maru 'A' machines reached the market in 1966, and gave remarkable results. The durability of the new bulldozers was twice that of the old models, and Komatsu accordingly lengthened the warranty period. An important tool called the Flag System for integrated control was established (see Figs 3.1–3.3). The second stage of the project was predictable – cost reduction. No stage in the design-to-production process was sacrosanct.

Purpose: To improve the quality of medium-size bulldozers to the level of competing machines within a short period.
(Cost and JIS may be disregarded for this purpose.)
JIS: Japanese Industrial Standard

Quality Target:
Targets for the following items were added to specifications:
(1) Durability (total hours until first overhaul)
(2) Availability

Fig. 3.1 Ⓐ *Project*

Results:
1) Durability doubled.
2) Guarantee period increased from 300 to 600 hours.
3) User claims reduced to one-third.
4) New product-development system was integrated.
5) Flag System in Komatsu Ltd was established.

Fig. 3.2 *Results of* Ⓐ *Project through TQC introduction and its activities*

32

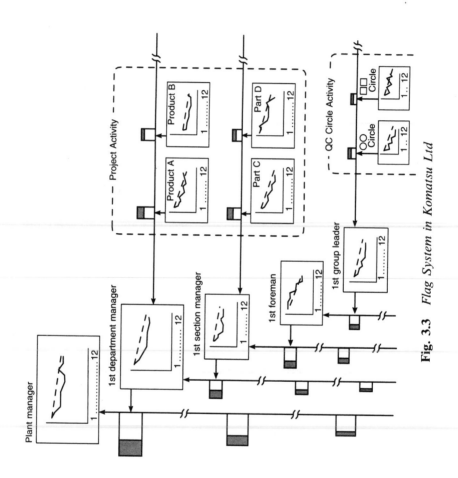

Fig. 3.3 *Flag System in Komatsu Ltd*

The double effect of high quality and reduced production cost meant that between 1965 and 1970 Komatsu market share in Japan actually increased from 50 per cent to 65 per cent despite the increased competition from Caterpillar inside Japan.

This multidimensional and sequential aspect of Japanese interpretation of Total Quality is often underrated by the West. It is frequently explained by devotees of Deming and Juran as Quality: Cost: Delivery, or QCD, as basic and equal aims, but Japanese pragmatism dictates that, for success, stages need to be given devoted concentration.

Although even today we succumb to the concept that TQC only readily applies to the production process, this short post-war sketch picture of Komatsu shows that TQC can be applied to all business processes, and initially can be interpreted into a long-term strategy of growth through quality. This translates TQC from the level of technique to philosophy. It came to represent a value system for workers and management alike. 'It is the spirit of Komatsu,'[2] said one top manager. 'For every issue or problem we are encouraged to go back to the root of the problem and make necessary decisions. Not only does TQC help us resolve short run management problems, it also lays the foundation for future growth. Thus it is the key to management innovation.'

The adoption of another Deming tool integrated quality into the management process, the PDCA cycle (Plan: Do: Check: Act) (see p. 137).

> A plan is made, it is executed, its results are checked and then new actions are planned. Every activity is based on this cycle, including company wide management control systems, production, marketing, and R&D. Because of this, the corporate ability to achieve the targets set improves. These steps also improve the workers' morale and management leadership.[3]

The starting point every year in Komatsu was the long-term plan of the top management team and the President's policy statement for the year. This was described as 'management by policy'. It provided the setting within which the elements of TQC and PDCA could operate. Moreover, top management were demonstrably operating the elements of Total Quality, not just providing a system for others to follow.

Over time, the products of this integrated system were seen, first, as tangible results of increased market share through quality improvement and productivity gains, leading to cost reduction, and secondly, the intangibles of better internal communication and the focus on clear, common goals (see Figs 6.7 and 6.8 on pp. 149 and 150).

DEVELOPMENT OF THE COMPANY

The twin themes for the 1960s were clear – upgrade the technology and revolutionise the quality. The first was pursued by commercial negotiations with Bucyrus-Eyrie and International Harvester, both of the USA, to achieve licensing arrangements on earthmover design, together with a similar agreement with Cummins Engine of USA for diesel engine technology. In parallel, the company established its first research and development laboratory in 1966 to focus on electrical engineering developments. (To give some idea of the recent proportion of turnover spent by Komatsu on R&D, see Fig. 3.4)

Exports

Having regained market share by the end of the 1960s, the focus shifted to exports where Komatsu had been relatively inactive. Sales

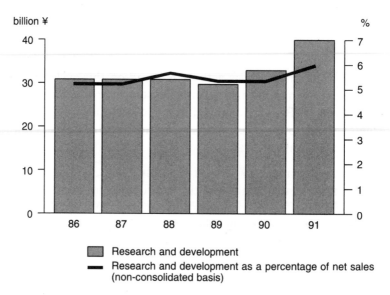

Fig. 3.4 *Research and development expenses*

and marketing outlets were established in the USA and Europe and new markets found in China and South America.

Export focus found its way back into product development and in the 1970s models were developed for the first time with export markets in mind (see Maru 'B' development) (see Figs 3.5–3.7), which contributed to an increasing external focus overcoming the previous introspection. It also closely followed TQC thinking, that of understanding customer requirements.

1. Period: May 1972–May 1976
2. Philosophy
(1) Improve the software to support product quality at the same time as improving the product quality (hardware) for overall satisfaction of customers.
(2) Collect and analyze live data (actual market data on reliability) from customers on the basis of the market-in concept to grasp the quality level of each of Komatsu products and competitors' products plus the quality level desired in the market.

Fig. 3.5 *Overview of* Ⓑ *activity (large-size bulldozers)*

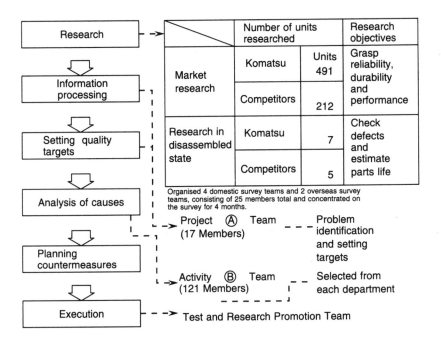

Fig. 3.6 *Steps in* Ⓑ *activities*

1. Quality of Products
Availability ratio	Up	3–5%
MTBF	Up	50–100%
Repair expenses	Down	30%

2. Integration of market reliability information system.

3. Komatsu market share up.

Fig. 3.7　*Results of* Ⓑ *activities*

Inward investment

The 1970s saw a new development, with efforts to penetrate the markets of less-developed countries (LDCs). The areas chosen were Latin America and South East Asia. Often the solution was to establish indigenous operations to contribute to growth of the domestic economies of these LDCs. For the first time, Komatsu developed the experience of overseas manufacturing operations. In these early days the local content of the products was low, with heavy dependence on parts exported from Japan in (KDK) knockdown kit form. These combined measures increased the ratio of exports to

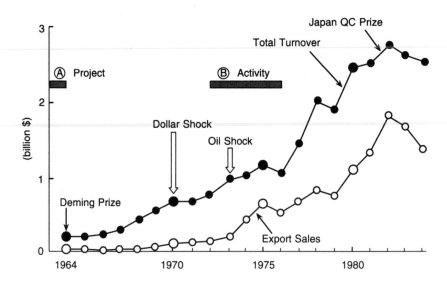

Fig. 3.8　*Business results: Komatsu Ltd*

total sales from 20 per cent in 1973, to 44 per cent in 1974, and 55 per cent in 1975 (see Fig. 3.8). This experience laid the foundations for the expansion of Komatsu's overseas manufacturing capacity into the industrialised world of the USA and the UK.

Increasing range and technology

Early investment in R&D was paying off in the late 1970s with extended ranges of equipment and the application of remote controls to earthmoving and mining equipment. The ambition was to become a 'full line' manufacturer in order to compete with Caterpillar. This followed the earlier marketing philosophy for which Komatsu became world famous. Entitled 'Maru C', it was dubbed 'Encircle Caterpillar'. Today, few would subscribe to this philosophy in Komatsu, seeing it as too aggressive for today's taste.

What was the motive?

An alternative explanation for the tactics against Caterpillar can be found in the Samurai strategy of the 'Five Rings'.

Of these five 'rings', the Ring of Fire philosophised that if you found an immovable object it was wise to work your way round it:

To injure the corners

It is difficult to move strong things by pushing directly, so you should 'injure the corners'.

In large-scale strategy, it is beneficial to strike at the corners of the enemy's force. If the corners are overthrown, the spirit of the whole body will be overthrown. To defeat the enemy you must follow up the attack when the corners have fallen.

In single combat, it is easy to win once the enemy collapses. This happens when you injure the 'corners' of his body, and thus weaken him. It is important to know how to do this, so you must research deeply.[4]

The parallel could relate to Komatsu's niche marketing strategy in the 1960s and 1970s in selecting relatively unapplied new technology, entering into licence agreements, and proceeding to refine, develop and manufacture in large quantities. The classic case was with the hydraulic excavators. The technology was undeveloped in the 1960s; Komatsu entered into a technology agreement with Bucyrus-Eyrie and by the 1970s had developed their own advanced and successful range. Komatsu UK at Birtley was established largely to give a foothold in Europe for this product, and by 1989 the world market had grown from virtually nothing in the early 1970s to 52,000 machines annually, representing a market on its own of £2.5 billion. Of this total, roughly half were sold into Japan and Japanese based design accounted for over two thirds of the total volume.

A less exciting theory is that the strategy of competing worldwide, increasing the range, concentrating on niche markets, and progressively globalising production is straightforward opportunism. What is clear is that this phenomenal expansion was founded on integrated TQC and what is now known as 'Lean Production' techniques. Also, the behaviour of Komatsu when faced with worldwide competition was consistent with the 'Yoshida' post-war doctrine of trading overseas, replicating the majority of blue chip manufacturers at the time:

> The doctrine, named after Shigeru Yoshida who dominated Japanese politics after the war, has four components: Japan's main goal should be *economic development to match the west*; it should be lightly armed and avoid involvement in international conflicts; to achieve this it should accept the political leadership and military protection of the US; Japan's diplomacy should be 'value free' to *allow it to trade with a wide range of states regardless of their political complexion.*[5]

The basic thrust towards overseas production was essentially to protect and enhance markets in the face of increasing trade friction between Japan, the USA and Europe. (See Figs 3.9 and 3.10, illustrating the recent growth of Komatsu Ltd.)

Japan comes to Birtley

> The lot of numbers were still on the walls, piles of dirt and debris were everywhere. Burnt-off holding-down bolts and holes in concrete were the only evidence of previously magnificent machine tools.

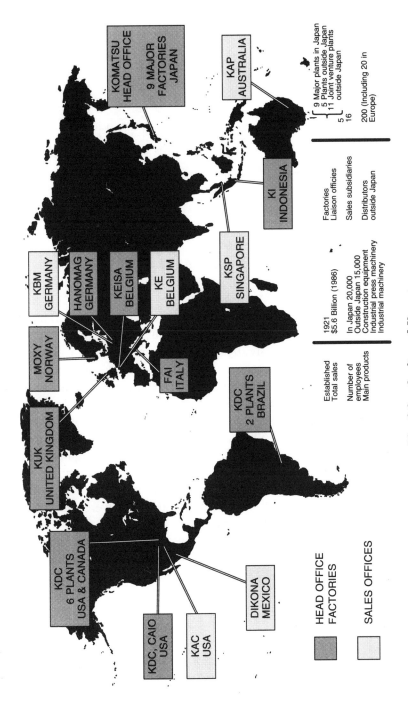

KOMATSU HEAD OFFICE
9 MAJOR FACTORIES
JAPAN

KAP AUSTRALIA

KI INDONESIA

KSP SINGAPORE

KBM GERMANY

HANOMAG GERMANY

KEISA BELGIUM

KE BELGIUM

MOXY NORWAY

FAI ITALY

KDC 2 PLANTS BRAZIL

KUK UNITED KINGDOM

KDC 6 PLANTS USA & CANADA

KDC, CAIO USA

KAC USA

DIKONA MEXICO

Factories	9 Major plants in Japan
	5 Plants outside Japan
	11 Joint venture plants
	outside Japan
Liaison offices	5
Sales subsidiaries	16
Distributors outside Japan	200 (Including 20 in Europe)

Established	1921
Total sales	$5.6 Billion (1986)
Number of employees	In Japan 20,000 / Outside Japan 15,000
Main products	Construction equipment / Industrial press machinery / Industrial machinery

HEAD OFFICE FACTORIES

SALES OFFICES

Fig. 3.9 *Outline of Komatsu*

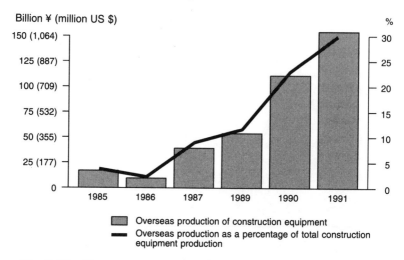

Billion ¥ (million US $)

Overseas production of construction equipment
Overseas production as a percentage of total construction equipment production

Fig. 3.10 *Komatsu overseas production of construction equipment*

It must have brought a wry smile to the faces of my Japanese colleagues to be offered a ready-made but ageing plant vacated some two years previously by their arch rival. The Caterpillar closure had left great bitterness within the local population. Some 1,500 jobs had vanished overnight without warning, when all the signs were in the opposite direction. In a perverse way, this eased the introduction of Komatsu – although the jobs in prospect were eventually only to exceed 500, it was at a time when local unemployment stood at 20–30 per cent – thus the prospect was significant.

The plant was depressing, and like a ghost town. Nothing had been touched since the withdrawal and plant auction. The lot numbers were still on the walls, and piles of dirt and debris were everywhere. Burnt-off holding-down bolts and holes in concrete were the only evidence of previously magnificent machine tools. We moved in without power, telephones or heating. At least some of the plumbing worked.

Why the UK?

The decision in 1981 to set up a manufacturing plant in Europe was an inevitable progression of Maru 'C', and with Europe looking like 'Fortress Europe', compounded by anti-dumping threats, it reinforced the decision. 'Closer to the Customer' was the TQC logic –

how can you build for European customers with all their varied requirements in an alien country 10,000 miles away? Critics will always point to the successful EC anti-dumping case by European manufacturers in 1985 against Japanese importers of hydraulic excavators and the rapid establishment of the Birtley factory in December 1985 to produce excavators in Europe. That is too simplistic, and whereas the anti-dumping ruling undoubtedly gave impetus, the decision in principle was made in 1981 with research into the merits and demerits of West Germany and the UK evaluated in the intervening period.

The UK was reputedly chosen because of language. The Japanese are taught English over a period of seven to eight years in high school. Until recently, English conversation was omitted, leaving the average educated Japanese with a superb knowledge of written English language, vocabulary, grammatical rules and literature, but no ability to speak conversational English; a possible throwback to isolationism?

However, when choosing between the UK and West Germany, the Japanese felt they had a good start in the UK. Other factors have emerged. Something odd like 'the island mentality' has surfaced in conversation. This is a 'sand through the fingers' concept, but has an emotional ring to it – the Japanese live on islands as do the British, thus there is surely some empathy there? More realistically, the compelling commercial arguments at the time were, first, the Thatcher government's clear signals attracting inward investment to the UK from Japan and, secondly, the trend among Japanese blue chip companies to commence investment in Europe via the 'offshore base' of the UK.

The UK is the 'The California of Europe' (Ex-Japanese Ambassador Chiba, 1989).

Ex-Japanese Ambassador Chiba said in 1989 that he saw the UK as 'The California of Europe' – not, he hastened to add, in terms of weather; but, as happened with Japanese investment in the USA, the first foothold for Japanese in Europe with the implication that further investment would then spread to the depths of the continent.

Why the North East?

Having decided on the UK in 1984, Komatsu began its search for a suitable site. Eleven locations were considered – all in development areas from Wales to Scotland. All were 'brown field', as opposed to the virgin or 'green field' site. To the Japanese, speed was of the essence. There was not time to plan, design and build a purpose-built factory – it had to be producing excavators within a year of purchase.

Almost at the end of their exhausting tour organised by the Invest in Britain Bureau, the Japanese team were shown the 750,000 square foot shell of the ex-Caterpillar plant at Birtley on sale from the then Tyne and Wear Metropolitan County Council. Although it looked depressing, the investigation team could see the possibilities.

Much frenetic activity and negotiation followed with well-publicised flights to Japan by the UK team from the DTI, North of England Development Corporation (forerunner of the Northern Development Company), Tyne and Wear CC, the trade unions and Gateshead Metropolitan Borough Council, in an effort to clinch the deal.

What struck the Japanese was the contrast between this remarkable show of unity[6] and their impressions of contemporary Britain as gleaned from the *Financial Times*, the most read European newspaper in the financial circles of Tokyo. Their abiding impression was of a nation of adversaries – right-wing central government against socialist local government. Trade unions in violent opposition to employers – witness the 1984 miners' strike: working practices linked to historical demarcation and class conflict, not flexibility and cost reduction.

The North East team got it right. They realised the Japanese were not just interested in the stark 'business case', they wanted emotional comfort on two fronts. They needed first to be clear that all parties agreed to their venture, and second, that they, the Japanese, were actually wanted in the North East.

Much has been made of the role of pump priming funds from government in attracting inward investment such as this. Important though these are, they have a marginal influence in the decision on a particular site; often it is the 'icing on the cake' rather than being a fundamental ingredient. For Komatsu at Birtley, the 20 per cent initial Regional Development Grant was not axiomatic, it helped clinch the deal.

Heads of Agreement

In December 1985, Managing Director Tetsuya Katada of Komatsu signed the Heads of Agreement with HMG Industry Minister Peter Morrison. In January 1986 Torio Komiya was talking to Executive Search Consultants Korn Ferry in London. He wanted a Head of Personnel for Komatsu UK in order to set up the site and to begin recruiting in the spring. For me, the timing was divine providence. The cold sweat of realisation that I was out of a job by the end of February was replaced by the warm thrill of a remarkable challenge that would begin in March.

The new dawn

Those early days were magic. With one employee, my secretary, and only two weeks to go before I was due in Japan, starting from scratch was exhilarating. We established early relationships with the local community, advertised for managers, bought cars, houses, basic equipment at breakneck speed. Differences between Japanese and British styles surfaced quickly. Before arriving in the North East I had already made contact with recruitment agencies in Newcastle known from my Wimpey days. Within two days of arrival I had a sheaf of CVs on potential secretaries. Una Morrison Recruitment recommended a managing director's secretary recently made redundant from Clarke Kincaid shipbuilders. I asked for her to start immediately on a temporary basis with a view to permanency. Hioki San, my Japanese adviser, was horrified. Surely, he said, I should see at least six to ensure the right choice. 'No time', I said. In the end I compromised, and we interviewed the one candidate, Janette Campbell, over dinner that evening. This was a decision based on a gut feeling that really paid off.

The frenetic activity mollified the initial impact of the poor conditions at the plant, although the North East weather came as a bit of a shock. I decided early on that we should have a policy of recruiting the unemployed whenever possible,[7] hence all vacancies were to be dealt with via Job Centres and the Department of Employment Professional Register for managers. I clearly remember my first visit to Washington Job Centre – wading through a foot of slush to see Harry Townsend (later MBE), the most helpful Job Centre manager I have ever encountered.

First trip to Japan

This was a time for long-term policy-making as well as the cut and thrust of setting up business. The foundations laid at that time produced success, and my first visit to Japan at the end of March 1986 triggered the joint vision that we evolved. The first impact was the discovery of the Japanese love for detailed planning. Every moment in three weeks, it appeared, had been planned and evaluated in detail. Bookings had been made for every evening and weekend, and I remember heaving a sigh of relief in the middle of the trip that tomorrow, Sunday, was a day off. This illusion was quickly shattered when my wife and I were told by Hioki San: You have not seen much of Tokyo, so we have arranged a sightseeing tour starting at 8.30a.m.!' The entertainment in Japan is legendary, and the Japanese, apart from their paranoia in their efforts to avoid offending anybody, are always anxious to know what you think. Hence, feedback and contribution is expected. However, at no point did anyone from the Managing Director down indicate what they thought was the personnel policy solution for the UK.

Having travelled widely between the plants in Japan and studied employment policies at the Corporate Headquarters, I was able to produce a crude analysis comparing the factors that have led to Japan's post-war industrial success and the potential agenda for us in the UK. This can be seen in Table 3.1.

This analysis turned out to be the vital stepping stone to positive change that formed the vision for Komatsu UK. The policy I put forward and that the Japanese supported was a pragmatic approach based on 'the best of both worlds'. If they ever had a blueprint for personnel policy, they never showed me. Mr Katada, then Managing Director of Komatsu Ltd, said when I visited Japan, 'You will see a lot of things that are attractive, but it does not mean you must adopt them in the UK.' I took him literally.

Certain key factors in Table 3.1 related to elements of the Japanese cultural profile which were clearly at odds with the British profile. It is no coincidence that the Japanese find team working and lifetime company loyalty come naturally, for it is deeply rooted in their history and culture (see Chapter 2). The British psyche, on the other hand, reflecting the Judaeo-Christian ethos, constantly lays stress on the individual.

Table 3.1 Factors for success

Japan	UK agenda
Focus on company/group	Focus on individual
Lifetime employment system	Applicable?
Seniority system	Applicable?
Company unions	Single-union agreements
Single status	Single-status/flexibility
Continuous development	Continuous development
Education and training	Education and training
	Reinforce role of
	supervision
Consensus	Communicate and involve
'Bottom up' reaction	Develop teams
Total Quality Control	Total Quality Control

These differences have fundamental implications for business practices. For the Japanese, competitiveness is reserved for 'the competition', redrawing the lines of 'them' and 'us'. The Briton's individual competitiveness can make him find it hard to accept or develop another's ideas, something the Japanese are past masters at. The Briton stands on principle, whereas the Japanese is the ultimate pragmatist.

The contrast between group-think in Japan and individualism in the UK has been discussed in greater depth in Chapter 2. It was to become a significant and continuing issue at Komatsu UK. Even when a teamworking philosophy was working well, individualism was always there under the surface, only to erupt when instinctive action was called for.

The key points that emerged from this process of evaluation were:

- Total Quality Control
- Single-union agreement
- Teams – supported by:
     single status
     reinforcement of supervisory role
     communication
- Continuous development, with long-term commitment
- Education and training

Total Quality Control

The Total Quality Control system, based on Deming principles, proved to be instrumental in the growth of Komatsu, and was to be the central company policy, permeating all aspects of policy. It would rely, however, on appropriate employment practices and a correct 'host' culture for its successful implementation.

Trade unions

I did not consider the Japanese company union system appropriate to the UK, but saw the single-union agreement approach as essential to ensure uninterrupted production, active participation, and to avoid damaging demarcation issues. I had to argue my corner in Tokyo over this issue. Komatsu had just set up Komatsu America Manufacturing Corporation in Chattanooga on a non-union basis, so why couldn't I do the same in the UK? I was not anti-union and believed that a stance for a non-union plant in engineering in the North East would only invite continuing friction. In any event, staff should be properly represented.

George Arnold and Joe Cellini signed the single-union agreement on behalf of the AEU in September 1986, the main features of which are included in Appendix 1 on p. 237. This agreement was based on experience of other successful plant agreements such as Toshiba at Plymouth and Nissan Manufacturing UK at Sunderland. I was closely advised at the time by the late Professor Keith Thurley of LSE, Dr Adrian Wilkinson of UMIST, and 'fellow adventurer' Peter Wickens of Nissan. The result has stood the test of time and is regarded as exemplary.[8] The AEU, on their own admission, learnt a great deal from the positive aspects of the Komatsu experience, which led them to negotiate more single-union agreements with other companies than competing unions have achieved. The downside, of course, was the jealous reaction within the TUC from those less successful or ideologically distanced from the concept.

Business objectives and people objectives

The analysis of Table 3.1 was extended to demonstrate the linkage for individuals to the policy on business objectives for Komatsu UK. We started with the business objectives of QCD (Quality: Cost: Delivery) and evolved the people objectives from there, not the other way around (see Table 3.2).

There is a distinctive difference between business objectives in Japan and the West. The typical British Chief Executive, when questioned, will define business purpose as making a sufficient profit to satisfy

Table 3.2   Komatsu UK employment policies

Objective	Policy	Method
High Quality	Best employees Development TQC	Thorough selection Training Quality Circles Motivation
Cost reduction	Continuous improvement Reduce inefficiencies	Involvement 'Bottom up' ideas 5'S' System
Reliable delivery	Uninterrupted production Constructive supervision	Single-union agreement Authority and responsibility
Safe working	Responsibility of each person	Good protection Education
Technical development	Close to customer Design development	High tech Engineering Close communications

shareholders. In contrast, his Japanese counterpart will state that business purpose is to produce quality, at low cost, and delivery on time. The unstated assumption is that, with these three things right, profits will automatically follow.

Teams

The part-British, part-Japanese compromise was exemplified in the working structures adopted for the new company.

The team system was seen as a key factor in a total quality culture, yet the British emphasis on individual development can be very destructive of team working. We laid great emphasis on our selection processes. People were told from the beginning that they would have to work in teams. We carefully selected people with the right attitude – that is, flexible and team-oriented. To me, that was more important than qualifications or experience. At the time, it turned on its head the sort of approach we were accustomed to in the UK.

The decision to locate in the North East was, among other things, to gain access to a pool of experienced people from shipbuilding and engineering. As stated earlier, I felt it was right that we recruited from the unemployed where we could, with unemployment running at 20–30 per cent in the region at the time, and mainly from the old engineering industries. The Japanese, although aware of the advantage of readily available skills, were anxious. Their research had told them that the North East was infamous for demarcation disputes and endemic strike action. They also felt that welders from the shipyards would be very rigid people. I was convinced they would be adaptable to flexible teamworking if we were thorough with our selection processes, created the right environment and delivered the kind of people development we were planning.

> 'You talked about flexibility at my interview, but I have only done three different jobs since – what about the other jobs I can do?'

My plan was to recruit team-oriented people through selection processes, and also to install a system of appraisal (see Appendix 1 on p. 227 for details) in order to encourage individual development, although annual meetings go against the pure Deming model. It turned out that our recruits were very adaptable. At the first six-month appraisal we had welders saying, 'You talked about flexibility at my interview, but I have only done three different jobs since – what about the other jobs I can do?'

Unlike most other Japanese implants, we decided to adopt the Japanese, originally Swedish, daily exercise routine. It was seen to be both an encouragement for health and safety and teamwork – after all, if the Managing Director is seen leaping up and down, the barriers soon get removed! My support for this initially was somewhat a trade-off for the agreement by Torio Komiya to my proposal for the absence of a siren (see p. 50). However, this exercise system has not stood the test of time and was quietly dropped in 1993.

SINGLE STATUS AND FLEXIBILITY

One of the biggest lessons learnt from Japan was the single-status concept. This is much more than a question of the works canteen. It means that, for example, that every single employee has exactly the same appraisal system and criteria whatever their function.

The reward structure also supported it; all employees were assessed on their performance and awarded increases in salary, over and above any baseline increment negotiated with the union. The same system and criteria prevailed from the shop floor to the boardroom. Demonstrating single status gives the precondition for flexibility. If people do not feel the threat of losing an employable skill, then resistance will disappear.

> 'No, please do not call them from the shop floor, they are too busy, please go and find them' (Torio Komiya).

Torio Komiya knew that active demonstration of this point was essential. He was famous at Komatsu UK for going to great lengths to show that the shop floor was where the money was made. If a member of the office staff tannoyed for someone on the shop floor to come to the office, he would find the caller and say, 'No, please do not call them from the shop floor, they are too busy, please go and find them!'

Also, in his avid interest in shop floor work, he would visit every station on the line each day. If he found a member of staff operating in an unsafe manner he typically would ask them, 'Tell me, have you a family?' The answer was inevitably affirmative. Torio Komiya would follow up with, 'Well then, you are precious to your family – please look after yourself', and would correct the unsafe practice.

He was the most respected Plant Director by a British workforce that I have ever worked with – a respect that spanned race, age and social background.

Supervisors

The team system was strengthened by the emphasis on ownership of the teams by supervisors and team leaders. As well as receiving training in basic management skills, supervisors and team leaders, assisted by the personnel team, made recruitment decisions. Thereafter they trained, developed and appraised the members of their team, thus creating a strong sense of ownership and responsibility. This followed extensive training in Japan, which always resulted in great enthusiasm for the new way of working. We made a conscious shift of emphasis from 'correcting and directing' to 'listening and learning' for supervision.

One of the very few disputes I had with Mr Komiya was over this very issue of trust and discipline. At the start he said, 'We must have a siren.' I imagine I responded somewhat aggressively: 'What on earth for?' 'How will our people know start and end of shift?' he asked. I asserted, 'We will have clocks on the walls; we will employ intelligent people; we will depart from clocking on and clocking off, but give supervisors the responsibility of managing their people.' 'Ah,' he sighed, 'when in Rome . . .' His voice trailed away. Later, he concurred that the system worked.

This system differed radically from classic British management practice, where supervisors have traditionally been ignored and left out of communications, decision-making and responsibility, and prevented from influencing the company. Subsequently, the NEDC report[9] on supervision has highlighted neglect in this area as being a major cause of industrial decline (see Fig. 3.11).

Communication

A briefing system was essential. The choice made was for five to ten minutes *each day* at shift changeover time. The TQC system relies on the Japanese concept of 'bottom-up' generation leading to innovation and continuous improvement, and on highly motivated individuals setting and maintaining their own standards. This process in turn relied on communication through the teams and Quality Circles.

Both the teams and the Quality Circles provide an arena for all staff to make a contribution to the running of the company. Komatsu didn't just depend on a few managers for their ideas. Equally, Quality Circles have taught that ideas do not have to be revolutionary to be

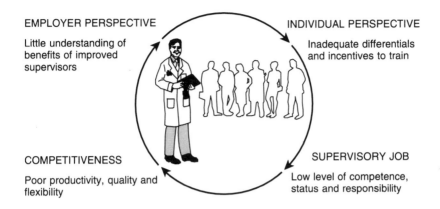

Fig. 3.11 *The vicious circle of UK supervision*

useful. Once again, the Japanese way of sharing and developing ideas in incremental stages through teamwork is the model. As in Japan, Quality Circles were encouraged, and by 1991 over 50 per cent of shop floor workers in Komatsu UK were actively involved in Circles (see Fig. 3.12).

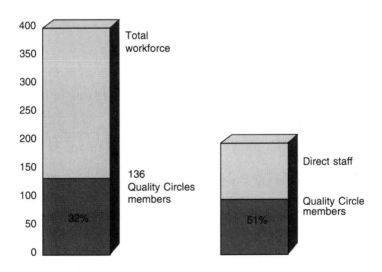

Fig. 3.12 *Quality Circle involvement, December 1991*

The question of motivation is directly linked to the real attention paid by all levels of management to the contributions from ordinary members of staff through the teams and Quality Circles.

The most powerful instrument in teamwork is for employees to see the results of their ideas. This is because of the natural cynicism throughout the typical British workforce that the hierarchy is not going to listen. 'If they do ask you, it's after the event and for lip service only.'

An example of this in practice resulted at Komatsu UK in a new system of team trainers: a welder said to his team leader at appraisal time that he would like to be involved in training. The team leader was gasping at the time, because he just could not cope with all the things he had to deal with, one of which was training his own team. So the welder received training in instructional skills, and the concept of team trainers was established. They could now take on youth training workers and train them, or, if there was a new development in welding techniques, this was mastered and then the team was taught. Not surprisingly, perhaps, these team trainers were often promoted to team leader.

Most importantly, the person who made the original suggestion had the experience of seeing that he could actually initiate and influence company policy. This way you begin to develop a culture where people feel they are not just coming to work to do up nuts or weld pieces of metal and to get paid at the end of the week.

CONTINUOUS DEVELOPMENT

Japanese management were very restrictive in the sense of limiting the numbers recruited. The first conclusion that sprang to mind was that this was just keeping costs down, but actually what they were saying was 'we have a commitment to the people we take on, we must meet that commitment, not just take them on to be laid off next year . . .'

In the first five years, with the workforce growing to 450, there were no lay-offs, nor was anyone put on short time. The Japanese Managing Director met everybody at induction, and made the point that if the company grows, you grow, and the company will grow *because* you grow. Employees then discovered it was not just words; that the systems are there to help them grow.

Horizontal or lateral development was encouraged, and we tried to get people away from thinking that the only progress is vertical.

Clearly, not everyone's going to become Managing Director. With flat structures and few layers, management therefore have to be much more imaginative about development.

Career development was promoted in an open-ended horizontal way, and appointments were made internally wherever possible. Supervisors and team leaders were all internal appointees. More importantly, though, there was a lot of interchange between departments. With retraining, people moved across into purchasing and production control, and a great number of highly technical jobs in design, for instance, were filled by painters and welders from the shop floor.

This sort of commitment bred the sense of security that was so desperately needed in a region like the North East, with its renowned unemployment record. Inevitably, some scepticism remained rooted in generations of on-off employment and was reinforced by the job losses that took place in 1992.

Education and training

The training policies reflected the long-term commitment to people at Komatsu and the innovative approach was exemplified in the presentation skills training made available to all employees.

We discovered that presentation and communication skills training was unexpectedly beneficial in confidence building. Over 50 per cent of recruits were previously unemployed, some of them having been out of work for three or four years. We wanted them to put across a quality picture to our distributors and customers, especially Europeans, who were very sceptical about this odd idea of a quality Japanese company setting up in the UK. Thus in 1986 these new recruits, following training in presentation, completely changed the view of these sceptics by demonstrating how good quality was to be achieved and improved upon.

Assertiveness training helped the team system work better. Sometimes a welder, for example, would want to make a suggestion to his team leader, who might have been busy or preoccupied. If he couldn't get his idea across he would then have gone away thinking it was a waste of time trying and the system would be demolished. Confidence building training enabled workers to push their ideas forward.

The appraisal system (see Fig. 3.13 above for the main features, and Chapters 5 and 6 for detail) identifies each individual's training

❄ All employees covered
❄ Same scheme for all
❄ Overall performance
❄ Self assessment included
❄ Open and agreed outcome
❄ Salary progression
❄ Career and training outcomes

Fig. 3.13 *Komatsu UK performance appraisal scheme*

requirements in terms of skill development, but furthermore each employee could engage in open learning and interactive video in a wide variety of subjects via the in-house Training Centre. The Training Centre's stated aims were to:

> Maximise the potential of each employee, to develop their skills and abilities beyond their immediate job to enable them to make a contribution at a higher level. It is an investment in Komatsu employees, both as individuals and as members of a quality workforce.

Over half the staff signed up for courses that are entirely demand-led and to be followed in their own time.

The staff development policy was seen as 'the release button' that enabled people to progress, overcoming the endemic British disease of classifying everybody into social and educational stratas – thereby limiting people and persuading them, very convincingly, that they themselves are limited.

What were the benefits of investing in people?

The benefits were clear: in the high levels of productivity, comparable with Japan, in the low sickness rate and minimal absenteeism and in negligible turnover of staff. In essence, it vitally improved the bottom line and made the company competitive and other people close to the business noticed the difference. We had suppliers who commented, 'We fish in the same labour pool as you do, but you seem to get a lot more out of your people – how do you do it?'[10] (See Fig. 3.14, which compares the result with the agenda set out in Table 3.1.)

THE AGENDA	THE RESULT
• Focus on individual	Annual career appraisal
• Single-union agreements	Flexible working practices
• Single-status flexibility	Single-status contract
	Same employment conditions for all
• Continuous development, education and training	Appraisal-led training
	Open learning facilities
• Reinforce role of supervision	No time clocks
	No docking for lateness
• Communicate	Daily and weekly briefings
• Involve	Advisory Council
	Quality Circles
• Development teams	Teamwork emphasis
	Team building courses
• Total Quality Control	Total Quality Control

Fig. 3.14   *In practice*

Effect on suppliers?

There were also examples where we sent some of our own people into suppliers in their annual shutdowns, because we needed additional parts. Komatsu staff actually produced more per man in that period, without having any localised induction, than those who regularly worked within those suppliers.

In fact, we took the lead from Japanese experience in this area too; they select their suppliers and sub-contractors in the same way that they select employees: on the basis of adaptability and trainability, not just pure cost at the beginning. We got to the point with suppliers where we were involved to the extent of enquiring how they trained their workforces. If there is another osmosis route for spreading the Investors in People ideas, it's through strategic partnerships with suppliers.

Supply chain management

The supply chain relationship warrants a study on its own. Suffice to say that the Japanese example was used here again, but with a realism that dictated that we could not replicate the intimate relationships achieved in Japan. However, we were able to encourage benchmarking between suppliers and Komatsu both in the UK and in Japan. We also trained Komatsu managers and those of suppliers together in order to increase the depth of understanding and working relationships. Such efforts achieved a 'family' relationship, where suppliers eventually contributed to product design and development.

Was it all sweetness and light?

The answer is regrettably, no. Achieving high-flown ambitions for the UK plant is relatively easy in the early stages when example, encouragement and, most importantly, money is coming in from Japan, combined with an enthusiastic workforce united by an expression coined at the beginning – 'there must be a better way of doing things'.

Tensions

In reality, internal tensions surfaced in the first two years, mainly as a result of misunderstandings. This applies to Anglo-Japanese relations in particular, because of the differing attitudes of Japanese and British managers. With hindsight, it is now clear that initial worries over shop floor resistance were misplaced. The real challenge arose from the fundamental differences in attitudes and thinking between UK and Japanese managers at understanding and working with these differences.[11]

By year 2, the objectives set at the beginning with regard to human resources had all been achieved. The single-union agreement with the AEU was in place and working, and the AEU now had in membership over 50 per cent of eligible staff. An excellent staff of 460 had been recruited, particularly locally in the North East, and initial training had been accomplished. Production of excavators had commenced to schedule and initial quality levels had been achieved.

As we have seen, the Japanese are famous for their simple but effective manufacturing systems. Komatsu UK followed a policy of gaining the best from both worlds in marrying Japanese investment with UK resources. We were still a long way from complete implementation, but the introduction of a highly disciplined approach to the UK shop floor was the least of our problems – what concerned us most were frequent 'misunderstandings', assumptions on both sides concerning behaviours that are then 'misread' by the opposite party in terms of his/her assumptions.

I have argued that it is very easy in one sense to understand Japanese success: simple manufacturing systems, total flexibility, good housekeeping, systems that make the individual responsible for quality, single status, and 'bottom up response'. All these could be translated into the Geordie culture with advantage, even when the labour force largely consists of unemployed skilled workers steeped in the history of depressed and declining heavy industry.

Need to understand the culture

What we also discovered is that although successful Japanese systems all appear to have an appealing logic, they cannot selectively be transplanted into the UK without a thorough understanding of the Japanese cultural support system that fathered them, and without a fundamental culture change occurring in managerial, supervisory, staff and worker roles.

Decision-making

The Japanese approach to 'consensus' appears like a breath of fresh air to British managers disillusioned by political gamesmanship and the adversarial approach. However, disillusionment soon sets in when they discover, in contrast to the super-efficient image of Japanese companies, that taking decisions, big or small, often seems to last for ever. Meetings happened, appearing to meander on with no obvious conclusion. The UK manager ends up perplexed and worried. What was the purpose of the meeting? What are we going to do? Has a decision been reached?

This is a big problem for British managers – how can Japan be so efficient when simple decisions take so long? The practice is of course that, despite the long gestation period for consensus, the end result is better because everyone knows of the build-up, was consulted, and is committed to rapid implementation. What is more, that particular British bad habit – 'let us consult after the decision has been taken' is made redundant. Instinctively in the UK we associate management with immediate individual action, convinced that speed is vital in decision-making and implementation.

What was the purpose of the meeting?
What are we going to do?
Has a decision been reached?
Don't the Japanese have families to go home to?

Overtime and family life

Another touchstone relates to dedication. In a start-up situation, where extra effort and flexibility is required, no one from an enthusiastic workforce objects to necessary overtime and weekend working. But when it is every weekend, every evening, and holidays are postponed, then the UK understanding wears thin. Don't the Japanese have families to go home to? Small wonder they gained the reputation of a nation of workaholics.

Individuals and groups

Individual responsibility and performance are clearly understood in the UK; it is how we are encouraged to grow. We also appreciate the concept of teamwork; however, we are 'jealous of our own patch' within the team. 'Tell me what you want done and leave me to do it' is a way of putting it in the vernacular. We expect individual accountability – that is, in performance terms, what we think we are paid for. Launch such logic into the Japanese system of group and corporate identity and responsibility and you get an inevitable clash. Even a UK manager who says that he is happy to give up the superficial trappings of status – wear a uniform, go to a single-status canteen, etc. – will bridle when there is repeated checking of the quality of his 'fact finding' by his peers or even junior people in his team. If he feels isolated he will take it personally. Repeated experiences of this can lead to a loss of self-confidence by UK personnel and concern over the real motives, and apparently aggressive attitudes, of Japanese management.

Building understanding

This problem was recognised early and, as it involved local managers, 'Japanese Familiarisation' courses were run to introduce UK personnel to Japanese language, culture and their approach to decision-making. At this stage, with the use of external consultants, participants studied systems that were inseparable from Japanese traditions and the UK concentration on individual responsibility and autonomy. We came to realise that the crucial contrast was between the fear in Japanese eyes of letting down the 'group' of peers, department or company and the assumption among many UK employees that they are not given 'real responsibility'.

However, it wasn't until a tailor-made seminar was held between British and Japanese managers that the fundamental underlying differences were voiced and acknowledged. For instance, on the subject of meetings, it became clear that Japanese and British wanted meetings for different things and that their expectations were poles apart.

To the Japanese management meetings are part briefing, part fact finding and part reporting. It is the start in decision making terms of consensus building or 'nemawashi'. Decisions, or even conclusions, are not expected. The chairman's role in Western eyes often appears non-existent and is rarely a controlling or orchestrating one. Traditionally, a summary or conclusion is not necessary because, with Japanese homogeneity, or 'sixth sense' (known as 'tummy speak' in Japan) all attending 'understand' what the outcome is.

Even allowing for converts to 'consensus management', it is not difficult to guess the reaction this experience created in UK management, who expected clarity of purpose of the meeting, direction and a summarised conclusion.

The discussion threw up another factor. Many of the Japanese managers were unhappy about the way meetings were habitually run in Japan and wanted a more Western-style approach. This led later to a joint Japanese/British workshop to decide on the rules for the conduct of meetings; behaviour that led to a 'charter' being adopted, basically adapting a Western-style framework with the objective of creating a hopefully undiminished consensus.

On the subject of high levels of overtime and the impact of this on family life, the workshop discussed the differences in attitudes between Japanese and British in terms of the alleged contrast between the dominant 'mother–child' relationship in Japan and the 'husband–wife' axis in the UK. It was argued that the tradition in Japan was that the overriding priority in marriage was the nurturing of children in the context of families based on arranged marriages. This allowed very considerable mobility of employees who were willing to separate from their families. Of course, the changes in equal opportunity in Japan that are currently occurring are beginning to challenge this whole assumption.

Regrettably, the Western understanding of the Japanese mind is still extremely limited. This has given rise to many irrational fears and misconceptions. I have not found the Japanese managerial systems or approaches difficult to understand; the problem lies in grasping the differences in *context*. As we have already seen, the Japanese are one of the most homogeneous races in the world. Although they originally received many ideas and values from other Eastern cultures, their deliberate isolation for 250 years developed a strong national identity and an innate sense of knowing what the other is thinking. Hence Japanese managers are often puzzled as to why we, the British, who like things spelled out in words of two syllables, do not appear to understand the drift of Japanese argument. It is, of course, equally true in reverse that the British managers and employees employ 'shorthand' in their verbal exchanges that contain connotations not really explained to the resident Japanese managers.

Whose language are we operating in?

Japanese expatriates who found English conversation difficult could be forgiven for lapsing into fluent conversation with their expatriate colleagues. However, British managers with whom they were supposed to be working ended up bemused, and not a little suspicious, and this was where paranoia would start – concerning decision-making, clout, who gets told first, and seditious rumour. Keith Tipping, then Production Director and now the plant's first British Managing Director, challenged Komatsu management in Tokyo to evolve a clear policy on the use of English and to stick to it!

Although they tacitly agreed at the time to use English exclusively, it took over two years to come to fruition – after Toshitaka Suketomo, board member of Komatsu Ltd, became Managing Director of Komatsu UK and had enough leverage in Tokyo to insist that faxes in Japanese from Tokyo to the UK would not be accepted!

Who is in the driving seat?

The phases of development of Komatsu UK were predictable. For the Japanese a time-honoured pattern would be followed. Just as we saw earlier in this chapter, for the parent company in the 1960s, quality and production were the priorities in the early years – quality to maintain the reputation and market share, and production, above all else to plug the gap caused by loss of Japanese imports to Europe following EC anti-dumping legislation. Further, the market in Europe was expanding at almost 20 per cent per annum to an incredible level of over 20,000 machines in 1989. Then recession set in. Priorities rapidly changed to cost reduction, while at the same time maintaining and improving quality.

New model development

In line with the philosophy of 'Closer to the Customer', elements of new model development were delegated from Japan to Birtley for initially adapting a new model to European requirements and later establishing a design and test centre to evolve the first new model ever to be developed and launched outside Japan.

These were exciting times. This gave the Birtley team the first taste of multi-discipline project working – simultaneous engineering – involving all stages of the production process in contributing to design and development. Individuals grew very rapidly and barriers were broken down.

Europe-wide production

Komatsu's plans for Europe were rapidly changing. For the next phase of market penetration it needed both to widen the range of European-produced models and spread the production base to overcome internal market friction between European countries. By this time the Japanese had come to recognise that removal of internal barriers within the EC was more conceptual than real. A further factor was the need to hedge against currency exchange fluctuations.

However, by 1990 Europe was suffering from over-capacity and speed of penetration was of the essence. The Japanese entered a new field – the joint venture. Two styles were adopted: a joint venture in Italy with an existing manufacturer to produce and jointly market mini-excavators, and a partial takeover of an ailing German manufacturer of wheel loaders. Following conventional industrial logic, the embryonic wheel loader production was transferred from the UK to

Germany. This regrettably reduced Komatsu UK to a one-product line plant and substantially reduced potential turnover. I was a lone voice in opposing this move as I believed it exposed Komatsu UK to the vagaries of a single economic cycle – and this decision certainly accelerated layoffs in 1992.

Top management in Japan and in Europe discovered a new problem: how to produce change in Germany with an existing indigenous team that does not see that there is anything they can learn from Japan! Attention drifted from Komatsu UK's problems to the wider scene in Europe.

Change in management

Internal management at Komatsu UK was now changing. The learning curve with the initial team from Japan had been achieved, but now, inevitably, top Japanese management moved on and was replaced by new expatriates from Japan whose priority was to make the company profitable with much lower volumes of production in a short time scale. The new incumbents were less concerned than the initial team with internal and external relationships and, predictably, took for granted the quite unique achievements to the UK in teamwork, flexibility and productivity.

Elements of British management sensed the opportunity for change and jockeyed for position in readiness for when the second wave of Japanese management migrated on, demonstrating the innate tendency for individualism and internal competition to dominate the agenda in the mind of the UK manager.

Recession and redundancy

The recession deepened in 1991 and predicted market demands fell steeply. The UK market shrank to one-third of its size in 1989. Job losses became inevitable and most of 1991 was spent devising measures to avoid redundancy. There was earnest consultation with the Advisory Council throughout this whole process Staff were successfully seconded outside the company – particularly to Tyneside TEC to help with the thrust of spreading the Quality Initiative throughout the North East; also natural wastage took its toll and the books balanced. The year 1992 showed even further falls in demand

and lay-offs and redundancies proved unavoidable. Both Japanese and British managers were divided on how to implement what turned out to be relatively modest losses (35 out of 400 permanent staff). I am pleased to say that the 'short, sharp shock' school lost, and that the job losses were implemented as fairly and gently as possible – with over 60 per cent of those departing finding alternative work in the space of four weeks.

POSTSCRIPT

Not surprisingly, this experience shattered the confidence of many Komatsu UK employees, who had given so much towards the successful establishment of what many hoped would provide 'jobs for life.' It shows, together with the experience of Nissan MUK in 1993 and as has also recently happened in Japan, that even well-run successful Japanese companies are not immune to market place pressures that eventually demand job cuts. The concept of life-time employment is changing in Japan (see Chapter 7). However, Komatsu UK has survived this experience and is holding its own in a fierce European market with gross over-capacity. It will be in good shape to take advantage of the upturn when it finally comes.

Catalogue of success

The impact of the dramatic downturn in 1991 an 1992 added an element of realism to a story of seemingly invincible success. This chapter cannot end without recognising the achievements of the UK plant that resulted from the enthusiasm and dedication of its work-force, supported by the teamwork – despite the acknowledged difficulties – of Japanese and British management and the almost unfailing patience of Tokyo. Some of the milestones were as follows:

- Achieved 60 per cent local content in 1987: 80 per cent by 1990
- Largest producer of hydraulic excavators in the UK (overtook JCB in 1989)
- BS 5750 accreditation 1990
- Queen's Award for Export 1991
- Investors in People 1991 (one of first 22 companies awarded – only other Japanese-owned company at the time was Nissan MUK)

- First ever Japanese-owned plant to design, develop and manufacture a new model outside Japan, 1992
- Achieved first profit in 1992

APPENDIX 1

TQC and Komatsu growth

1961	→	1991
$168m turnover		$6bn turnover

1960   Japanese government remove trade barrier
1961   TQC system introduced
        Maru 'A' project started
1963   Caterpillar forms joint venture with Mitsubishi in Japan
1964   Komatsu awarded the Deming Prize for quality control implementation
1967   Komatsu Europe established (Sales and Marketing)
        TQC activities extended:
          – Policy management
          – Cross-function TQC structure formed
          – QC circle activity encouraged
1972–6 Maru 'B' project for export growth
1976   Dina Komatsu Mexico (2nd plant outside Japan)
1979   Licence agreements for production in India and China
1981   Komatsu awarded Japan Quality Control Prize (only one of 8 companies in Japan)
1982   Komatsu Indonesia (3rd plant outside Japan)
1985   Komatsu America Manuf Corp Established (4th plant outside Japan)
1985   Komatsu UK established (5th plant outside Japan)
1988   Komatsu Dresser
        Joint venture with Dresser Industries
        Joint venture with FAI of Italy for mini excavator production and sales
1989   Controlling interest in Hanomag of West Germany for wheeled loader production
        Establishment of Komatsu Europe International to coordinate European operations

Komatsu UK production levels top £100m – largest producer in UK

1990 Komatsu UK BS 5750 accreditation

1991 Komatsu UK: Queen's Award for Export

Komatsu UK: Investors in People Award

1992 Komatsu UK introduces wheeled excavator to the market.
First model ever to be designed, developed and manufactured outside Japan

Komatsu UK achieves first profit

NOTES

1. Harvard Business School study paper U385-277, 1985 p. 6.
2. Ibid., p. 13.
3. Ibid., p. 13.
4. Miyamoto Musashi, *A Book of Five Rings*, originally written in 1645. Translated by Victor Harris, published by Fontana, 1974.
5. *Financial Times*, 25 January 1993.
6. The foundations for this relationship had been laid over many years by NEDC, TWCC and Gateshead MBC.
7. T. Cowley-Bainton, M. White, *Employing Unemployed People: How Employers Gain*, PSI study of Komatsu for Department of Employment, published 1990.
8. Industrial Relations Review and Report, May 1987.
9. NEDC, *What Makes a Supervisor World Class?*, Engineering Skills Working Party 1991.
10. This quotation became the slogan for Tyneside Training and Enterprise Council in encouraging employers to raise standards.
11. This issue is now generally seen to be crucial in all Japanese companies in the UK. See the discussion in Chapter 5.

4 How Can Your Company Achieve Best Practice?

Konosuke Matsushita, who founded Matsushita Electric, chillingly said:

> We will win and you will lose. You cannot do anything about it because your failure is an internal disease. You firmly believe that sound management means executives on one side and workers on the other, on one side men who think, and on the other, men who can only work. For you, management is the art of smoothly transferring the executives' ideas into the workers' hands.

AN INTERNAL DISEASE AND AN INABILITY TO CATCH UP?

'You won't do it anyway'

In 1984, as part of the National Quality Campaign in the UK, a group of people representing management, banking, purchasing and media – called the Pacific Basin Study division – visited Japan to study the importance of quality management and business success. During their visit they asked a leading Japanese economist why Japanese companies had been so open about their techniques and secrets of success – weren't they afraid the West would catch up? His reply was succinct and fatalistic. 'Because,' he replied, 'it would take you ten years to get to where we are now, and by that time we shall be even further ahead. And besides,' he smiled, 'we know you won't do it anyway.'

That was ten years ago. What progress in the West has been made since then? World-class companies have emerged in the West, some achieving the prestigious Baldridge Award or the new European Foundation for Quality Award. However, they are but a handful.

The Womack, Jones and Roos[1] study (see Chapter 6) has shown that 'Lean Production' standards are not confined to Japan. However, the plants that have achieved the standards of quality and cost

66

outside Japan that are equivalent to the best in Japan are, by and large, Japanese implants in North America and Europe.

If it is clear that for survival in worldwide competition 'Lean Production' standards or their equivalent have to be achieved in all industries (unprotected by trade barriers), how is it that so few Western companies are achieving world-class standards?

The search for the reasons for Japanese industrial supremacy has occupied brilliant minds for many years in the vain attempt to explain the success away and provide ammunition in the war of words over international trade that can only get worse as the issue of Japanese trade surplus and imbalance in the world economy increases.

The search is better directed at the following question:

> 'If it is now demonstrated that the fundamental ideas of TQC/ Lean Production are universal – applicable anywhere by anyone – why is it that the West seems incapable of revolutionising its industrial performance?'

The problem of introducing new technology into Europe is not new. Henry Ford introduced mass production between 1908 and 1913 at his Highland Park plant in Detroit, in 1911 he opened an auto-assembly plant at Trafford Park near Manchester, UK,[2] to overcome transport limitations and eventually trade barriers.

To start with, all went well as Ford attempted to replicate the mass-production system he was perfecting at Highland Park. Initial resistance from craft workers concerning deskilling was overcome, and by 1915 American managers at Trafford Park reported that productivity was comparable to that at Highland Park.[3]

However, a number of factors, including Henry Ford's voiced views that America should stay out of the First World War, caused a sharp drop in demand for Ford products in the UK. Trafford Park ran at a fraction of its capacity and Detroit seemed to lose interest:

Not surprisingly, factory performance seemed to deteriorate steadily. None of the English managers shared a conception of management that was compatible with mass production. The idea of a manufacturing career beginning on the shop floor with hands-on management was unattractive to middle-class Englishmen, who emerged from an education system that steered them toward the Civil Service, the Law and other types of high level administration. They didn't want to get involved with the nitty gritty of running anything. Rather, they wanted to delegate operational details, just as they did with the Empire. . . . Consequently, managing the shop floor soon became, by default, the responsibility of the shop steward . . . Ford abandoned Trafford Park in 1931.[4]

Reading this in 1994 it occurs to me that the attitudes and ambitions of English managers are remarkably resistant to change, as even today the UK government tries to find an explanation for the paucity of engineering graduates interested in entering industry!

Oliver and Wilkinson[5] have compared the reported success of the introduction of Japanese-style production systems in UK-owned companies and Japanese-owned companies in the UK. Their conclusion is that unless these production systems are matched with the introduction of Japanese-style personnel systems, problems will arise.

DO WE NEED A CULTURE CHANGE?

In essence, my own empirical experience supports the Oliver and Wilkinson thesis. However, I would argue that for successful transplantation of these ideas, a major shift in cultural attitudes is essential. This shift in attitudes must span top to bottom of the organisation, involve radical change in the relationships within the company and, increasingly, also with those outside companies and organisations it deals with.

To quote Womack, Jones and Roos again:

> Our studies of plants trying to adopt lean production reveal that workers respond only when there exists some sense of reciprocal obligation, a sense that management actually values [skilled] workers, will make sacrifices to retain them and is willing to delegate responsibility to the *team*. Merely changing the organisation chart to show 'teams' and introducing quality circles to find ways to improve production processes are unlikely to make much difference.[6]

This implies a major shift in attitudes, giving mutual support within such companies, which in turn will affect relationships outside – such as those with suppliers, trade unions and the wider community.

THE LADDER OF ORGANISATIONAL BEHAVIOUR

John Nirenberg of the National University of Singapore, in his important article in *The Journal of Managerial Psychology*,[7] produces a hierarchy of organisation behaviour, which, like Maslow's hierarchy of human needs (A. Maslow, *Motivation and Personality*, Harper and Row, 1954), suggests that there are a series of socio-behavioural components that an organisation must understand for it to be able to carry out its mission effectively. He suggests four steps on the ladder of organisational behaviour (see Fig. 4.1)

This theory is rooted in the validated work of Burns and Stalker,[8] arguing that organisations develop structures that reflect the conditioning of the market place and the external pressures on the enterprise. The situation for so many organisations today is that the external environment, i.e. increased competitiveness, privatisation, pressures on public-sector finance and performance, and so on – *demand* radical changes in internal performance, which in turn

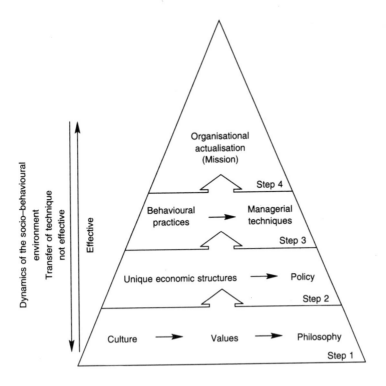

Fig. 4.1 *Ladder of organisational behaviour*

Step	Japanese Examples		Attention of management writers	Probability of successful transplantation of techniques to other socio-behavioural environment when starting at this	American Examples	
Step 3	Lifetime employment	Quality Circles	High	Low	Stable employment	Participative management
Step 2	Mutual indebtedness Indebtedness Boss–Employee Commitment	Peer pressure	Limited	Limited	Social/ psychological contact	To make a difference Negotiated agreement
Step 1	Groupism – place in world	Mutual obligation	Low	High	Individuality	Self-actualisation

Fig. 4.2 *Management examples related to the ladder of organisational behaviour*

demand radical changes in practices and techniques that cannot be achieved without changes in culture, values and philosophy.

What Nirenberg's ladder also shows is that the usual mechanism used by executives – a new mission statement followed by top down initiatives – is doomed to failure unless the host culture is changed. Nirenberg expands the point in Fig. 4.2, giving management examples related to the ladder of organisational behaviour.

Nirenberg's precondition for the successful transplantation of techniques is for 'groupism' and mutual obligation to be the foundation stones. He postulates that failure in the attempted transfer of Japanese management technology is the inability to change the underlying steps in the ladder of organisational behaviour. He gives the following example:

Malaysia articulated a 'Look East' policy in 1980 to learn from the Japanese experience and imitate some of their practices. In that regard, Malaysian style sogo shoshas, or trading companies, were formed after the Sumitomo and Marubeni models. Not having considered the underlying cultural reasons for the success of the Japanese and how they might differ from Malaysians (and for a host of other reasons as well) the Malaysian sogo shoshas were doomed. As one Malaysian researcher noted, '. . . these institutions are not only quite irrelevant but also quite impossible to duplicate in the Malaysian economy'.

Once again there was a rush to adopt a technique without considering its underlying socio-behavioural properties . . . the level of trust and co-operation need to operate within the sogo shosha framework is not part of the Malaysian economic experience.

CULTURE SHIFT

There is a universal need for organisations to analyse current and desired future culture. The trend today within companies is away from what Dr Charles Handy[9] nearly twenty years ago termed 'power' and 'control' and instead there is a move towards 'achievement' and 'support' – termed a 'commitment culture' by Richard

Walton,[10] more recently, as opposed to what he, Walton, termed 'command and control'.

This demand for a culture shift is not necessarily a product of responding to a perceived need for an 'enabling' environment for introducing such things as TQC and Lean Production. It is a product of a number of trends in society that are joining forces in an almost accidental fashion to produce unprecedented external constraints.

Lean Production and TQC lead to a need to use employees' minds, not just their hands. It undoubtedly can increase pressure and demand on workforces and initially they may be unprepared for this; also they may resist if they do not see the change as being in their interest. In today's fast-moving global market place there are few protected areas, and dominance by the consumer will mean that all companies will have to compete on these terms:

- Technology shifts mean that life cycles of products have shrunk unbelievably in recent years, so simultaneous or concurrent engineering is not a shining exhibition piece, but obligatory for companies that wish to survive. Vertical barriers and 'silo' mentalities have to go. Further, as disciples of re-engineering would point out, computing power can now be distributed throughout the organisation
- Individuality will increase in the long term. It was possibly accelerated by the Thatcher years, but it is here to stay for people desire to control their own destinies. Respect for authority is on the wane and there is an understandable desire for work to be subservient to life rather than the reverse

This last is a stimulus for re-engineering, flattening hierarchical structures, reducing middle management and devolving responsibility down the line, quite apart from the commercial pressures we started with.

The new role for the supervisor or team leader, long overdue, has so much more value added by him motivating his new-found team and also gaining job satisfaction into the bargain. This is a product of the growth of individualism and at last recognises that people doing a job actually know more about that job than anyone else!

This release of energy relies on both the framework of *formal relationships* to be effective, for instance, between the company and the union(s) representing the employees, and also on the *face-to-face relationships between people.* This raises the issue of teams, team roles and team building.

The word 'quality' has not been mentioned in this context. This, as discussed in Chapter 1, is now taken for granted. If you do not produce good quality you cannot even start to compete.

Having established that we are on an inexorable path towards culture change because of pressures that will not go away, we can either lie back and think of England, as it was, or make the decision to participate. Culture change that transforms formal and informal relationships implies a major shift in mutuality. The extremes between Japan and the West are illustrated by Nirenberg's third diagram (Fig. 4.3).[11]

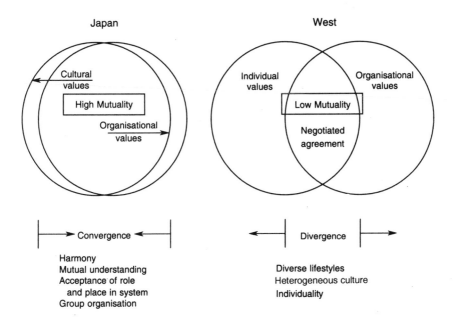

Fig. 4.3 *Contrast of organisational–individual values in Japan and the West*

COMMAND AND CONTROL TO COMMITMENT

It is worth recognising the change of shift in attitudes and modes of working that are implicit in the change from command and control to commitment.

For management

Need to know principle	→	Consult employees and trade unions, communicate the vision, keep communicating
Correct and direct	→	Listen and learn
Blame culture	→	Support
Consult if we have to (afterwards)	→	Consult widely beforehand and incorporate views
Control everything, especially meetings	→	Encourage responsibility to perform as a team
Defend your function	→	Demolish vertical barriers
Nail individuals, pigeonhole others	→	Accept responsibility for making things happen

For employees

Do what I am told without question	→	Do what it takes to achieve goals that I share with the company[12]
I have a job, I get paid	→	Feel responsible for success of the total enterprise and know how I must contribute = empowerment[13]
Don't argue, we know our place	→	Question assumptions, agree on the focus,[14] influence company policy and practice
I can choose my friends: not those I work with	→	Work as a team, understand what others bring, aim to balance and maximise the outcomes
Don't change, I know where I am	→	Flexibility leads to more variety and knowledge
Suffer in silence, otherwise I may be out of a job	→	Manage stress – feed back to the boss problems that you can't solve
It's just a job	→	Have fun

For trade unions

Defend your membership in an adversarial fashion	→	Understand the issues, work for your membership by aiming for

to the last

Priority of membership   →   the long-term success of the
numbers – compete with   company and employees
predatory trade unions   Long-term interest of members
Listen to the disaffected →   is satisfying job with a future;
dinosaurs (they shout   forget artificial divisions
loudest)   These are not the members
                               for the future; recognise changing
                               roles at work and changing role
                               of trade unions

Don't listen to management; → Share information –
they are about to hoodwink   after all, you both have an
you   investment and interest in the
                               enterprise

All should be paid the   →   Embrace flexibility
same, irrespective of   performance appraisal and merit
ability and contribution   pay within context of equal
                               opportunity

For supplier relationships

Arm's length   →   Integrate.
don't let them talk to   inform – open book accounting;
each other   arrange supplier days
It's all in the contract. →   Mutual understanding, long-term
Price is the final arbiter –   relationship, shared problems and
we will dispense when it   solutions
suits us
The price is cost plus   →   The price is the market price.
margin   Let's help you reduce
                               manufacturing costs

Hedge bets by doubling   →   Reduce to single source where
up on suppliers   possible
Can't trust delivery,   →   JIT (Just in Time) responsibility
therefore forward order   for on-line on-time delivery
with a buffer stock   passed to supplier
We are the final   →   Integrate and delegate design to
manufacturers, and   suppliers – they have to make the
know what the customer   parts/supply the service and
wants, so we must design.   contribute to the end quality

Suppliers do as they are
told, otherwise where does
responsibility lie?

For the relationship with the wider community

We only need to keep them   →   We have a responsibility to the
at arm's length – they should   community in which we work
be grateful that we are
providing employment

We suppose someone should   →   Networking is important.
provide a link – in case   If we link with education, we
of crisis   could improve the intake

Defensive PR   →   It is important that the
     community understand the
     business and its needs, and that
     we understand them

No time   →   We should contribute to
No money   community needs both in
No interest   money and time – from all levels
     in the company (it helps with
     employee development)

We have nothing to offer   →   We should promote quality as a
     philosophy in the community –
     we depend on a quality response

TWIN DILEMMAS

Two contradictions emerge from this analysis. I dealt in the same
breath with the inexorable growth of individualism and, on the other
hand, the necessity for people to work in teams. Indeed, the oft-
quoted contrast in this book is between the destructive nature of
Western individualism and the benefit of Japanese team working.

    The second contradiction is that I stress the need for controls,
conformance and standards to produce consistently high quality, and

at the same time encourage delegation and flexibility which, un-bridled, will be liable to produce the opposite.

The first 'contradiction' is not such a contradiction in practice. Management in 'Lean Production' environments need to encourage teamworking and an increased amount of creative input, but within terms of reference that are consistent with commercial goals. In other words, encourage individual creativity, but not to the point where it damages teamworking. There is potential for genuine employee involvement because it places responsibility on to those directly involved in production and allows employees and their elected representatives influence over hitherto forbidden areas, such as:

- New technology
- Product changes
- Organisation structures
- Work methods
- Facility layout
- Environment
- Training

However, the mode is different, as illustrated on p. 74. The involvement is not in the old adversarial mode of resisting such change, but to facilitate changes for the benefit of both employees and the company.

Visitors at Komatsu UK often challenged the contrast between the strong emphasis on teamworking and the system of individual appraisal (see Chapter 5 for details), which would seemingly militate against teamworking – 'How can you achieve team spirit when different members of the team end up on different rates of pay as a result of their individual appraisals?' In fact, this seeming contra-diction was only theoretical, since one important measure in the performance appraisal was, 'Do they work well in teams?', again encouraging individuality, but not to the point of damaging team-working.

This apparent conflict has been discussed in a Japanese context by W. Ouchi,[15] and he also concludes that any conflict is resolved by including teamwork ability and quality of relations with subordinates in personal assessments.

The second contradiction is an apparent conflict between control and commitment. In companies where quality and cost are para-mount, jobs are broken down into clearly defined, short-cycle, repeatable elements which, after much evaluation, must be performed in a specific way. This is often called the 'standard operation', which is known as the best method of doing the job to give maximum quality and productivity within safety considerations. Any deviation will lead to lower quality, higher cost and possibly unsafe working. Operators must be trained to perform these tasks without deviation. Flexibility of the actual manufacturing process is not encouraged, however attractive the concept.

In the early days at Komatsu UK, in order to encourage flexibility of working and break down a few barriers, we rotated workers on the shop floor between quite distinct functions, e.g. welding to assembly, and vice versa, on a continuous basis. The concept was great, but difficulties emerged. Soon we were less ambitious and rotated on a short-term basis *within* teams where there was sufficient knowledge, training and control to ensure repeatability. Also, significantly, changes were then within the control of the team leader and not a policy foisted on him from above. Rotation between teams and functions still took place but was based on longer time spans, prearranged training and agreed patterns. Here control and commitment are not incompatible. Control is demonstrated by repeatedly producing quality and productivity and commitment of management is shown by allowing team leaders and production management to 'own' the effective operation of their processes. Teams respond with commitment by effective production and influencing policy and practice through team meetings and quality circles.

Do other observers believe we need fundamental culture change to implement TQC?

Masaaki Imai, in his book *Kaizen*, quotes Professor Michael Haley of Vanderbilt University Owen Graduate School of Management, who concluded, following a visit to Japan, that TQC in Japan, as I would argue in the Komatsu example, is applied as a complete corporate strategy:

> To be implemented the strategy must become concrete to everyone in the organization. Therefore, long-run strategies must be translated into short-run plans and objectives which are clear and actionable.
>
> The principles of total quality control provide the necessary structural framework to help both the employees and management

communicate and decide how to improve the quality and productivity of work.

Thus, total quality control as a corporate strategy inevitably involves such areas as improving communication and labour–management relations, as well as revitalizing organizational structures.

But above all, most importantly, total quality control as corporate strategy must deal with people. Its net results are more productive workers, more efficient managers, improved communication and more effective organisation. Better and competitive products are the result of better people and better management and not vice versa.

Imai continues:

Corporate strategy should not be monopolized by a handful of top management executives. It must be spelled out in a form that can be understood, interpreted, and carried out by everyone in the company. As Haley stated, 'It must be a basis of communication between all individuals of a business organisation. The strategy must relate to their needs and motivate their performance – getting everyone to participate positively needs the right climate or corporate culture.

Creating a cooperative atmosphere and corporate culture has been an inseparable part of KAIZEN programs. All the KAIZEN programs implemented in Japan have had one key prerequisite in common: getting workers' acceptance and overcoming their resistance to change. Achieving this has necessitated:

1 Constant efforts to improve industrial relations
2 Emphasis on training and education of workers
3 Developing team leaders among the workers
4 Formation of small-group activities such as QC circles
5 Support and recognition for workers' Kaizen efforts
6 Conscious efforts for making the workplace a place where workers can pursue life goals
7 Bringing social life into the workshop as much as practicable
8 Training supervisors so that they can communicate better with workers and can create a more positive personal involvement with workers
9 Bringing discipline to the workshop'.

All of which, when we compare with the typical Western enterprise, add up to a fundamental culture change.

Oliver and Wilkinson, in *The Japanization of British Industry* (p. 84), conclude:

> Japanese success with JIT and Total Quality management may be seen as a consequence of an effective fit between Japanese production systems and Japanese personnel priorities, supplier relationships and so on – the whole system being supported by an appropriate set of social, political and economic conditions.

> 'If there is a "secret" to Japanese success, we suggest that it lies in the synergy generated by a whole system, and not, as some have suggested, in specific parts of the system' (Oliver and Wilkinson).

They continue on p. 88: 'If there is a "secret" to Japan's success, we suggest that it lies in the synergy generated by a whole system, and not, as some have suggested, in specific parts of that system.' As for successful implanting of these ideas in the UK, Oliver and Wilkinson conclude (p. 277): 'Japanese direct investors *are* bringing with them to the UK many of the manufacturing and personnel practices that they use in Japan. That is, "adaptation" to the local environment does not necessarily entail the abandonment of the essential elements of the Japanese approach to manufacturing.'

We need a creative crisis to change?

Visitors to Komatsu UK sometimes came with a preformed explanation for the apparent success, determined to carry it away undiluted by what they saw. Typically they would say: 'It is easy for you, you started with a blank sheet of paper, a semi-green field site, with people who were unemployed and desperate for a job – small wonder they complied with what you wanted. You could not apply this in a "brown field" organisation with a deeply rooted culture.' Inevitably, there are grains of truth in the critique; however, it is far too deterministic.

'It is easy for you, you started with a blank sheet of paper . . . you could not apply this in a "brown field" organisation with a deeply rooted culture.'

First it wasn't that easy, as was demonstrated in Chapter 3, for, despite a backcloth of unemployment, new recruits brought the baggage of experience and attitudes of previous employment into the workplace. Further, the threat of unemployment providing compliant attitudes soon disappears in a company that is trying to encourage perspectives of a long-term career.

Secondly, others have demonstrated success in the 'brown field site' situation. An example in the North East of England has been S.P. Tyres, originally Dunlop, who were subject to a reverse takeover by their original Japanese subsidiary Sumitomo in the 1980s. Sumitomo kept the same British management, workforce and trade unions that had previously been operating in its British plant, yet nevertheless produced the same sort of dramatic results that were achieved at Komatsu UK in the same area.

Outside Japanese control, the startling example of transformation of Rover under the previous ownership by British Aerospace is there for all to see. Admittedly, the catalyst for workshop change has been Honda, but the stimulus has come from British management, who have made clear efforts to change the culture. Bartodo, quoted by Oliver and Wilkinson,[16] indicates a shift in management style from directive and controlling to 'facilitation, guidance and training of subordinates in a fluid interacting environment'.

Ford had rather earlier inside experience of Japanese management techniques, almost by accident in the late 1970s. In 1979 it acquired a 24 per cent stake in Mazda. Mazda had itself gone through a major crisis in the 1970s because of the need to abandon the thirsty Wankel engine as the basis of product strategy. It had extensively adopted 'Lean Production' learning from Toyota at the time.

The acquisition of the Mazda stake enabled Ford executives to gain full access to the Hiroshima production lines. 'They discovered that Mazda could build its 323 model with only 60 per cent of the effort that Ford needed to manufacture its Escort selling into the same market segment.'[17] In addition, quality was better, new product development time was much lower with less effort, and supplier relations much smoother.

This conversion on the road to Damascus occurred at a time of mounting crisis for Ford, as it rapidly lost market share in the early 1980s and losses were threatening the survival of the company. This created what Womack, Jones and Roos term a creative crisis.[18] This is when employees at all levels are ready to stop thinking about how to advance their careers or departmental interest and to start thinking about how to save the company, and therefore their jobs.

During the 1980s Ford implemented many elements of Lean Production and, despite many setbacks, the results were demonstrated in the market place. Whether the transformation at Ford was deep or long-lasting enough, only time will tell. However, the example is apposite.

Western business needs a *creative crisis* in order to indulge in the complete leap of faith to TQC or Lean Production.

What are the elements of culture change?

On p. 72 I talked of the twin needs for formal relationships to be effective (e.g. between company and union) and also the face-to-face relationships between people. Hence the issue of teams, team roles and team building. Implicit in this is the need for top management to demonstrate their participative support for such changes. This is the most difficult area, and requires wearing a hair shirt *with sincerity.*

This in fact means demonstrating by example. Visitors to Nissan MUK in Washington, Sunderland, are taken aback to find the British Chief Executive, Ian Gibson CBE, occupying a desk in an open-plan area with no partitions, seemingly no privacy and certainly no difference in status. We followed a similar path at Komatsu UK and as well as having open-plan areas we insisted on the wearing of standard uniform. Directors and managers parked their cars with everyone else's – those who arrived last were liable to greatest exposure to north-east weather!

The first Managing Director, Torio Komiya, recognised how important this issue was. Faithful to single status, we had very carefully adjusted working hours so that there was basically no difference in start, finish and break times between shop floor and the office. However, as soon as the staff canteen was in operation, it was clear that the office staff were at a disadvantage, for they had to walk through the factory to gain access to the canteen – and at 1200 hours they naturally found a large queue of shop floor workers had beaten them to it!

Without consulting anyone, the office workers on their own initiative naturally regulated their time, putting off lunch until 1215 hours and returning at 1300 hours, fifteen minutes later than the shop floor. British managers were staggered when Torio Komiya raised the issue at the weekly managers' meeting, insisting that office workers should be back at their desks by 1245 hours like everybody else! We thought that was altogether unreasonable. However, Torio Komiya's point was as follows. What does it look like, he said, to the shop floor workers if office workers pass through their working area fifteen minutes later than they knew they had to start work! Demonstration is therefore vital.

Expectation of privilege is deeply ingrained in British management and will continue to be a major inhibitor in implementing TQC and Lean Production and, importantly culture change.

Formal relationships have to at least be embryonically right before such major change can happen. Trade unions need to be convinced of the critical nature of the changes just as much as management. The extracts from the Komatsu/AEU agreement in Appendix I(iii) show the degree of mutual understanding achieved from the outset. Much care was taken to get the environment right – we even had a large round table especially made for the Advisory Council meetings.

Face-to-face relationships are somewhat different. In this sense, the task at Komatsu UK was easier. All entrants had gone through an elementary form of psychometric testing and were judged to be 'good at working in teams', 'enthusiastic', and with 'a positive attitude'. That at least gave us a starting point. In applying for promotion, further in-depth tests were carried out, giving information that can be used to predict future team working performance.

My belief is that the changes talked about in this book are so fundamental that, over a period of time, whole 'brown field' organisations need to find out a lot more about their current and potential face-to-face relationships for successful transformation. This means widespread use of psychometric or personality tests, definition of team roles, team building and personal growth.

This is precisely the pattern we followed within Northern Electric plc, where I was engaged in assisting with a major culture shift with the aim of producing a world-class organisation to replace the public-sector bureaucracy that existed prior to privatisation (see Chapter 5 for more detail).

Accepting this intrusion into British personal privacy was no mean task, especially when it needs to be applied top down and to people occupying *existing* roles, not just applying for new ones! However, if we are to make the shift from specialism and sanctity of professionalism to interactive group working where the mode changes from tasks in sequence to pooled project management activity, then how people will work together, or not work together, needs to be anticipated and built upon.

What about the service and public sector?

The cited history and experience of TQC and Lean Production is unashamedly in manufacturing. Can the principles be applied in other industrial sectors, or even in the public sector? Fortunately, the answer is yes, judging from the experience of others and my own more recent involvement.

Masaaki Imai cites an example that applies to all businesses with a large customer base. On pp. 54–5 of *Kaizen*,[19] he reprints the case history of a study by Ricoh Company Ltd on 'Shortening Customers' Telephone Waiting Time' in the main office of a large bank in Japan; banks are not particularly well known for efficiency in Japan. Following classic use of cause and effect diagrams and analysis of 'Reasons why callers had to wait' using Pareto diagrams, a number of countermeasures were introduced that caused failures to plummet from 351 to 59 in comparative periods before and after the self-imposed countermeasures. Many other such examples can be quoted that illustrate that TQC can be integrated into the strategic renewal of the service sector.

In October 1992, in addition to my role at Northern Electric, I became part-time non-executive Chairman of the Gateshead Hospitals NHS Trust. I am therefore very interested in whether Total Quality can apply to health care today. In 'Curing Health Care',[20] one doctor speaks of a visit to a company practising Total Quality principles in the USA:

> Visit any such company and there are lots of surprises in store. The employees at all levels, like the clerk just mentioned, seem to value data about their own work. They seek such data; they collect them as part of their jobs; they interpret them; and they use them daily. For them, 'management reports' are a service, not a surveillance system.

This active use of information is only the beginning of what is new. Ask the employees about the purpose of their company, and you may be surprised to discover that they have detailed knowledge of it. You will find a consistency of vision up and down the hierarchical ladder; people know their jobs and know why their jobs exist. They are also aware of their inter-dependencies. Employees in manufacturing areas understand the work of support services; the business office understands the front line; the design people understand production, and production people speak regularly with designers. You will have a hard time finding people who blame each other for their troubles at work.

Ask the employees who their customers are and they will tell you clearly. Ask them what the customers need and they will tell you that, too, since they have asked the same questions themselves and actively sought the answers.

Ask workers chosen at random when they last served on a quality improvement team and they are likely to say they are on one now. In the team, they meet regularly with people from other departments and other organisational levels in order to accomplish a specific, time limited goal, for which the team was created by a management council: to improve a particular process on which quality depends. The team members have received specific training in quality improvement methods; they have learned how to define problems, create hypotheses, collect data, analyse the data, and design and test remedies. They are making their own work, and the work of others, better. (A nurse looking at this situation said, 'I get it. In this management system everyone has two jobs: their job, and the job of helping to improve their job!')[21]

[The nurse said]: 'I see I have two jobs – one to do my job, the other to improve my job!'

Ask them how the company can afford to give them the time to serve on teams and they will ask how the company could afford NOT to.

Not surprisingly, morale is high. The company can report steadily decreasing employee turnover ever since it got serious about quality improvement, and the unions, instead of obstructing change, are helping to lead the effort. The employees are sharing financially in the growing profits of the company; but, as you study their faces, you will begin to wonder if it really IS profit and income that these workers are enjoying so much.

The short answer is that although the application is not quite so clear as in manufacturing – yes, these principles can be applied in service and public sectors to advantage.

How do you keep the momentum up?

How do you open the eyes of the blind?
Benchmarking is the key. The earlier examples of change being transferred globally, even back to industrial pilgrimages to the Highland Park and Rouge plants in the USA from 1915 onwards, all resulted from benchmarking.

Toyota's pre-eminent position can be traced back to benchmarking that preceded Ohno's radical changes to production methods in Japan. Womack, Jones and Roos have put this critical issue rather succinctly:

> There are only two ways for lean production to diffuse across the world. The Japanese lean producers can spread it by building plants and taking over companies abroad, or the American and Europeans can adopt it on their own. Which of these methods proves dominant will have profound implications for the world economy in the 90's.[22]

'There are two ways for Lean Production to diffuse across the world. . . . Which of these methods proves dominant will have profound implications for the world economy in the 90's' (Womack, Jones and Roos).

Understanding the stimulus for benchmarking

There are two basic reasons: achieving and maintaining competitive edge and learning from comparable situations to solve problems and involve people.

It used to be a basic belief that you did not let your competitors into your factory or plant because they were all potential industrial spies. The practice is different today. A mutuality has emerged, tinged with globalism, that has as a basic philosophy that we are all seekers after truth and that the receiver of the benchmarking team is as likely to learn as much as the visitor.

Today in world-class companies you will find universal enthusiasm for benchmarking exercises, which often employ teams at a great variety of levels in the organisation. So what is the real gain? The answer is a different perspective that can help the visitor perceive routes to success otherwise not conceived or thought possible.

Benchmarking is a good technique, but it needs careful planning and follow-up to achieve proper results. For instance:

- What are the objectives?
- Which are the target companies?
- Who should go? At what level? What mixture?
- What will it cost?
- Use of the results?
- Who will champion?

Looking outside the box

Many executives have a horror of their staff spending time outside their company, geographic region, industry or country. It smacks of time wasting spending unnecessarily, or simply diverting from the *real* job.

Traditionally benchmarking exercises were not encouraged, and those that did happen were either at executive level (an unchallengeable privilege) or with IT specialists, for example, where few professed to understand or challenge. The results of the former were rarely successful without follow-up because the 'Executive Tour' is inevitably short, only skin deep and in the nature of a PR exercise rather than investigative work. Apart from such exercises, most companies were naturally parochial.

As we have seen, the stimulus has been the Total Quality Movement and the culture change this has brought about within all sectors. It has created a common cause that companies can identify with, quite independent of competition. As referred to in Chapter 3, it can be encapsulated by the quotation of one of the suppliers in the North

East to Komatsu, who came to see me concerning the way we did things: 'We fish in the same labour pool as you do – how is it that you get so much more out of your people than we do?'. This quotation has become an oft-used symbol of benchmarking in the North of England. The quality theme that underpins the experience has been used to encourage widespread benchmarking between businesses and business sectors under the Quality North banner promoted by the Northern Development Company (successor to the North of England Development Corporation).

To overcome the natural inertia of parochialism, a catalyst is needed to show that the gains are there. The demonstration effect is powerful, but a commonality of experience must be shown. The biggest boundary historically is one of industrial sector. Traditionally, managements have shouted loudly that *our* industry is different – bigger problems, other industries are irrelevant or unhelpful. Add to this the horror of dealing in detail with the competition and you are frozen in aspic.

All industries employ people; labour costs have risen; manning levels have become an issue of the 1980s. Quality has moved from specialist assurance and control to the impact people can have in quality improvement. The concept of labour has moved from command and control of compliant hands to using the intelligence of the whole system; to use a succinct phrase: 'With every pair of hands you get a free brain'.

'With every pair of hands you get a free brain'.

Further, for world-class companies the global village has become true. They are part of an integrated system of global manufacture, sourcing components on a variable basis dependent on exchange rates, quality outcomes, raw material and labour costs. Their suppliers are integrated, not at arm's length and, maybe for some, benchmarking starts here.

Learning from within the supplier chain

The change here has been particularly rapid. Ten years ago talking to suppliers was taboo in manufacturing – and it is still so in utilities and many sectors of public service. It was questionable because it could be seen to interfere with the contracting process – giving the inside track to preferred suppliers and stopping the free market. The EC Utilities Directive, effective from January 93, would seem to discourage privatised utilities in the UK from intimate relationships with suppliers. Yet to rely on contractual negotiations and arm's length monitoring to give synergy is totally inadequate in world-class terms. Manufacturing has embraced this; the service and public sectors have yet to become as flexible.

The best example of how this works comes from Japan, where Komatsu suppliers belong to a club called the Midori Kai, which meets collectively with their main customer (Komatsu) at regular intervals to understand the changing demands made on the business overall, how the suppliers can help, and indeed how Komatsu can help suppliers. With Komatsu as the catalyst in organising mutual 'swops' of information, visits between firms are arranged, and once a year a worldwide tour of plants outside Japan and *their* suppliers is arranged (with the usual dose of frenetic sightseeing and photography thrown in!).

The result is one of integration and responsiveness. Adversarial stances and bouts of arm wrestling at contract renewal time are avoided, since with 'open book' costing and frequent visits on the basis of mutual help, the bottom line for all parties is known.

Few have reached this intimacy outside Japan. Japanese subsidiaries in Europe and the USA have made a start. With Komatsu and Nissan in the UK, Supplier Development teams have been active for some years. Here the benefits of benchmarking have been for the supplier, with most of the learning on a one-way basis, because of the customer's more advanced development in quality, costing and people systems.

Improvements can benefit customers, suppliers and sometimes the competition. In the early days of Komatsu UK, purchasing specialists discovered a well-made, economical cab heater in the UK for supply to the UK plant, which was then used as an imported component to Japan for assembly into Japanese-built machines and was then further marketed via the trading company to competitors in Japan. Why help competitors in this way? Answer: the greatly increased volumes mean lower unit costs in the longer term.

Another initiative was to organise visits to Japan for suppliers of the UK plant. Such was the interest that the suppliers paid their way, with the hosts in Japan finding the entertainment and escort costs. It was an important confidence booster, as the universal conclusion by the suppliers was 'there is nothing that their suppliers do in Japan that we could not achieve at home'.

Is it a necessary prerequisite to have the Japanese example and stimulus? Thank goodness, no. A home-grown example of mutual exchange was the Supply Chain Training Initiative of British Steel which commenced in 1990. The concept was for joint training of managers whose only link was to work for a company involved in a supply chain for British Steel. In 1992, British Steel won a National Training Award for this pioneering work.

The chains set up were:

British Steel Plates Teesside Mill	British Steel Tin Plate	British Steel Strip Products
↓	↓	↓
Steel Stockholders	Carnaud Metal Box	Rover Group
↓	↓	↓
Komatsu	Nestlé	Mann Egerton

Managers from each company joined a workshop that stimulated further benchmarking exercises.

The last point concerns the power of benchmarking to put across messages. I recall a series of incidents in the early days of Komatsu UK when a supplier of profiled (i.e. cut) plate continued to deliver out-of-tolerance pieces despite the usual feedback, complaints and emotion generated at a high level. It became apparent that even with clear messages, the critical nature of dimensions was not understood at shop floor level. On the advice of a Japanese expatriate, the Komatsu UK Quality Circle from the fabrication shop, made up of Geordie welders, visited the suppliers' plant to discover that their 'colleagues' knew the plate was destined for a 'big machine', therefore 'out of tolerance' must be acceptable because components could be 'made to fit'. The situation did not recur.

> . . . the Komatsu UK Quality Circle from the fabrication shop, made up of Geordie welders, visited the suppliers of profiled plate concerning out of tolerance deliveries. The fault did not recur.

Staff development as a by-product

It may not be the prime objective, but participation in a benchmarking exercise can accelerate the development of people in an unprecedented way. Staff become ambassadors for the company overnight. Responsibility for representing externally can be thrust upon relatively junior levels on return. Parochialism and the 'confined box' can be converted into apostledom without a blinding flash of light. With time, the whole organisation can become outward looking from an introspective past.

Examples of benchmarking exercises

Komatsu UK
The experience of benchmarking was unusually widespread, but relatively unstructured. Teamworking, Quality Circles and supplier chain contacts encouraged the stimulus for benchmarking down the organisation on a continuous improvement basis. This meant that Quality Circles often at their own instigation set up benchmarking exercises with available contacts, starting inside the company and extending to relevant examples outside. A Quality Circle facilitator provided networks, sharing of information and encouragement. In purchasing, the regular meetings with the 'family' of suppliers gave opportunities for comparing best practice.

Quality North Campaign – Northern Development Company
In 1989 I was asked to speak at the Great North conference on Quality on the process of implementing Total Quality at Komatsu UK based on the system developed from three decades of experience in Komatsu worldwide. At the time, I had also been involved in the establishment of Tyneside TEC and we had determined that Quality was to be our central theme. The North was in many ways a Quality region and I suggested to the then Marketing Director of the Northern Development Company, David Williams, at this event that I could lay down a challenge to the North to become the Quality North, encouraging its business to adopt Total Quality both within and between its partners. He readily agreed. He wrote a paper for the Newcastle University Conference on Total Quality in 1993. I will let him take up the story:[23]

'I had never heard of Total Quality Management four years ago. It sneaked up and surprised me during a conference under the Great North banner at Wynyard Hall in 1989. I would not describe my conversion in terms of a flash of blinding light; rather it was a roll of drums and a crash of cymbals. What stirred within me belonged less to the spirit of Saint Paul than to the coarser grain of Phineas T Barnum. I was inspired by the thought that this quality thing was a great marketing opportunity.'

'Just as many companies – perhaps most – who strive for accreditation to BS 5750 do so because it will look good on the letterhead, so I felt I could use the "quality" tag in my task of promoting the Northern region. I suppose it was a typical marketing man's response. In advertising, where mediocre claims to excellence are an everyday phenomenon, the word 'quality' has been debased by over-use. In this case, however, I felt we could add substance to the claim, as some Northern companies seemed to be ahead of the game in quality management. For example, in 1989 all three winners of the British Quality Awards – ICI, British Steel and 3M – were located in the region. We were also rapidly gaining a reputation as the preferred European location for Japanese industry (in fact, by 1993 over 50 Japanese companies had settled in the North East) and it was clear the Japanese were setting the pace in TQM, not only for themselves but for their suppliers.'

'What struck me was the opportunity this provided to position the region as a quality leader in international terms, to "badge" it distinctively with a quality branding, and to underline the clear competitive advantage to be enjoyed by a business locating here among such illustrious company.'

'It looked like a firm basis for a marketing campaign, until market research suggested otherwise. We conducted a survey among Northern firms at the end of 1989 which asked them about their commitment to quality and teased out evidence about actual quality practices. As words cost no effort, commitment was in the high nineties, but it was not generally reflected by positive action, which sat in the low forties. The region had further to go than I imagined.'

Thereafter, the slogan for Quality North was developed by major employers who benchmarked amongst themselves: 'Think Quality; Deliver Quality; Promote Quality'. The campaign was launched in June 1990; 2,000 organisations were involved by the end of 1992;

3,000 by the end of 1993. Benchmarking was encouraged in delivering quality.

Year 3 Flagship Projects included:

- Quality Benchmarks
- Quality Improvement Exchange
- Partners in Quality
- Supplier Chain Initiative
- Quality North Open to View

All examples of benchmarking have been extracted from the wide range of activities.

One of the most significant developments is the Quality Improvement Exchange, which has established a team of regional facilitators (Quality Champions within their own organisations) to promote inter-company exchange visits by improvement teams. Komatsu UK were one of the first to participate, and now Northern Electric is an enthusiastic supporter. The scheme provides the opportunity for existing teams to learn and report on initiatives that can be used in their own workplace, and to encourage new improvement groups.

So what are the tangible results from all this? In terms of formal quality accreditation, the region has made significantly more progress over the last two years than any other region in the UK (source DTI of UK government). It has certainly raised the perception – 93 per cent of top managers in the North are now operating or developing TQM processes. In another report, the CBI has shown that Northern UK companies are better managed than their Southern counterparts!

Northern Electric

Northern Electric is one of twelve regional electricity companies within England and Wales, and its main business, the supply and distribution of electricity, is regulated by the Director of Electricity Supply through the Office of Electricity Regulation (OFFER).

Northern Electric plc was floated as a privatised company in 1990 after a period of forty-three years as the nationalised North Eastern Electricity Board. The company currently purchases electricity from generators via the National Grid and supplies it to over 3 million people in an area of 5,600 square miles stretching from York in the south to Berwick in the north. There are nearly 1.5 million customers, turnover from all sources is £1bn, and the company employs just under 5,000 people. A separate retail business with over fifty high street shops and superstores sell a wide range of domestic electrical goods and provides a point of contact for customers of the main business.

Northern Electric also has interests in other related businesses, the main areas being a 15 per cent share in Teesside Power, a new gas-fired power station on Teesside, and a 10 per cent share in Ionica, a recently formed telecommunications company as well as Gas (R&P) J.V. with Neste Oy, the Finnish State oil company.

I was appointed Director of Personnel in 1992 and took over among other things, the Quality Improvement Programme, which had been running for over two years.

The relevance to benchmarking lies partly with the link with the Northern Development Company Quality Improvement Exchange. There are other aspects, particularly in the area of electricity supply, where Northern Electric regularly benchmarks on a worldwide basis with utilities in the USA, Japan, Australia and elsewhere, usually based on technology, customer service standards and information technology. The benefit to Northern Electric of the Quality Improvement Exchange has been for the local Quality Work Groups (similar to Quality Circles) to gain confidence and encouragement from similar groups, often in unrelated industries. They have found similar objectives in other companies to those at the heart of the Quality Improvement Programme:

- improving levels of customer service
- providing a focus on customer needs
- increasing efficiency by improving systems and reducing waste
- assisting the development of a new culture
- helping create market leadership

They have found similar problems and solutions in the introduction and energising of such initiatives. By benchmarking with other companies from other sectors, Northern Electric Quality Work Groups have 'plugged into' solutions that would otherwise not have been obvious, and thus gained important infectious enthusiasm.

> One sceptical participant in a Northern Electric benchmarking team suddenly discovered how real the support was when she compared her experience with the paucity of help available to other companies benchmarked.

Gateshead Hospitals NHS Trust

Gateshead Hospitals comprises Queen Elizabeth and Bensham Hospitals, a 487-bed district general hospital offering acute and rehabilitation services with a turnover of £35m and 2,000 staff.

Team building weekends for Executive and Non-executive Directors early on led to the establishment of project teams. One of these has had the task of linking with a 'first wave' trust – the South Tees Acute NHS Trust – to benchmark on their progress on Total Quality.

One of the main benefits of the NHS reforms is the opportunity given to hospitals to create a corporate and unified approach. Quality has its role in this, and to match with a pioneering example is clearly important.

Although it is as yet still early in the life of the Gateshead Hospitals NHS Trust, there is little doubt that our approach to Total Quality at Gateshead will be based on such benchmarking exercises, and as a by-product it ensures that Non-executives, Executives and specialist staff link together on the development of strategy and policy formulation.

Keeping it going

Continuous improvement is never-ending, as should be the search for new solutions. Benchmarking is not only here to stay, but will be the key to energising more and more of the productive workforce.

NOTES

1. J. Womack, D. Jones and D. Roos, *The Machine that Changed the World*, Rawson Assoc., 1990.
2. Ibid., p. 228.
3. W. Lewchuck, *American Technology and the British Car Industry*, Cambridge University Press, 1988, p. 157.
4. Womack, Jones and Roos, op. cit., pp. 250–1.
5. N. Oliver and B. Wilkinson *The Japanization of British Industry*, Basil Blackwell, 1992, pp. 84, 88, 277.
6. Womack, Jones and Roos, op. cit., p. 99.
7. J. Nirenberg, 'Understanding the failure of Japanese Management Abroad', *The Journal of Managerial Psychology*, 1987.
8. T. Burns and G.M. Stalker, *Management of Innovation*, Tavistock Publications, 1961.

9. C. Handy, *Understanding Organisations*, Penguin, 1976.
10. Joan Woodward, *Industrial Organisation*, Oxford University Press, 1965.
11. Nirenberg, op. cit.
12. See Michael Hammer and James Champy, 'Bell Atlantic Experience', *Re-engineering the Corporation*, Nicholas Brealey, 1993.
13. Ibid., p. 169 – Hallmark Cards Experience.
14. Ibid., p. 145.
15. W. Ouchi, *Theory Z: How American business can meet the Japanese challenge*, Boston, Addison-Wesley, 1981.
16. Oliver and Wilkinson, op. cit., p. 100.
17. Womack Jones and Roos, op. cit., p. 237.
18. Ibid., p. 238.
19. Masaaki Imai, *Kaizen*, McGraw-Hill, 1986.
20. P. Berwick, A. Godfrey and J. Roessmer, *Curing Health Care*, Jossey-Bass, 1990, pp. 18–19.
21. Ibid. p. 46.
22. Womack, Jones and Roos, op. cit. p. 240.
23. J.F.L. Chan (ed.) *First Newcastle International Conference on Quality and its Applications*, Penshaw Press, 1993, p. 53.

5 What is 'World Class'?

This is not a case of just going and working for a foreign company. This is a case of assisting a foreign company to have a base in the UK which will, in fact, revolutionize the attitudes in British industry. If it doesn't then I don't believe we [the British] have an industrial future.[1]

WHAT IS 'WORLD CLASS'?

What does a 'world-class' company look like? What is our measure? Is it just a showpiece? Does it guarantee success?

In Japan, the measure has been the Deming Award; in the USA, the Malcolm Baldridge Award; in Europe, the EFQM Award. Not all winners of such prizes have subsequently been commercially successful. The majority of the successful companies in Tom Peters's work *In Search of Excellence* in the early 1980s are now out of business or in deep trouble. Similarly, in the UK, winners of the Queen's Award for Export and for Technology often seem as vulnerable to market failure as also-rans or non-entries. This much is clear: awards do not guarantee commercial success. Clearly, if the award has synergy with business purpose, then it can be helpful. If it amounts to a deflection from the corporate purpose, it can even be counterproductive.

So is it possible to conclude what the features of a 'world-class' company are?

As acknowledged in Chapter 1, *quality* has to be the entry point for world-class companies. It has to be the qualification for entering the competition – not an end in itself. Achieving it, however, leads on to other features of world-class companies to which we will return in this chapter.

In the long term, *cost* is not exchangeable for quality. More and more consumers expect high quality *and* low cost – not as previously, when it was universally accepted in the West that quality cost more. The systems detailed in Chapter 6 show that quality can be achieved without increasing cost – and often, in fact, *lowering* cost can be combined with improving quality, providing another entry point for meeting the competition.

Delivery on time is now a minimum acceptable level. The insistence by Japanese implants of JIT performance from European suppliers came as a shock to indigenous companies in the 1980s and their achievement was a severe disappointment to the Japanese (see PSI study, Chapter 7). There is little doubt that the majority of Western industry still operates on the 'buffer stock' principle masking dysfunction in a 'sea of inventory' (see Fig. 6.9 on p. 156). Thus, for long-term survival, industry in Europe and the USA has to regard delivery on time as another entry point.

Continuous Improvement is both a means to achieving:

- High Quality
- Low Cost
- Delivery on Time

and to advancing beyond the 'entry points' towards increasing market share; higher profitability, achieving customer 'delight'; and long-term viability.

What is the key to continuous improvement? As in Chapters 2 and 6, Step Change has its place in increasing competitiveness, but continuous improvement is vital for an inbuilt momentum for effective change. This cannot be achieved without individual and team motivation.

What policies do world-class companies pursue to achieve the necessary contribution from employees? My conclusion is that they need to:

1 *Ensure mission, vision, values and objectives* for the company are dovetailed into individual and team plans and objectives. (See Policy Deployment Chapters 3 and 6).

2 *Ensure effective communication* throughout the organisation. This goes beyond a cascade of management information to efficient feedback from employees and, importantly, *across* the organisation – breaking down the 'silo factor', which usually militates against horizontal links. This policy usually has synergy with product development or cross-functional project working to give such non-functional structures purpose.

3 *Establish systems to consult widely* before taking decisions and to 'demonstrate' the use of employees' views in the end result. In Japan, the twin systems of 'Nemawashi' and 'Ringi' (described in Chapter 2) ensure thoroughness, albeit in a ponderous, undy-

namic way, thus giving the feeling of 'drift' and not management control. The contrast with the West is stark.

Brian Johnson, Purchasing Executive of Toyota MUK, has said: '[In Europe] it was ten minutes to make the decision, ten to implement it and three months to correct it. In Toyota there's three months' discussions, ten minutes to approve it and no time correcting it.'[2] In the same way that the combination of continuous improvement and Step Change can give the West a competitive edge, so a marriage of consensus with focused decision-making can again supply 'the best of both worlds'.

4   *Encourage equal opportunity.* Much of the achievement at Komatsu UK was to uncover the hidden potential among employees who felt there was no real future. There are four dimensions to this:
   (a) ensure selection and promotion decisions are both fair and seen to be fair;
   (b) demonstrate that the company is running a meritocracy and that excellent performance is recognised;
   (c) encourage development by getting employees close to their managers, so that the overall relationship is jointly examined – not just the process of task giving and achieving;
   (d) promote equal opportunity in training by self-analysis, manager nomination and open learning. In short, a lifelong learning culture.

5   *Defeat the 'vertical progression is good: horizontal moves are bad' syndrome.* During my early career as a civil engineer in the fast-moving construction scene in the 1960s, project managers expected to be promoted, or given larger jobs to manage, every eighteen months or so. Being 'moved sideways' or into another function was often viewed as failure or being put into a 'graveyard slot'.

With today's flat structures in companies, vertical progression is less available and, further, management needs to be broader based in terms of skills and experience. Horizontal development must now be seen as the norm, not the exception or the avoidable.

The blue-collar equivalent is the issue of multi-skilling. Here again, traditional defences are raised – are craft skills being watered down; are we producing a 'jack of all trades' who masters nothing? Resistance is due to the fear of losing security. World-class companies need to tackle the underlying fear and to demonstrate that multi-skilling enhances job opportunities and gives alternatives rather than lessening security.

6 *Create a new role for management.* Much has been devoted to the need for empowerment of the shop floor. Total Quality and Lean Production all enhance 'bottom up' contribution. The new role of the supervisor has been recognised, and many see the revolution in contribution at this level as the key for further progress in companies that aspire to be world class.[3] Teamworking further integrates the supervisor and teams. This progress at the bottom end of 'flattened' organisations increases responsibility and self-management, but conversely leaves 'middle management' nervous and insecure – what is their contribution meant to be? Many of them were promoted to the position on the basis of technical qualifications and experience, only to find that they are primarily expected to be responsible for motivating those they manage when previously this was the province of the personnel specialist!

In *Managing Managers* by Snape, Redman and Bamber, the authors show that this group has suffered from 'benign neglect':

> Thus the manager's role is being transformed, particularly for those at middle management level. The new role places greater emphasis on leadership, teambuilding, and the development and motivation of staff. Increasingly, managers are being expected to take greater responsibility for H.R. issues, including appraisal, development and rewards. All this demands new skills, many of them concerned with the management of people, rather than with technical production-related matters.[4]

Apart from the forces tending to cause the decline in middle management, the authors point to the counter-argument that a new role is being found in some companies where such managers are empowered themselves as a result of new technology, devolved authority and the encouragement of entrepreneurial risk taking.

'Managers were walking the halls asking: "What is my job?"'
'I can count on one hand the number of executives who have adopted a new style of empowerment' (James Champy).

James Champy, co-author of *Re-engineering the Corporation*, talks of re-engineering middle management:

> I recently visited a company that had structured its work around self-managed process teams. Managers were walking the halls asking: 'What is my job?'
>
> The answer is that it is nothing like the job they had before. No more close supervision of workers, no more focus on data irrelevant to running the business, no more energy spent on defending turf. The role of managers becomes one of empowerment – providing workers with the information, training, authority and accountability to excel in a re-engineered business process . . .
>
> . . . Managers periodically must inspect the work, measure the performance of the process and its contributors, and coach the workers to even better performance . . .
>
> . . . Managerial styles. Shedding the traditional 'command and control' model for one of 'lead and enable' is proving a difficult transition for most managers. Many continue to bark orders and micro-manage people in whom they have vested new decision-making authority. *I can count on one hand the number of executives who have adopted a new style of empowerment. . . .*
>
> . . . In this new team environment, behavioural knowledge and skills become crucial.
>
> Successful managers will be masters at getting people to work effectively together, managing conflict and being effective coaches. Knowledge of the content of the job is no longer the overriding requisite for promotion.[5]

Other research shows the middle management group to be critical to success. In a recent research paper, Nick Oliver[6] surveyed fifty-three Japanese manufacturers operating in the UK in the early 1990s and the results were compared with an earlier survey in the mid-1980s. He concludes that the manufacturers were less optimistic today about the potential success of Japanese management practices in the UK than they were in the earlier survey. Employee diligence and differences in 'ways of thinking' between Japanese and local employees were the most frequently cited internal problems. The problem of differences in 'ways of thinking' centred mainly on British middle management not understanding or not being understood by their Japanese counterparts and superiors. While not knowing the internal problems of the companies surveyed, I would conclude that this is very similar to the 'culture gap' that we discovered in Komatsu between British and Japanese managers (see Chapter 3).

The Japanese ambassador to Britain, Mr Hiroshi Kitamura, has commented recently on the performance of British managers in a competitive world:

> In order to combine science with technology, and technology with innovation, it is important to promote people to top management with a thorough understanding of technology. . . . He had detected 'something of a shortfall in middle management'. . . .
> The development of human resources in this stratum of management is surely of critical importance in boosting corporate competitiveness.[7]

Japanese implants are not guaranteed success, for Japanese management practices are not automatically absorbed by Western employees. Failure is usually associated with Western managers not understanding or adopting the new role and, equally, Japanese managers not facilitating such changes. In my experience, it takes a great deal of time and patience because the cultures are so far apart (see Chapter 2). I do not conclude, however, that it is unachievable – indeed, many successful examples show that it both does work and can be made to work.

CULTURE CHANGE

It is clear from this analysis, regardless of whether we are talking of green field sites with strong Japanese input or existing Western companies in manufacturing or services sectors, that to achieve world-class performance a major culture shift is required to ensure that change happens at *all* levels.

The issue of culture change being crucial for the successful adoption of world-class systems is supported by Oliver and Wilkinson.[8] The following table from their 1991 survey, illustrates the obstacles to change in UK companies.[9]

Culture and its change is in the hands of management. I argue that obstacles 1, 3, 5 and 7 can be aggregated to show that in this survey 60 per cent of the obstacles for removal lie in management's court, and it is up to management to persuade for the rest!

> Culture and its change is in the hands of managers . . . 60 per cent of the obstacles are in management's court, and it is up to management to persuade for the rest!'

Obstacles to change in UK companies

		Number of citations as:			
		First Obstacle	Second Obstacle	Third Obstacle	% of Total
1	Existing culture	17	–	–	27
2	Unions/demarcation	6	3	–	14
3	Lack of support at senior levels	7	2	–	14
4	None	8	–	–	13
5	Attitudes of middle management	4	2	1	11
6	Attitudes of labour	–	3	2	8
7	Lack of Resources/ Investment	3	2	–	8
8	Technical Constraints	2	1	–	5
		(47)	(13)	(3)	(100)

NORTHERN ELECTRIC – A CASE STUDY IN CULTURE CHANGE

In Chapter 4, Charles Handy's work on changing cultures was referred to and the need to ensure that the framework of *formal relationships* was effective (for instance, between the company and the unions representing the employees); also, the *face-to-face relationships* between people were looked at. This highlighted the importance of teams, team roles and team building.

When I arrived at Northern Electric a Quality Improvement Process had been in place for nearly two years, so the language of quality was known – the focus was much more on the customer and 'getting it right first time' following the Crosby pattern. However, culture had not markedly changed from the days of public ownership and quality exhortation was seen as very much 'top down'.

Putting a strategy in place

My starting point was to establish and gain top down commitment to strategy for employee relations, and to link the company mission statement and values to the results we needed in terms of flexibility and multi-skilling.

The starting point: Northern Electric mission statement

'Northern Electric's mission is to achieve high standards of service and efficiency, and to operate our business in an enterprising and innovative manner so as to create value for our shareholders, customers and employees.'

Company values – already established by the Northern Electric Board of Directors

- Quality
- Caring Concern
- Efficiency
- Innovation
- Teamworking
- Integrity
- Enterprise

With this material as a foundation we went through a process involving management and unions to establish the following:

Employee Relations Strategy Statement

'Northern Electric's future depends on the contribution of all employees focusing on continuous improvement and on our ability to work as a team.

'We are committed to an open management style with the aim of producing the best informed, trained and motivated team to satisfy our mission statement.'

This Employee Relations Strategy was then set against the company values as set out above:

QUALITY
- Aim to achieve culture change through full participation in the Quality Improvement Process

CARING CONCERN
- Aim to achieve mutual trust and common interest
- Aim for mutual understanding and respect for the individual
- Caring approach to employees
- Openness in communication

EFFICIENCY
- Staff need to understand the demands on Northern Electric and can take advantage of the opportunities provided for the company
- Aim to reach a culture that motivates staff where achievement is valued and rewarded
- Training and development of staff is vital to improve the performance of the individual and the team
- Openness in communication

INNOVATION
- Aim to use talent and initiative as well as skills and experience

TEAMWORKING
- Our aims as a team are to:
    provide customer satisfaction
    achieve growth in profit
    give a sound investment for shareholders

INTEGRITY
- Equal opportunity to obtain the best match for Northern Electric and the individual
- High standards in safety and preventative health care
- Northern Electric respects the right of employees to belong to trade unions. We will provide necessary facilities for recognised trade unions to represent members' interests

ENTERPRISE
- Managers will be accountable to the Executive for their performance in managing people. Managers' aims will be to develop the strength and commitment of their teams

Company bargaining

Having agreed this strategy, the next task was to get the *formal relationships'* right. Post-privatisation, the regional electricity com-

panies took the opportunity to leave nationally bargained arrangements and set their sights on achieving locally negotiated agreements
with the recognised trade unions. At Northern Electric we were
considerably more ambitious, and aimed at attaining a 'single
table' agreement combining the status quo of the three existing
arrangements – one for industrial staff (electricians, fitters, etc.),
one for clerical and professional grades, and one for power engineers.
The logic being that we had one opportunity to produce a focus in the
agreement on the company and staff as a whole, enabling the
elimination of barriers in the future.

The four main existing trade unions were keen to see a single table
approach to local negotiations, and so began the long drawn-out
process of dovetailing three sets of elaborate and detailed terms and
conditions into one new local agreement.

From a pay viewpoint, the key issue was to assimilate the overlapping grading structures into one to enable greater flexibility, easier
progression, removing barriers, and the labels of distinction between
employees. Also, the opportunity was taken to buyout inappropriate
payments.

To communicate or not to communicate

We thought the process would take about six months. However, the
difficulty and length of the negotiations over the following eighteen
months showed how ambitious we had been! The disparity between
planned and actual length of negotiation caused acute problems in
communication. With an intensive period of six months in prospect,
we agreed with the trade unions at the outset that it was wise to ban
communication to employees while ideas and substance were fluid,
and only to inform when something solid was agreed – preferably at
the end. This turned out to be a mistake. First, the negotiations
became protracted since various groups were being asked to yield
long-held privileges and benefits, and secondly, when we were able to
communicate, both the company and the unions found staff difficult
to convince because they had been left out of the formative argument
that had gone on for months. 'Why change?' was the response, 'the
company is doing well'.

Changing attitudes

I found changes in the attitudes of both the management and union
teams were the first things that needed to be achieved. They had been

used to the highly formalised arrangements at national level, where they were supporters and implementers of long-winded set-piece negotiations. Now we had to *explore* jointly with the trade unions locally, without restrictive frameworks, what were the right solutions for both company and employees. Their zenith was in terms of discipline – the serried ranks of employers and unions lined either side of a long table when only one of each side would speak on behalf of the rest (most outcomes having been determined in the corridor beforehand!).

I felt we could make no progress like that. At the first opportunity we broke both phalanxes into working parties or teams to come up with solutions to specific areas. At first, all four unions wanted to be in on every team; also, management distrusted the idea of delegation, fearing loss of control. Over a period of months the policy worked, although the tensions between the unions stayed right through to the end with the inevitable ghost of unions competing for membership peering over the shoulder.

A new role for middle management

When we finally communicated to staff, a break with the past was also required. The pattern of communicating change had been for a Board director known to employees to address mass meetings to ensure credibility and a degree of trust. Small wonder that middle management felt it had no role in communicating over key issues. These managers were to be the 'New Communicators'. They were all briefed on the substance of the agreement and I gave them, without penalty, the option of not selling the agreement if they were not convinced themselves – none declined, but many appreciated the choice.

They then briefed staff twice on the need for change and the agreement, and also saw each individual who had queries. Our problem was that the agreement was supported by only two unions out of four. However, having gained the support at ballot of the two unions representing the majority of staff, the remainder conceded as a result of time and persuasion.

The lesson for me was reinforcement of the knowledge that middle managers must play their part in such communication, owning the message, and that the process gives them a major boost in confidence with, moreover, confirmation of a critical role.

A joint commitment

That such a pioneering agreement was achieved was in no small part due to the commitment of the Chairman of the trade union side, David Harrison of the AEEU, in holding often disparate factions together, and also a result of the support I received from the negotiating team.

Northern Electric employees are now on the new arrangements, which involve working much more flexible hours to suit customer needs.

Costs are likely to reduce as flexibility and teamworking increase. Vitally, the agreement is a flagship to enable and facilitate change in other ways throughout the organisation.

Organisational development

The second task was to tackle the 'face-to-face' relationships between people in the organisation. A process of 'Organisational Development' was started by Tony Hadfield, then Managing Director, which was to be totally different from the bi-annual reorganisations to which Northern Electric and its predecessors had been accustomed. These previous reorganisations had been typically 'structural' – purely changing reporting links responsibilities, office and depot locations, and so on. Tony Hadfield knew that we also had to change values and 'processes' as well as the knee-jerk reaction of altering the organisation chart. The theme was *consultation, listening* and *evolution*. This meant changing the way work was tackled – moving away from a sequential operation to project teams and a great deal more flexibility. Multi-skilling and teamwork is easier to achieve with blue-collar workers – here, though, we were tackling the bastion of professionalism among the white-collar staff. As successive government ministers have found, the more intelligent and qualified their staff are, the more difficult it is to weld them into teams and to break down barriers that have been erected to protect!

Experiential learning

We determined on a process of self-discovery. With the help of external consultants – John Redpath and Kelvin Cox of CPCR in Newcastle – we started to use a culture questionnaire (designed by Roger Harrison) at Executive level and then progressively down the organisation. This questionnaire is based on Charles Handy's work

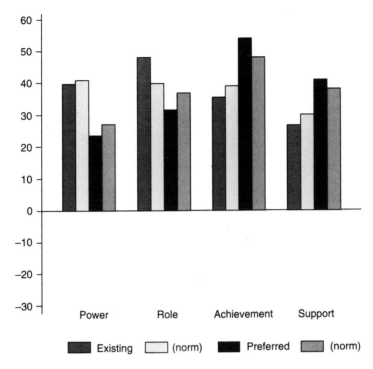

Fig. 5.1 *Northern Electric plc: Organisation Culture*

(see Chapter 4), a self-analysis of where the organisation culture is seen to be and of where individuals would wish it to be. From this, a pattern emerges. (See Fig. 5.1 for results and Appendix II for an explanation of the elements of culture.)

What culture?

Northern Electric is typical of most bureaucratic organisations in that 'power' and 'role' are seen as dominant and again, typically, employees of whatever level wish to see a diminution of these two preferences towards 'achievement' and 'support' (for definitions, see Appendix II). It is easy to explain existing culture in that, in the public sector, accountability ultimately to a Secretary of State engendered a 'power' preference; and in electricity supply, where it is vital to follow set-down procedures for safety reasons, 'role' is clearly highly valued. Post-privatisation and with more emphasis on individual and team contribution, recognition and reward is expected, and the shift in terms of aspiration to 'achievement' and 'support' is healthy.

As we worked down the organisation and included lay trade union representatives, the astonishment grew that aspirations at each level were broadly the same as those of senior management and the Executive. At the same time, individuals were encouraged to participate in further self-analysis that they could share with their colleagues. This time it concerned personality questionnaires or well-validated psychometric tests such as the Myers-Briggs Type Indicator (MBTI) and Cattell's 16PF (Personality Factors leading to Belbin roles). Participants were successively asked to form their own project teams in workshop conditions using such new-found knowledge, and discovered that the two dimensions they were used to from the past – qualifications and experience needed the third dimension of preferred team roles and personality factors to define competences and accurately predict that the team would work together effectively and produce results.

Engineers, who previously did not regard themselves as managers, suddenly produced joint solutions to live commercial projects that their bosses were still tussling with! Similarly, a degree of realism emerged from trade union representatives that astonished senior management. The realism was there anyway, of course – what was released was a commercial focus, teamwork and better *communication*.

The Lewin model for change

The last catalyst for change used in development workshops was the Lewin model[10] applied to the Northern Electric Change Effort. The model shown in Table. 5.1, setting a matrix of the need for a transition over time of 'unfreezing' the organisation, 'moving', and subsequently 'refreezing' to ensure a new culture was embedded against levels affected, such as *individual, systems* and *climate* (Table 5.2). I used the same formula to map past, current and planned changes in Northern Electric to form our own matrix. This was useful in a number of ways. First, because the process of change was clearer in separate phases over time and the various change programmes could be seen in context and they formed a logical pattern – those affecting individuals; structures and systems; and climate and culture.

The last is vital. Change in culture must underpin other changes, for otherwise employees see change as a threat rather than an

Table 5.1 *Lewin's change model: unfreezing the organisation*

Levels of change	*What is meant*	*Unfreezing*	*Movement*	*Refreezing*
Individuals	Skills, values and attitudes	Reductions in numbers Development Involvement	Demonstrate new skills New supervision	Make behaviour patterns secure against change Commitment in line with new values
Structure and systems	Pay systems Reporting relationships Work design	New agreements Experiential training programmes	Changes in reward systems Reporting relationships	Ensure delivery supports rhetoric Performance appraisal
Climate or culture	Openness Conflict management Decision-making	Providing feedback on employees' views	More trust and openness	Committed to use databased feedback on climate and management practices

Table 5.2 *Applying Lewin's model to Northern Electric Change Effort*

Levels	Unfreezing 1991–3	Movement 1993–6	Refreezing 1995 onwards
Individual	Downsizing of workforce Change in management team Mission statement and values Customer-driven aims	Personnel and others as change agents New team leader roles 'Colleague' style Performance appraisal to link corporate and individual aims	Make behavioural patterns secure
Structures and systems	Use of project teams OD concepts ABB/ABM introduction	Single-table agreement Project management – OD Experiential training – ODW Reduction in layers – OD Total logistics **ABB/ABM**	Ensure delivery supports words
Climate/Interpersonal style	Redefining of the business (Customer-driven, not pass the costs on) Quality Improvement Process Communication improvements Top management commitment OD consultation	Communicate and convince Match agendas Employees 'own' company aims Top down to bottom up Feedback on staff views and participation Demonstrate change from the top	Identity – new Workwear for staff? Continued use of databased feedback on climate and management practices

opportunity, often because the context is not understood. Many companies appear to follow a 'flavour of the month' approach to change, and multiple initiatives do not seem linked or within a logical pattern. This leads to loss of confidence and changes often reach saturation level.

We were reaching saturation point in 1993, but the use of the Lewin model helped us put the myriad projects into context and showed the overall pattern, with the vital issue of culture change underpining everything.

As I left Northern Electric, this process was still continuing, with its designed outcome aimed at achieving the culture change necessary to achieve the features of world-class companies highlighted at the beginning of this chapter.

GATESHEAD HOSPITALS NHS TRUST – A CASE STUDY IN THE PUBLIC SECTOR

The hospitals (Queen Elizabeth and Bensham) became an NHS Trust on 1 April 1993 under the well-publicised government reforms, making the Trust into a 'provider' unit of 487 beds with a full range of secondary care services designed to meet the needs of the Gateshead and surrounding districts' population (250,000).

It is still very early in the life of the Trust to be talking of substantial changes being achieved. However, the issues of culture change, quality approaches and performance improvement are just as valid as in Northern Electric or Komatsu.

There is certainly a 'creative crisis' in health care today that transcends national boundaries, as all countries struggle with aspirations of higher quality, demands on services, hyperinflation in drugs and other medical costs, while trying to contain public expenditure on health.

The biggest opportunity for 'provider' units under the UK reforms is to produce better care with similar resources through better management. For the first time they can achieve a corporate focus for the hospital. Previously, the focus was undiluted specialism where it was almost coincidental in which hospital the care was provided.

The various interest groups – doctors, nurses, administrators – have developed separate cultures in the health service to such a degree of dysfunction that this has only been overcome by the dedication of staff to patients on a vocational basis.

The new structures of Trust Boards, Clinical Directorates and Nurse Managers mean that a wider participation is possible in running the hospitals and in deciding on priorities with limited resources – just as in the Northern Electric example one quickly discovers that structural change is not enough. Process must be used to facilitate changed attitudes. We have discovered in Gateshead that a process of understanding and communicating the changing roles is fundamental. Clinical independence is deeply rooted in centuries of medical and surgical practice and the boundaries of a normal hierarchy did not exist – what has mattered has been the views of the Royal College and that of their peers. Modifying deference to the Royal College to accommodate the views of a new untried non-medical Trust Board is not a step to be taken lightly!

Similar tools towards team working, self-analysis and self-discovery are being used, as in Northern Electric, with very positive results. The policies associated with world-class companies pinpointed at the beginning of this chapter are just as valid aims for Gateshead Hospitals as for the manufacturing and service sectors.

The pivotal role of management change

The NEDC studies on the role of supervision (see Chapter 4) demonstrated the key role that supervision must play in achieving empowerment, teamwork and the 'bottom up' response at the production end of enterprises. There is little doubt that supervision has been an area of profound neglect in the past and that the potential for growth is enormous. However, as we recognised earlier in the chapter, acceleration for the first line supervisor can mean alienation for the middle manager already besieged by technology, delayering and lack of involvement. Snape, Redman and Bamber[11] point to the need for a new approach in managing the middle manager, and for them in turn to adopt the approach in managing their subordinates.

> Middle managers can make or break planned changes in culture by cynical attitudes, obsession with status, or simply acting as observers rather than full participants.

They point out that there is an implicit view in organisations that managers can look after themselves. They quote Longenecker and Gioia:

Senior managers seem typically to believe that managers are autonomous, self-starting and self-directing individuals, or they would not be managers – a belief that governs their approach to managing their managers. This belief also leads to dysfunctional attitudes such as 'benign neglect' and the 'let them sink or swim' mentality'.[12]

The elements of the new system of managing managers should embrace the 'HRM cycle' defined by Devanna, Fombrun and Tichy.[13] This has four 'generic functions':

Selection
Rewards
Appraisal
Development

Snape *et al.* concentrate on the application of the HRM cycle to managers, and that, I agree, is valid. I wish to pursue the logic further and postulate that this process can give a new role to managers that is proactive and formative in promoting change.

Just as supervisors are key in promoting TQM and empowerment at the 'sharp end', and can thwart these changes by not enthusiastically participating in teamwork, middle managers can make or break planned changes in culture by cynical attitudes, obsession with status, or simply acting as observers rather than full participants.

There is little doubt that if the 'HRM cycle' is applied genuinely to these managers and if they find it successful, then they will in turn use it to promote cultural change throughout the organisation.

SELECTION

Taking the 'HRM cycle' as defined, I do not propose to dwell on the issue of selection except for two issues. First, to advocate the use of validated psychometric tests operated and interpreted by professionals to help management get it right. These tests do not make the decisions: they *aid* the decision-making and give some (usually) very accurate prediction of preferred individual and team roles, and measures of performance. Because of the expense, a full battery of tests tend only to be used for higher-paid jobs, or at the final shortlist stage. At Komatsu and Northern Electric we obtained good results from a limited range of simple inexpensive tests that can be used more widely, such as 16PF, verbal, numerical and abstract reasoning tests. The most important step, in my view, is to make management comfortable in using the tools and to give appreciation knowledge so that the methods are valued and used to supplement judgement in selection, team building and development.

The second issue is to ensure management ownership in selection. This means involving all levels of management right down to first line supervisor in the process of recruitment. This will often be an unusual experience for them. I recall in the first four months after the Komatsu UK start-up recruiting supervisors, the majority of whom had previously been unemployed, and passing a mound of application forms for team leader positions to them on their first day. The reaction was one of astonishment. They had never been faced with such a task. In their previous experience, all that had been done by the Personnel Department!

This experience of first line supervision focusing on new competences is corroborated in Oliver and Wilkinson[14] who give a quotation from a team leader, in an unnamed company, who has been charged with recruiting operators into his team:

> I personally wasn't interested in what they'd done before. Obviously that came into it, but that wasn't what I was after. What I was after was people with the right attitudes . . . as I said to [the assistant personnel manager] you could almost forget the job spec. and write attitude . . . a guy came in for an interview and sat down and said, 'I've been with the company for 38 years, I'm not the fastest guy in the world and I'm not the best operator in the factory, and I never will be the best operator in the factory. But I tell you what – I'll do whatever you want me to do. I'll help you in every way I can. I'm always here. And I'm never late.' I said, 'You've got yourself a job'.

REMUNERATION, REWARDS AND RECOGNITION

One of the most controversial areas in human resource management is the issue of pay.

Does money motivate, or is it like providing a canteen – brickbats when it's wrong, silence when you have got it right? Are incentives helpful, or do they attack quality and raise costs?

Historical perspective

Remuneration yesterday had the theme of order and structure. At best, the policies were designed to produce a defensible situation, often on a national basis. Complicated grading structures emerged linked to highly defined job specifications, which over the passage of time led to inflexibility and pay related to qualifications and length of service. Increments happened just as long as the employee turned up for work and was still breathing. Such practice produced hierarchical pay structures. These did not reward performance, were inflexible, inflationary and still exist in many areas today.

For blue-collar workers, the same hierarchical structures did not exist but were often inflationary because of poorly managed incentive schemes or skill-based rewards, where individuals could accrue incremental pay rates unrelated to the task in hand. The failure of such nationally negotiated schemes in the building industry, for example, has led to wholesale labour only subcontracting with its attendant problems of quality, safety, control, lack of training and costs.

When tax rates were high imaginative fringe benefit schemes abounded, distorting pay structures and causing untold administrative complications. The theme was to attract, retain and motivate; rather than reward. The company car, pensions and canteen facilities are the long-term survivors from a Jurassic age, despite the persistent attacks on the first.

In the past we paid because we had to, the system was often unrelated to what was effective at local levels, and became inflexible and inflationary; in short, unsuitable for today's business.

Pressures on pay

Competitive pressures on business have pushed pay up the agenda – not for the old reasons of attraction and retention, but in relation to reducing costs and improving performance.

Payroll costs have become an increasing proportion of total costs. Outsourced materials and components have forced pay to have a higher focus as added value has fallen. Lean production techniques have put the spotlight on manufacturing costs. Overhead burdens have been isolated and seen as not value added – in line for eradication, subcontracting, or at least the subject of cost reduction. As manufacturing has declined and the service sectors have increased their proportion of the whole, payroll costs have become the dominant issue.

Many companies have redefined core activity with new concepts of who is permanent and on a pay structure, and who is on the fringe or temporary and dispensable. Career-related pay structures look outdated. Charles Handy talks of the Shamrock organisation with dispensable elements – a process of fragmentation rather than integration.

'Flattening' the organisation has become conventional wisdom if only in terms of desire to replace the old cumbersome hierarchical structure. Clearly, if layers are removed that saves cost; however, flatter structures can mean a different approach to remuneration. Pay structures can be released from the bondage of supporting incremental progression and better value for money can result.

Trends

In the 1990s we can view the pay question in a totally different context. The employment infrastructure is now so radically different. Replacing the acceptance of full employment as a goal from previous decades, we are now forced, whether we like it or not, to recognise that high levels of unemployment are here to stay in the industrialised West.

Economic cycles appear to be less under control by governments than ever they were. The recession in the early 1990s has been followed by a slow, patchy recovery, and fiscal policies today do not allow for the Keynesian philosophies of the past to hold sway in accelerating from the trough. The goal is, of course, maintaining low inflation. Low inflation, at last achieved, again puts the pay question in a different setting. For the first time almost in living memory, management have been able to ask, 'Why do we need an annual pay round? Do we need to increase pay at all?'

The added value of each employee now becomes the focus. The impact of quality programmes, Lean Production and re-engineering processes mean that the question of numbers and pay becomes central. But how is management able to differentiate? Subcontracting work out is simple, but this purely passes the nub question of policy over pay to someone else. For competitive advantage, the subcontractor has to solve the pay equation instead.

This trend has provided the focus on achievement and commitment by employees, giving a theory of convergence in personnel policies. Previously, appraisal systems were related to career development and setting up proper means of communications between managers and subordinates – both still valid stimuli. Now, though, to support an achievement and commitment culture, appraisals support pay policies and practice, giving the key to performance-related pay that can be truly individualised, defensible and not inflationary.

Along with flatter structures, the trend towards breaking down the barriers between employment groups continues with the 'holy grail' of single status being the goal for many. This again attacks hierarchical structures and demands few incremental differentials and a farewell to payments related to status quo as opposed to contribution.

The last significant trend is that of local pressures. This started as a political aim in the UK in the 1980s, but now has its place in conventional wisdom. Local bargaining is seen as better *per se* than national arrangements – more in touch with what is needed, facilitating local change, and – above all – cost effective. In short, giving value for money.

Opposing theories on pay

Does money motivate, or does it play a passive role? The debate has a tenacity that is unrivalled in the personnel field, and one that has not been deflected by changing management theories, styles and practice.

Typical opposing rhetorical questions that illustrate the polarised positions are:

- How else do you reward for good performance?
- How else can you ensure the targets for the individual are what the organisation needs?
- How else can you improve productivity and ensure value for money?

As opposed to:

- Would you work twice as hard as you do now if you were paid twice as much?
- Isn't the process of top down targets reinforcing command and control and the 'pleasing the boss' syndrome?
- Don't incentive schemes work against quality?

The theory of motivation tends to be against the concept of pay as a motivator – for example, McGregor's Theory X and Theory Y and the strongly held views of the late father of TQC, Dr Edwards Deming, that both appraisals and incentive-based pay work *against* producing good quality and lowering costs.

Yet the conventional wisdom is to move to performance-related pay more to attack the rigidities of the old hierarchical pay structures than anything else. It is seen as increasing insecurity of pay rather than actually rewarding.

Motivation

In truth we must see pay as a *recognition*, not a *reward*, and that it is only one of a large range of factors that contribute to employee motivation.

However, our managers, if they are to use pay to motivate by recognition, need to understand the arguments, participate in and promote the scheme that is in line with the culture and objectives of the organisation.

APPRAISAL

This is another controversial HRM tool for which there are as many advocates as doubters. However, the tide of opinion certainly favours appraisals as contributing in the following areas, which link back to many points on our list of policies for world-class companies at the beginning of this chapter:

- *Integration of mission, vision, values and objectives.* Appraisals, properly run, can ensure employees know of company business plans and can see how these policies reflect in their own personal and team objectives. (See principles of UK Investors in People; also, policy deployment in Chapters 3 and 6).

- *Effective communication vertically/laterally.* The face-to-face nature of appraisal should act as a catalyst to resolving problems and enhancing performance. It enables conflicting perspectives under the surface to be aired and resolved.

An example of this at Komatsu UK was of the welder who said at the start of his appraisal interview with his team leader that he was glad of the opportunity, since he was sure that the team leader thought little of his performance as he was often banished to the Rework Section in his work. Astonished, the team leader replied that the welder was sent to operate, check and adjust because he was the *best* welder on the team and could work without supervision! A simple but true example that is often typical.

- *Systems of wide consultation.* Not perhaps a main role of appraisal, but one that can be used to check that routine consultation is working properly.

- *Equal opportunity.* Demonstration of meritocracy should be an outcome of appraisal, provided the information is effectively used in development.

  Life-long learning: a product of appraisals must be training and development. If manager and managed agree a plan for training and development, then a future perspective is provided. However, this plan must be used, otherwise credibility vanishes.

- *Encourage 'horizontal' career development and multi-skilling.* 'No holds barred' discussions can allow thoughts on development to germinate and the fear of leaving an established career pattern can be mollified.

  I gave the example in Chapter 3 of the welder at Komatsu who pointed out at appraisal that there were many more jobs he could do than the three types he had had in the previous six months!

- *Create a new role for management.* In running appraisals, the 'new manager' is empowered and able to devolve authority, and automatically owns the system. However, he *must* be appraised himself.

  This may sound an obvious point, but both Western and Japanese managements find this harder to do the further up the recipient is in the hierarchy.

- *Key issue of culture shift.* The body language of being on the same side of the table, sharing the same piece of paper, openness, a show of vulnerability by the manager, all speak volumes.

Developing close links between employees and managers is, perhaps, the most crucial contribution of good appraisal. Run properly, it can demolish barriers and provide realistic views for all participants.

Of all the systems that we developed in Komatsu UK it was the most time-consuming, but the most rewarding. Managers and supervisors spent two to three hours preparing to interview their staff, who in turn prepared through self-assessment. This culminated in an hour-long appraisal interview.

The system owed nothing to Japan or Deming, but was right for the UK, innovative in including blue-collar workers, and gave a major contribution to enhanced performance.

The detail of the Komatsu UK Appraisal Scheme is in Appendix I(ii). However, the outline is as follows:

Komatsu UK – Performance Appraisal Scheme

From 1987, an innovative Appraisal Scheme was established; this was linked to pay for all employees no matter what job they did. It was controversial, since it apparently flew in the face of the theory of quality control and the issue of incentives opposed by Dr Edwards Deming.

The features of the Appraisal Scheme were:

- All employees were covered
- The same simple scheme applied to all
- The factors to be measured were *not* physical output measures, but concerned the overall performance in the job
- Self-assessment was included
- Manager and managed agreed the outcome
- The link to pay provided salary progression, i.e. it was not a cash bonus
- Improved performance was necessary to warrant an appraisal award, i.e. not at the level attained last year
- Career and training issues would be pursued by management with employee input

The process of the Appraisal Scheme development was interesting. Naturally, I was in a hurry to get something off the ground in early 1987. I felt an off-the-shelf scheme would not work; it had to have local management ownership. We needed to train managers and supervisors in appraisal techniques, so Fred Thomson of Commu-

nication and Employee Relations Training (Human Resource Consultants) suggested a workshop that both trained the managers and
supervisors, and also designed the scheme at the same time. The idea
was brilliant, the effect was workable – management owned the
system.

The outcome was rewarding, but remained controversial. Staff
found it difficult at first to relate the emphasis on teamwork to the
outcomes of individual incentives, especially when they had been used
to collective group bonus schemes in their previous employment. The
pay link gave stimulus to managers to operate the appraisal scheme
effectively and integrated the issues of performance, future objectives,
training and career development. Staff also found the self-assessment
form unhelpful, so in the spirit of continuous improvement some
twelve months later we invited the Advisory Council, the forum for
negotiation and consultation, to redesign the forms to reflect their
concerns. Other modifications to the system followed, giving the
system a long-term viability – unusual for Appraisal Schemes.

The Industrial Relations Review and Report commenting on the
Komatsu system in May 1987[15] said, 'The breadth of the characteristics covered by this process is striking. Items include not only the
more conventional one such as job knowledge, quality of work, work
rate and reliability, but also others such as flexibility, adaptability to
change, determination, teamwork, personal contact skills and activities "beyond the contract" [See Appendix I (ii)]. . . . appraisal is
completed jointly by the person being assessed and the reviewer and
considers the former's strengths, weaknesses, future work preferences
and development needs.'

Oliver and Wilkinson's research shows that the breadth of appraisal characteristics used by Japanese companies in the UK is generally
extensive. They quote analysis by Yu and Wilkinson[16] of thirteen sets
of appraisal documentation which demonstrated a mix of task
performance indicators and subjectively assessed personal characteristics, as they claim is found in the 'satei' system in Japanese
companies in Japan (although in the Komatsu case, no use was
made of Japanese experience in designing the UK Appraisal Scheme).

Their analysis (Table 5.3) shows the frequency of use of such
criteria:

My conclusion is that effective appraisal needs to include the
factors, both objective and subjective, that are important for overall
job performance, and the system should be linked to recognition and
be 'owned' by all.

Table 5.3   *Appraisal criteria at thirteen Japanese companies in the UK*

Criteria	No. of companies Using criteria
Teamworking, ability, co-operation	11
Self-organisation, problem-solving skills	10
Leadership, persuasiveness	9
Attendance, punctuality	8
Quality of work, efficiency, productivity	8
Communication skills	7
Job knowledge	7
Accuracy, attention to detail	7
Attitude, motivation, loyalty	7
Creativity, initiative	6
Flexibility, adaptability	5
Quality of work	5
Ability to work under pressure	4
Enthusiasm, willingness to work	4
Safety, housekeeping	4
Reasoning, analytical skills	4
Persistence, determination	3
Work skills	3

TRAINING AND DEVELOPMENT

Historically training and development in industry has followed the cultural pattern set by the educational establishment – along lines of class and specialism. Hence, only certain groups of employees were seen to be worth training, and then only in specialist subjects.

For those at the bottom end, training was in craft skills for life; thus they would plateau in their early twenties with no additional training for the next forty years.

Graduates, as the potential elite, were to be given continuous training in their specialism so that they had engineering, accountancy or computing in concentric rings in their trunk of knowledge with, at best appreciation-level knowledge of the other functions that made up a commercial enterprise. No wonder this was a breeding ground for the 'silo' mentality and an ability for character assassination of other functions.

Lastly, at the point where these ingrained specialists were promoted to the level where they had to understand the business, there was a perceived need to broaden their perspectives and make them into generalists.

In short, training and development was seen as a cost only to be incurred when absolutely necessary. The contrast with Japan is interesting. As we saw in Chapter 2, the Japanese education system is conformist, but produces a high-quality product for the vast majority of participants. Despite the mix of public and private schools and ranking of universities, it is relatively classless and based on meritocracy. There are virtually no business schools in Japan, little vocational training outside companies, and professional qualifications as we know them in the West are not valued.

All vocational training and development is done within the enterprise, and most of it 'on the job' rather than the Western preference of 'off the job' or formalised chalk and talk courses. The West rejected 'on the job' (OJT) in the 1960s as liable to be passing bad habits on (sitting next to Nellie) instead of recognising that if Nellie is trained to train, the student can absorb 80 per cent of what they are taught, not 20 per cent as in the typical classroom. The West is totally obsessed with qualifications – any training must have an MBA, MSc or NVQ label, otherwise it is worthless. In Japan, qualifications do not enter the argument – the measure is 'Does the individual's performance improve as a result of the training? Does it ensure his integration into the company?'

> 'Senior managers in Japanese organisations . . . are moved laterally into different functions throughout their careers as part of a carefully planned development programme extending until retirement.'

As Snape, Redman and Bamber have said:

Senior managers in Japanese organisations are experienced in many facets of the business; they are multi-skilled and well able to take a realistic and holistic view of the organisation for the purpose of long term planning. To acquire this wide range of expertise, managers are moved laterally into different functions throughout their careers as part of a carefully planned development programme extending until retirement.

Since much of the managerial training in Japan occurs on the job, senior managers are deeply involved in developing their less-experienced colleagues. Mentoring is common. Japanese managers may spend up to 30% of their time educating less experienced colleagues. The culture of the organisation supports management development throughout the person's career and at all levels this sort of involvement is expected, not resented as an intrusion.

In Japan it is in the interests of managers to immerse themselves completely in the culture of the organisation, to perform appropriately and to maximise their promotion prospects. Western managers by contrast, typically do not expect to remain with the organisation for their entire career, so it is in their interests to retain a degree of critical detachment from it.[17]

LESSONS FOR WESTERN MANAGEMENT

With this stark contrast, are we so far behind that we cannot catch up? I do not believe so: Western managers can excel. What is needed is to use them as agents for cultural change, while they are being trained themselves.

- They must *own the process* and the content of training. Experiential learning in peer groups can achieve this method of self-discovery, as with the Northern Electric example given earlier in the chapter.

- They must receive *mentoring and coaching*. This is not a new concept, but rarely formalised. It has depended on the individual manager's enthusiasm for the task. It can sound patronising, and cynics will rarely accept it at face value. Managers must receive it themselves and be trained to use it.

- Training and development must be seen as an *investment, not a cost*, giving long-term returns.

- The company should inculcate a *lifelong learning* culture to encourage a thirst for learning, rather than 'I-have-status-because-of-my-experience-and-length-of-service attitude.'

- It is essential to force the pace on *team building and team training* activities, which become harder the higher up the organisation you go. The process will not be taken seriously unless very senior management and the top of specialist trees participate.

- Management must ensure that *all levels participate* in relevant training and development, particularly in relation to cultural change – the bottom line is that all have to contribute to it.

- Lastly, organisations need to achieve an *integrated approach for training and development* plans that give training needs for the individual from appraisal, but that clearly link to the organisation's mission, vision, values and objectives.

WHICH WAY?

Three choices for Western management:
- Blind faith
- Ruthless exploitation of the market
- Long-term competitive approach

The conclusions are now clear: companies exposed to global competition have three stark choices today. They may:

- Continue in their old ways in the hope that their previous competitive advantage is not eroded by the competition (blind faith).

- Pursue exploitation by sharper macho management for short-term advantage. The emphasis will be on catch-as-catch-can leadership, divide and rule, subcontracting everything that moves on a purely short-term commercial basis, relying on lowest cost and contract terms for maximum advantage (ruthless exploitation of the market).

- Emulate world-class policies. This analysis has shown that emulating world-class production systems on its own almost inevitably leads to failure. World-class personnel systems must *precede* or be at minimum in parallel to the planned introduction of new production systems. The bottom line is that Western business must effectively implement culture change of the type described as a prerequisite for world-class aspirations (long-term competitive approach).

CAN YOUR COMPANY DO IT ON ITS OWN?

A company that aspires to world-class standards can clearly follow the process of achieving quality, cost and delivery as defined, embrace continuous improvement, mobilise its management as described within this chapter, and empower its employees; however, in today's globally sourced market the end product is often a combination of components from many suppliers. Your company may be world class in many respects, but if your suppliers, or your suppliers' suppliers, do not share the same aspirations, the end product will not be world class.

ENHANCING THE SUPPLY CHAIN

Supplier development is vital – Japanese companies have only achieved their pre-eminence through an integrated approach with suppliers. Their cultural background helps, of course, because of the web of interdependence that grows naturally in Japan, which gives both growth and protection to the various tiers of subcontractors.

It should be recognized that Japanese style production systems inevitably increase mutual dependency. The thesis of Oliver and Wilkinson's work is: 'that Japanese manufacturing methods dramatically increase the interdependencies between the actors involved in the whole production process, and that these heightened dependencies demand a whole set of supporting conditions if they are to be managed successfully'.[18] Their conclusion, and mine, is that these supporting conditions, both inside and outside the company, are characterised by high-trust relations. This is so far away from the instinctive approach of many in Western management as to appear almost unbridgeable at first sight.

The West cannot totally emulate the Japanese system, nor would it wish to, because of the almost total dependence that the system encourages; however, some aspects are essential candidates for transfer.

● *Selection of suppliers*. Select as you would an employee, based on whether they appear keen to improve and are trainable and adaptable

– after all, what you ask them to make today may not be your requirements next year. As with employee selection, go for single sourcing, recognising the parting of the ways with normal practices and the implications of this policy. The contrast is made by Oliver and Wilkinson:

> High dependency on suppliers is implied when a policy of single sourcing is involved. Some organisations are willing to heighten their dependency on suppliers via long-term contracts for instance, in return for promises – and performance to match – regarding quality, delivery and price. Others prefer to take advantage of the competition between suppliers, constantly playing each off against the others. In the latter case, supplier characteristics are not a cause for concern, only the cost of the goods.[19]

Such policies cannot be in isolation from the culture that exists elsewhere in the enterprise. Ford, in 1988, provides an example of what can happen if policies are out of step inside and outside the company.

In February 1988 Ford UK suffered their first national strike for a decade over an offered package that included, among other things, new flexible working practices. Ford was spurred to make changes in work organisation to increase efficiency, largely in the face of Japanese competition. The initiative in the UK was in parallel with other moves by Ford to introduce similar Japanese-style management practices in the USA, Australia, Belgium and Germany.

The effects of the UK strike were felt almost instantly. The day after the start of the strike, Ford announced that 2,000 workers were to be laid off in Genk, Belgium. Within a few days, 9,700 had been laid off at Genk, 1,500 at Düren in Germany, and production cut at Saar Louis. The immediate effect was due to stocks being at a minimum because of JIT implementation, and consequences across Europe were due to the policy of single sourcing of suppliers that had been followed from the early 1980s. As Oliver and Wilkinson comment:

> the move towards just in time production had greatly increased the dependency of the company on its employees' goodwill and willingness to work. . . . Ironically, it was Japanese style production integration that gave workers the ability to hit Ford so hard in their resistance to Japanese style work practices.[20]

- *Open communication.* Treat suppliers as extensions of the company, so that longer-term issues that affect your company are communicated early to suppliers. Open-book costing is to be encouraged so that manufacturing inventory and overhead costs are jointly examined rather than determined by bouts of arm wrestling in negotiations.
- *Product development.* Involve preferred suppliers in the design of future products – again it helps the 'buildability', quality and profit contribution of the final product, as well as reducing the product development cycle. (See Fig. 5.2 for a diagrammatic representation of the difference between integrated and sequential product development.) The former involved simultaneous engineering and is possible in a company that has successfully attacked the 'silo' mentality and also uses its suppliers' product development 'brains', as well as their manufacturing ability.
- *Train supplier teams* together with those of the client company for greater understanding and synergy. I referred under the heading of benchmarking in Chapter 4 to the supply chain teams Komatsu UK joined, initiated by British Steel from 1990 to 1992.

Because of these compelling reasons (as mentioned in Chapter 4), I believe the EC has introduced a counter-productive measure with the Utilities Directive, which, although designed to open up competition, actually militates against utilities establishing long-term dependency

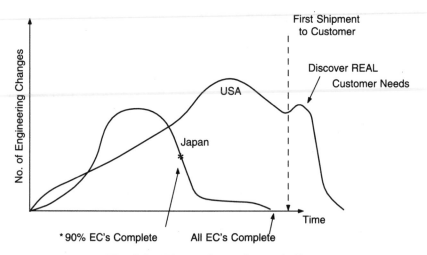

Fig. 5.2 *The product release challenge*

relations with their suppliers by insisting that all potential purchases over a certain level be open to public tender.

THE WIDER COMMUNITY

Michael Porter in his acclaimed book *The Competitive Advantage of Nations*,[21] postulates that regional or national economies need 'clusters of excellence' in terms of businesses that can create synergy to transform the local balance of payments situation. In regions where there is an aspiration for rapid economic growth, leaving the synergy to direct relations between client and supply companies, may not be fast or universal enough. In the North East of England, various initiatives have been aimed at raising the general level of appreciation and implementation on quality, for instance (see the example described in Chapter 4 under the theme of benchmarking for quality).

In order to convert the faint-hearted an enigmatic and outspoken businessman, Karl Watkin, Chairman of Crabtree of Gateshead (printing machinery manufacturers), launched what he termed as the 'Manufacturing Challenge' for the North East in January 1993. Karl produced some targets to galvanise the thinking. His words were:

Aim to double manufacturing output and treble exports from the region in ten years.

The means was to be business-to-business support and benchmarking, so that resources were pooled through brainstorming at a series of workshops and events where manufacturers large and small met with service and public-sector providers to find ways of creating synergy to promote regional growth.

To date, the success has been to introduce many thousands of separate local businesses to the process and to create a catalyst bringing the great variety of economic agencies together to focus on shared targets. For instance, the Manufacturing Challenge was embraced by the Northern Development Company responsible for encouraging inward investment; regional and national offices of the Department of Trade and Industry and blessed by the Rt Hon Michael Heseltine, President of the Board of Trade; the Training and Enterprise Councils; the Confederation of British Industry; the banks; the universities and colleges of further education, together with local government and endorsed by Sir John Harvey-Jones, ex-Chairman of ICI and management guru.

The support is important and a recognition of mutual dependency between manufacturing and the North East economy, but results in terms of growth is what is being looked for.

One key supporter of Manufacturing Challenge is Robin Mair, Managing Director of Black and Decker in Spennymoor, County Durham. His reason for 'signing up' was one of 'self-interest'[22] – because of competition from abroad, 'the likes of which we have never seen before', . . . he was concerned about what he called quite astonishing development taking place in the Pacific Rim. To meet such a challenge, North East manufacturers would have to:

- Equal the best in the world on service, quality and cost
- Achieve competitive edge through developing a technological base
- Dramatically shorter lead times for product development, as well as creating new products
- Achieve better management of supply chains through larger manufacturers giving better assistance to smaller suppliers

These comments come from the Managing Director of a world-class plant in the UK that is outstripping comparative European performance. Later in January 1994, it was announced that Black and Decker were to close their Limburg factory in Germany and concentrate their European tool-making operations at Spennymoor.[23]

At its own initiative, the North is now formulating an economic agenda for the next decade and building such foundations:

- To identify complementary clusters of excellent businesses as a platform for growth (on the basis of a range of shared character-istics, e.g. market orientation, technology and production meth-ods, skills required, etc.)
- To 'embed' existing inward investment and ensure related busi-nesses gain from the systems they bring
- To focus on high value added for longer-term growth and earnings potential
- To focus on the vital role of the small- and medium-sized business sector (SMEs) for growth in turnover and jobs

- Encourage mutual support and exchange of experience among all companies – embracing benchmarking, demonstration, advice and good practice
- To focus on creativity and technology throughout a lifetime of learning embracing initial education and on going training.

The clarion call to businesses is to be commited to the Manufacturing Challenge objectives and to undertake a cultural change in each business to gain contribution and commitment from all involved – central to the theme running through this book. The attraction is the encouragement given to local business that may shrink from risky exporting unless helped. If we return to the Japanese parallel, then small but growing Japanese businesses would never have ventured outside Japan or become associated with large-scale production without the growth of dependency relations with larger companies, the banks and trading companies that now form such an intricate and apparently impenetrable web to the outsider.

In Western society it is not appropriate or helpful to suggest imitating such claustrophobic relationships – we have to find our own solution to suit our own culture.

I would argue that such moves of self-help and growth of mutual dependency are vital if we are to change from having the isolated world-class company in our midst to a world-class regional and national economy.

NOTES

1. The author quoted by N. Oliver and B. Wilkinson in *The Japanization of British Industry*, Basil Blackwell, 1992, from the BBC TV documentary *Bulldozers: Chopsticks: and Newcastle Brown* (1987).
2. Brian Jackson, Purchasing Executive, Toyota MUK, quoted in *Financial Times*, 10 April 1991.
3. See NEDC report, *What Makes a Supervisor World Class?* Engineering Skills Working Party, 1991.
4. E. Snape, T. Redman and G. Bamber, *Managing Managers*, Basil Blackwell, 1994.
5. *Financial Times*, 14 January 1994.
6. Judge Institute of Management, University of Cambridge, *Making it in Britain? Japanese Manufacturers in the UK in the 90s*, 1992/3.
7. *Financial Times*, 9 December 1993.
8. Oliver and Wilkinson, op. cit.
9. Ibid., p. 174.

10. Kurt Lewin, 'Group Decisions and Social Change' in *Readings in Special Psychology*, Holt, Rinehart and Winston, 1958.
11. Snape *et al.* p. 10.
12. C. Longenecker and D. Gioia, SMR Forum 1991.
13. M.A. Devanna, C.J. Fombrun and N.M. Tichy, *A Framework for Strategic HRM: Strategic Human Resource Management*, John Wiley, 1984.
14. Oliver and Wilkinson, op. cit., p. 160.
15. Quoted in ibid., p. 227. Also see Appendix II.
16. C. Yu and B. Wilkinson, 'Pay and Appraisal in Japanese Companies in Britain', *Japanese Management Research Unit Working Paper No. 8*, Cardiff Business School, UWCC, 1989.
17. Snape, Redman and Bamber, op. cit., pp. 91–2.
18. Oliver and Wilkinson op. cit., p. 68.
19. Ibid., p. 87.
20. Ibid., p. 113.
21. M. Porter, *The Competitive Advantage of Nations*, Free Press, 1990.
22. Reported in *Newcastle Journal*, 19 January 1994.
23. *Sunday Times*, 30 January 1994.

6 'Japanese' Management Techniques

Western management is continually bombarded with the latest technique from Japan, often via the USA. Managers are exhorted to change rapidly in the 'nanosecond nineties'[1] or be overtaken. We are reminded that 'Survival is not compulsory',[2] and that all we took for granted before is about to be stood on its head. It is easy to feel inadequate in a situation where you are encouraged to grasp the latest panacea that will accelerate your business into the world-class league. So what route should change management follow? Total Quality Management or Lean Production? Or should we 're-engineer' our companies? Are they names for the same thing, developments of each other, or totally separate? Do we have a hope of successfully introducing these techniques in the West, or do we need an Eastern culture to make them work? Do we need to change the culture of our organisations first to ensure these new ideas take root and flourish?

Before these questions are answered, we need to see where some of the ideas started, how they have been applied, and how they developed.

TOTAL QUALITY CONTROL (TQC)

The late W. Edwards Deming is seen as the father of Quality Control (according to Japanese Industries Standards (Z8101 – 1981) definition, Quality control is a 'system of means to economically produce goods or services that satisfy customer requirements'). When Deming introduced QC to Japan in 1950, it was to improve product quality by applying statistical tools in the production processes.

Dr J.M. Juran brought a wider definition of QC in 1954 to Japan – the concept as a vital management tool for improving managerial performance. Between them, Deming and Juran elevated QC from application of statistics to an all-pervading management philosophy. What they found in Japan was totally the right climate for growth.

135

All aspects of Total Quality – Just in Time, Kanban (explained on pp. 156–7), Poka-Yoke – flourish under the umbrella of another term now in daily parlance – Kaizen, which literally means improving on goodness.

Why all these confusing terms? In fact, is important to understand why such systems and slogans have had such impact and why Deming and Juran's ideas took off.

The climate was right

Here the role of Japanese culture and value systems was vital and irreplaceable. The first value system is the 'group-think' instinct explained in Chapter 2 – a function of weather and history in Japan. Japanese do not think they lose kudos by sharing ideas, or evolving solutions in a group. By contrast, in the West each person looks for the credit in initiating change and is therefore reluctant to share. Also, we do not credit people with less education than ourselves or those lower in the organisation with having any *ideas*.

The second value system is the *process*-oriented way of thinking in Japan versus the West's *innovation* and *results-oriented* thinking.

After many years Western management gurus are realising the value of *process* in a rapidly changing business world. To focus purely on end-results gives no credit where major effort has been made often fosters the individual often against his peers and sometimes even the corporation.

The third value system is the distinction between gradual and step change. In Japan, gradual change has always been the norm. Hence the Kaizen (incremental change) instinct is strong in Japan and correspondingly weak in the West. Conversely, step change is often welcomed in the USA and Europe – it is seen as decisive, clinical and, more importantly, individuals can be identified with it.

The fourth value system is the renewal instinct. Visitors in Japan are often staggered by the short design life of buildings and facilities. This, I believe, is another product of the environment in Japan – the Earthquake Syndrome. The Japanese are conditioned to rebuilding from scratch – when something is outmoded dispense with it – do not make do and mend.

Lastly, the Japanese were desperate to succeed, and saw themselves under siege by the USA in particular, as we saw in Chapter 3.

KAIZEN

For Japan, systems of Total Quality Control, QC Circles, Zero-Defects and so on neatly fitted within an instinct for gradual, incremental, group-based activity.

What started as an imported technique of statistical control from the USA mushroomed into a new way of management.

The contrast in concept between the West and Japan could not be more stark. Masaaki Imai, in his book *Kaizen* (1986), distinguishes between job functions (as shown in Figs 6.1 and 6.2).

Imai points out that for Kaizen to work in an organisation it must be applied at all levels (see Table 6.1, and further contrasts Western innovation and Kaizen in Table. 6.2). Kaizen or continuous improvement is not a system, but a catalyst or environment for Total Quality.

QC systems have been devised for achieving *continuous improvement*, such as the Deming Cycle. This started life as a continuous process of

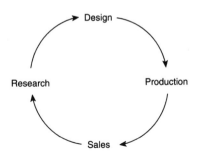

to emphasise the need for constant interaction between these functions to achieve better quality that satisfies customers.

The concept was broadened to apply to any process – as in:

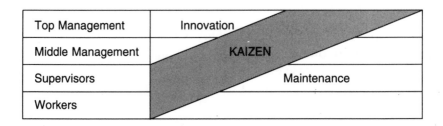

Fig. 6.1   *Japanese perceptions of job functions*

Top Management	Innovation
Middle Management	
Supervisors	Maintenance
Workers	

Fig. 6.2   *Western perceptions of job functions*

The customer is defined as the next stage in the process.

Juran developed this concept into the Quality Spiral to illustrate that improvement as three dimensional.

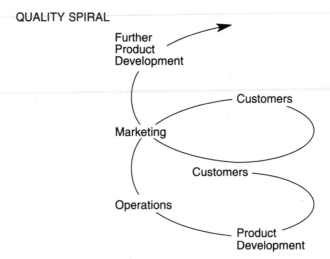

(See Fig. 6.3 for TQC in Komatsu using the same logic.)

Table 6.1   *Hierarchy of Kaizen involvement*

Top management	Middle management and Staff	Supervisors	Workers
Be determined to introduce Kaizen as a corporate strategy	Deploy and implement Kaizen goals as directed by top management through policy deployment and cross-functional management	Use Kaizen in functional roles	Engage in Kaizen through the suggestion system and small-group activities
Provide support and direction for Kaizen and by allocating resources	Use Kaizen in functional capabilities	Formulate plans for Kaizen and provide guidance to workers	Practise discipline in the workshop
Establish policy for Kaizen and cross-functional goals	Establish, maintain and upgrade standards	Improve communication with workers and sustain high morale	Engage in continuous self development to become better problem-solvers
Realise Kaizen goals through policy deployment and audits	Make employees Kaizen-conscious through intensive training programmes	Support small-group activities (such as Quality Circles) and the individual suggestion system	Enhance skills and job performance expertise with cross-education
Build systems, procedures and structures conducive to Kaizen	Help employees develop skills and tools for problem-solving	Introduce discipline in the workshop	
		Provide Kaizen suggestions	

Table 6.2   *Features of Kaizen and innovation*

		Kaizen	*Innovation*
1	Effect	Long-term and long-lasting, but undramatic	Short-term, but dramatic
2	Pace	Small steps	Big steps
3	Timeframe	Continuous and incremental	Intermittent and non-incremental
4	Change	Gradual and constant	Abrupt and volatile
5	Involvement	Everybody	Select few 'champions'
6	Approach	Collectivism, group efforts, systems approach	Rugged individualism, individual ideas and efforts
7	Mode	Maintenance and improvement	Scrap and rebuild
8	Spark	Conventional know-how and state of the art	Technological break throughs, new inventions, new theories
9	Practical requirements	Requires little investment but great effort to maintain it	Requires large investment, but little effort to maintain it
10	Effort orientation	People	Technology
11	Evaluation criteria	Process and efforts for better results	Results for profit
12	Advantage	Works well in slow growth economy	Better suited to fast-growth economy

Inspection was considered an unnecessary overhead and the slogan became 'build Quality into the process'.

Quality Control Circles (QC Circles are defined as a small group that voluntarily performs quality-control activities on the shop floor) emerged in Japan in 1962. It is important to see the QC Circle in context. It is only *part* of a company-wide programme, not TQC in its entirety.

Enthusiasts in the West have tried to embrace QC circles as a stand-alone system and have usually ended up disappointed. Their attraction was a potential means of employee involvement and, whereas the Japanese can point to countless thousands operating in manufacturing, service and public sectors of Japan, their achievements do not dwarf the mainstream TQC activities in corporations.

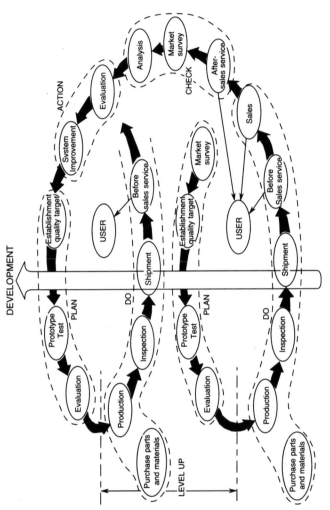

Fig. 6.3 *Total Quality Control in Komatsu*

The term 'Quality Control' in the West implies a narrow issue of measuring product quality. This has not been the practice in Japan, as seen in the Komatsu example in this chapter and also in Chapter 3. Often, at best, Western observers have seen TQC as an excellent system for shop floor organisation in manufacturing, not as it can be perceived – integrated with long-term company strategy and radically changing the roles of top management right down to first line supervision.

Further, managers in the West have seen TQC as a means of reinforcing discipline and have latched on to such concepts as 'Right first time' and 'Zero defects' as commands from on high rather than stages on a journey for the whole organisation – top management included. Again, this gap is due to the difference between a process-oriented culture and the familiar results-oriented culture.

Masaaki Imai[3] points out that the process-oriented manager puts a high value on:

- Discipline
- Time Management
- Skill Development
- Participation and Involvement
- Morale
- Communication

In other words, such a manager is people-oriented.

TOOLS OF QUALITY CONTROL

Deming and his colleague in Japan, the late Professor Kaoru Ishikawa, developed the seven tools of Quality Control:

- Pareto diagrams
- Cause and effect diagrams*
- Histograms
- Control charts
- Scatter diagrams
- Graphs
- Check sheets

---

*Also called the 4'M's or Ishikawa diagram (see Fig. 6.4 as applied to Komatsu UK assembly quality).

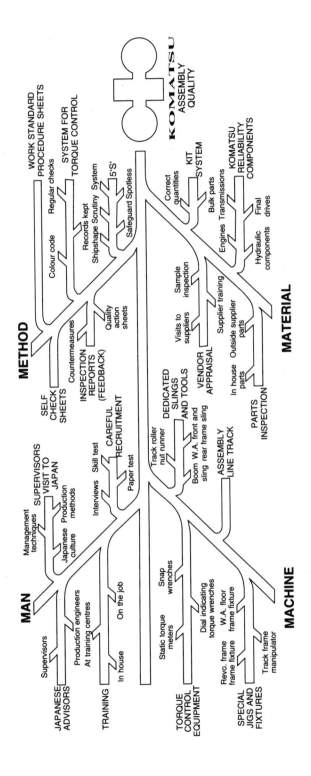

Fig. 6.4 *Effect of 4M on assembly quality*

Ishikawa went on to develop a three-pronged formula for promotion of TQC:

- Mass Education
- Simple Tools
- Teamwork

which led him to be an enthusiast for Quality Circles. He realised that Quality Control was all about Quality of People, and coined the phrase: 'Quality Control starts and ends with education'.

Imai talks about the three building blocks of business being Hardware, Software 'Humanware'[4] and that TQC starts with humanware. He makes the point that unless management gets the relationship right on the last point, no real progress can be made with the first two.

VISIBLE MANAGEMENT

The essence of Kaizen is to communicate targets, measurement, analysis and achievement. Visible management is the concept of displaying data in a very visible manner in or adjacent to rest areas or places of work. Examples are:

- Quality
- Cost
- Delivery
- Training
- Accident levels
- Attendance

Self-discipline or 'housekeeping' is another visible demonstration. In Komatsu UK, we adopted an approximate translation of what is known as the 5 'S' System (see Fig. 6.5).

Japanese	Literal meaning	Komatsu UK adoption
Seiri	Discard the unnecessary	System
Seiton	Put things in order	Shipshape
Seisou	Clean up/Find defects	Scrutiny
Seiketsu	Personal cleanliness	Spotless
Shitsuke	Discipline	Safety

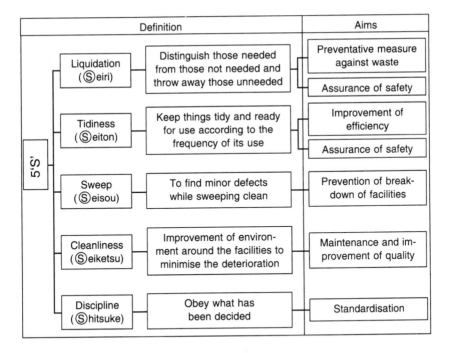

Fig. 6.5 *Definition and aims of 5'S' system*

THE FUNDAMENTAL NATURE OF TQC TO BUSINESS SUCCESS

Here again, a stark contrast can be found between Western and Eastern attitudes.

BUSINESS PURPOSE
IN THE WEST: SUFFICIENT PROFIT TO SATISFY
SHAREHOLDERS
IN JAPAN: QUALITY, COST, DELIVERY

When asked about priorities for the business, the typical Western Chief Executive has been known to answer, 'First and foremost to make profit, to satisfy my shareholders'.

His Japanese counterpart, schooled in TQC, is likely to say, 'To satisfy my customers with quality, cost and delivery'. The inherent belief, borne out by the facts, is that profit will automatically follow.

Professor Imaizumi of Musashi Institute of Technology states that the basic elements to be managed in a company are:

- Quality (products, services and work)
- Quantity, delivery (time)
- Safety
- Cost
- Employee morale

Therefore the difference arises in the focus for the role of TQC between the West and Japan. Deming recognised the change had to be fundamental:

> Solving problems, big problems and little problems, will not halt the decline of American industry, nor will expansion in use of computers, gadgets and robotic machinery. Benefits from massive expansion of new machinery also constitute a vain hope. Massive immediate expansion in the teaching of statistical methods to production workers is not the answer either, nor wholesale flashes of quality control circles. All these activities make their contribution but they only prolong the life of the patient; they can not halt the decline. . . .
>
> Only transformation of management and of Government's relations with industry can halt the decline.

TQC UPSTREAM AND DOWNSTREAM

TQC philosophy dictates thoroughness – digging for the root cause of problems using a cause and effect diagram and repeated questioning, even if it means stopping production. Otherwise, immediacy takes over and a 'fix' is employed.

Downstream is typified as 'the next process is the customer'. This we employed to great effect in Komatsu UK, getting individuals who reported to differing team leaders to establish customer–supplier relationships and mutual responsibility. The logic was also employed in supply chain relationships, not just to improve supplier performance – often the client is at fault.

SUPPLY CHAIN MANAGEMENT

The logic of Kaizen in improving supplier relations is based on better systems and communication.

The thrust changes from a macho arm wrestling negotiation to:

- A definition of optimum inventory
- Developing additional supply sources for faster delivery
- Improving order placing
- Improved quality of information to suppliers
- Better physical distribution systems
- Understanding suppliers' internal requirements

To bring suppliers and distributors further into the 'family', special awards were given to suppliers and distributors, based, for example, on:

- Policies and management systems
- Quality assurance
- Cost control
- Delivery
- Technology and development
- Education and training
- Safety and environmental control

CUSTOMER ORIENTATION

This is the fundamental of TQC, which must start at the top.

Komatsu Ltd's goal was: 'Satisfying Komatsu's worldwide customers through rational, cost-conscious research, development, sales and servicing'. This implies that it was necessary for management to involve customers in the business by ensuring dialogue – and not just with the sales force.

KAIZEN AND TQC OVERCOMING THE SILO FACTOR

Most corporations operate like efficient vertical storage silos, performing well in a downward compartmentalised fashion. All would admit that horizontal links between functions are much more difficult.

As TQC has come to include cost reduction, quality assurance, volume management and so on, it has given the opportunity for a horizontal extension of TQC and a breaking down of departmental barriers.

Over time this exercise has led to another management discovery, that of 'Simultaneous' or 'Concurrent' engineering in terms of accelerated product development – multi-functional teams co-operating throughout the process of product evolution.

For business in the West simultaneous engineering is the most powerful tool to overcome the 'silo factor' that affects all organisations.

Cross-functional TQC was practised at Komatsu, focusing on QC integrated in the way illustrated in Fig. 6.6.

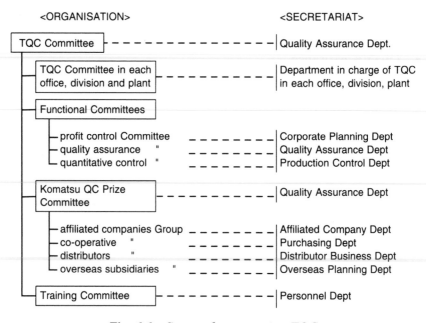

Fig. 6.6   *System for promoting TQC*

POLICY DEPLOYMENT (OR MANAGEMENT BY POLICY)

This is a rather quaint phrase to describe the role of top management in setting the scene for TQC throughout the company. It is a clear demonstration of the integration of TQC into company goals and avoids the concept or impression of TQC being applied as a control mechanism for the lower orders.

'Policy' encompasses the range of annual, medium- to long-range plans and is expressed as a cascade from top management down, but only after deep consultation throughout the organisation.

The nature of the plans tend to be more abstract at the top level, percolating to more concrete and specific goals at production level. Prioritisation is arrived at by Pareto analysis. Typically, the statements gravitate as below:

Top Management: General statement of direction for change (Qualitative).

Division Management: Definition of top management statement (Quantitative).

Middle Management: Specific goals (Quantitative).

Supervisors: Specific actions (Quantitative).

(See Figs 6.7 and 6.8).

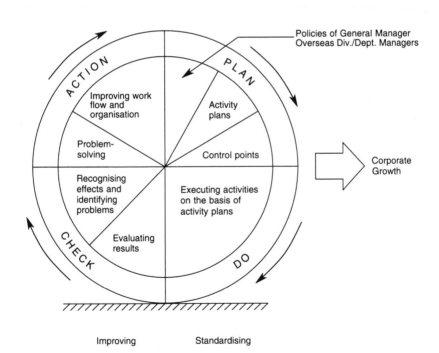

Fig. 6.7 *Concept of management by policy*

150

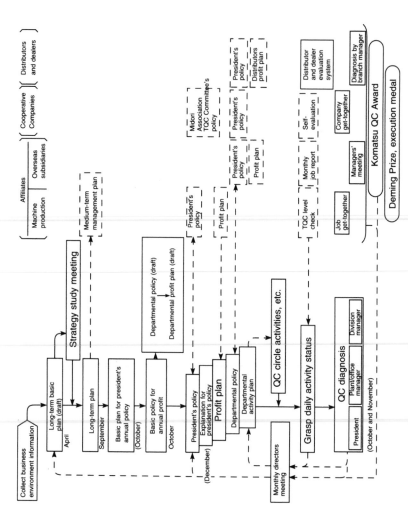

Fig. 6.8 *Policy development system*

This practice for each plant in Komatsu was typically contained on one sheet of A3 (see Fig. 6.8), fitting succinctly the President's policy for the year in the top left-hand corner, cascading through the levels to the specific goals for the department on the right-hand side. We at Komatsu UK needed no convincing of the logic of UK 'Investors in People' criteria in 1990–1, which prescribes that company and business objectives should demonstrate a link with the objectives for the individual!

Before leaving the subject of Quality Gurus, I must acknowledge the limited nature of this short exploration. I have concentrated on the *developed* lessons from Deming, Juran, and Ishikawa, all within the umbrella of Kaizen as a philosophy, because I believe that these are the most applicable areas for the West.

I have cheerfully bypassed others who have contributed a great deal to aspects of the Quality Movement but who, in my view, have not had as fundamental an impact.

Examples of such people are:

Shigeo Shingo, whose notable contribution was something odd called 'poka-yoke' or 'mistake proofing'. Devotees are quite happy for workers on their own volition to stop the production line whenever a defect occurs, define the cause, and prevent the recurring source of the defect. This is achievement of 'zero defects' by good engineering and process investigation (see Lean Production on pp. 152–8 for application of this principle).

Philip Crosby, whose claim to fame is to have been the most effective marketeer of Quality Management approaches worldwide with an exhortation/slogan emphasis on 'Do it right first time' and 'zero defects'. His approach is typified as top down with management setting the tone on quality and workers following their example; while employees are consulted, the initiative comes from the top. Regrettably, many managements have seen this as useful reinforcement to 'command and control' structures.

Crosby defines Four Absolutes of Quality Management:

1 Quality is conformance to requirements.
2 The system for quality is prevention.
3 The standard is zero defects.
4 Measurement is price of non-conformance.

Armand Feigenbaum, a little known contemporary of Juran and Deming. He originated the term Total Quality Control, requiring the

involvement of all functions in the quality process, not just manufacturing. TQC is seen by Feigenbaum as stimulating and building up
operator responsibility and interest in quality. Quality is viewed as
the single most important force leading to organisational success and
company growth in national and international markets.

Dr Genichi Taguchi is famous for his development of quality
methods in *design* rather than *production*, and relates to the
'optimisation of the product and process prior to manufacture'.
Quality is defined in seemingly negative terms, i.e. 'the minimum
loss imparted by the product to society from the time the product is
shipped'. Such losses can include rework, scrap, maintenance costs,
down-time and warranty claims, and also costs to the customer
through poor product performance and reliability, leading to further
losses to the manufacturer as his market share falls.

Taguchi methodology is fundamentally a prototyping method that
enables the engineer or designer to identify the optimal settings that
will enable consistent manufacture to produce functionality for the
customer.

Claus Møller, famous for his 'Time Manager' trade mark and his
devising of the change programme 'Putting people first', initially for
Scandinavian Airline Services, then British Airways, which he later
adapted for Japanese culture at the request of Japan Airlines.

This approach to quality in organisations is holistic and focuses on
the need for time management in order to help avoid situations that
lead to stress, tension and failure.

LEAN PRODUCTION

A new term has come to embrace the impact of new methodologies –
in particular, in the realm of car production. Lean Production is seen
as the successor of mass production or Fordism. The term was coined
by John Krafick of the International Motor Vehicle Program, which
produced the MIT study *The Machine that Changed the World*.[5]
(Krafick originally devised the term 'fragile production' to indicate
how delicate the balance was, but was persuaded by his colleagues to
adopt 'lean' as a more acceptable term.)

Lean Production is 'lean' because it requires less of everything compared with mass production, typically:

- Half the human effort in the factory
- Half the manufacturing space
- Half the investment in tools
- Half the engineering hours to develop a new product in half the time.

Also, it requires keeping less than half the needed inventory on site, results in fewer defects, and produces a greater and ever-growing variety of products.

Taiichi Ohno

The credit for the results of this integrated approach must go to another Japanese, Taiichi Ohno, who was not a guru, but a humble production engineer who had the job of putting Toyota on its feet (or maybe wheels) in 1950.

His colleague, Eiji Toyoda, joined a succession of industrial pilgrims and visited Ford's Rouge plant in Detroit, where he was suitably impressed by size and volume, but not by the vast waste (or 'muda') in the system. Copying mass production from the USA was not for them.

Ohno's contribution was an ability to see radical improvement opportunities in the opposite direction of conventional wisdom. An example quoted by Womack, Jones and Roos is of the revolution Ohno brought about in die changes for pressings. The economies of scale dictated for Ford that press lines should stamp out over a million parts per year continuously because of the disruption caused by a simple die change. The design volumes of this system were far too large for Toyota at the time, so Ohno concentrated on developing simple die changing techniques and training production workers to do their own die changes. 'By the late 1950's he had reduced the time required to change dies from a day to an astonishing 3 minutes and eliminated the need for die change specialists'.[6]

As a spin-off, he discovered it was actually cheaper per part to make small batches of stampings than to run off enormous lots. First, because small batches eliminated the need to carry the cost of large inventories. Second, making only a few parts before assembly caused stamping mistakes to be shown up instantly.

Muda

In these two important ways, this process eliminated waste (or muda) which became Ohno's battle cry, but this philosophy created a need for a very skilled and motivated workforce to control quality and respond rapidly to changing demands.

Toyota, in common with other Japanese manufacturers, had suffered the economic crisis of the late 1940s caused by the occupying Americans' credit restrictions. This caused massive lay-offs and prolonged strikes, but brought about the birth of a new labour deal. The product was what the world now associates with Japan – first an undertaking by employers to supply lifetime employment, and secondly, pay was related to age and seniority. In exchange, complete flexibility of labour was agreed to by the trade unions. Hence the environment for enhancing workers' skills was created, thereby gaining the benefit of their knowledge and experience.

Ohno in the 1950s implemented much of the prescription we have seen earlier in this chapter. Workers were grouped into teams with a team leader, rather than a foreman, who would do assembly tasks and fill in for absent workers.

Team roles

Team roles were enhanced with housekeeping (see the 5'S' system on pp. 144–5), tool repairs and quality checking. Time was set aside for group discussions and how to improve (forerunners of Quality Circles?). Kaizen techniques were applied in collaboration with the production engineers.

Poka-yoke

Gaining the inspiration from Shigeo Shingo, the principles of poka-yoke were applied to reduce rework dramatically. A pull cord was placed above every station on the line with an instruction to workers to stop the line immediately if a problem emerged that they couldn't fix.

Ohno also has the credit for the 'Five Whys' – the investigative system referred to earlier, where production workers are taught to trace systematically every error back to its ultimate cause (by asking 'why' as each layer of the problem was uncovered) and then to devise a solution so that it would not occur again.

Ohno looked outside the factory in his hunt to reduce waste. Supplier relationships were transformed in order to reduce inventory in the process, improve quality, speed up delivery, increase flexibility and to involve suppliers in the design of components. Suppliers were actually encouraged to talk to one another in order to improve quality and design.

Ohno's other lasting achievement was to develop the Just in Time system, known as Kanban in Japan. (See Figs 6.9–6.12 to illustrate the effect of JIT through Kanban – literally a card system to call up inventory when it is required.) This was an effective system to co-ordinate the flow of parts within the supply system on a day-to-day basis. The essence is that parts are only produced at each previous step to supply the immediate demand of the next step. This move not only eliminated the need for inventory or buffer stocks, but also showed up any inefficiencies in the system – thereby causing production to stop. Then the inefficiencies were tackled, not kept under the surface of a sea of inventory (see Figs 6.9–6.12).

Who is lean?

Womack, Jones and Roos point out that with the diffusion of these ideas throughout the world, particularly via Japanese 'implants', that 'we have to stop equating Japanese with lean production and western with mass production'. Their results not only show dramatic differences in performance between 'lean' production plants and 'mass' production, but also demonstrate large variations in efficiency in Japan and high levels of performance outside Japan where 'Lean' Production' is successfully implanted.

> '. . . workers respond only when there exists some sense of reciprocal obligation. . . . Merely changing the organisation chart to show "teams" and introducing quality circles to find ways to improve production processes are unlikely to make much difference' (Womack, Jones and Roos).

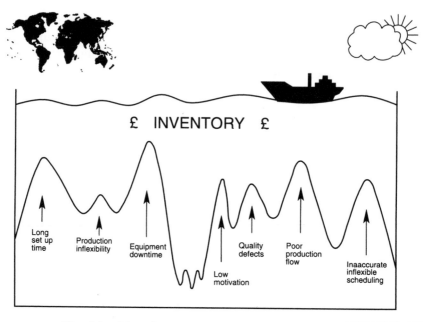

Fig. 6.9 *Manufacturing yesterday: a sea of inventory*

Make on a timely basis.

– What is wanted

– When it's wanted

– In the quantity that is wanted

> The basis of the Toyota
> Production System,
> developed by Taiichi Ohno

Fig. 6.10 *Just in Time manufacturing*

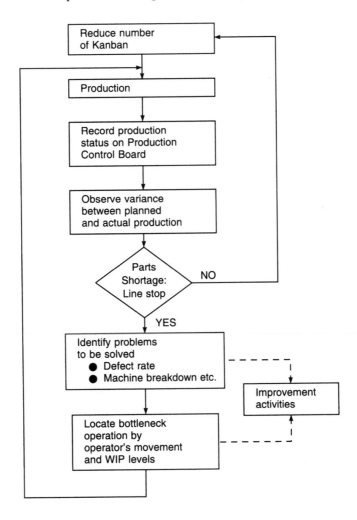

Fig. 6.11   *Using Kanban for continuous improvement*

Conclusions on Lean Production

Lean Production is not a substitute for TQC: it uses and builds on the thinking and systems evolved by the Quality theories in that:

- it boosts the tasks and responsibilities to workers actually adding value on the line
- it has a system of detecting defects that quickly traces any problem to its ultimate source

- it requires good, immediate communication (see
  visible management earlier in this chapter), so teams can respond
  quickly

Womack, Jones and Roos conclude that on a worldwide basis:

> workers respond only when there exists some sense of reciprocal
> obligation, a sense that management actually values skilled work-
> ers, will make sacrifices to retain them and is willing to delegate
> responsibility to the team. Merely changing the organisational
> chart to show 'teams' and introducing quality circles to find ways
> to improve production processes are unlikely to make much
> difference.[7]

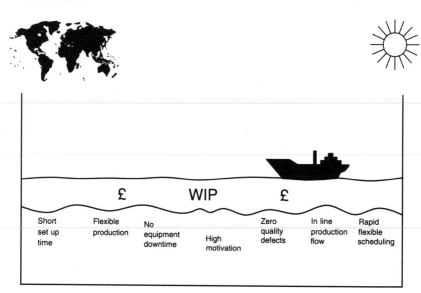

Fig. 6.12   *World-class manufacturing: Just in Time production*

PROCESS RE-ENGINEERING

The advocates of Business Process Re-engineering (BPR) will quickly
assure you that this is not another idea imported from Japan. So why
is it included in this chapter? It is simply because it is as fundamental
in its change process as the earlier examples of TQC and Lean
Production, in that it encourages management to rethink their
businesses.

Also, it illustrates a major shift in thinking in the West that I believe has been inspired by the opposites highlighted earlier in the chapter when we focused on the contrast between Japanese process-oriented thinking and Western results-oriented approaches.

In *Re-engineering in the Corporation*[8] by Michael Hammer and James Champy, they discover that, 'It is not products but the processes that create products that bring companies long-term success' p. 25. Hammer and Champy argue that re-engineering is necessary for corporations because of the speed of growth of the 3'C's:

- Customer expectations
- Competition
- Change

The authors see this as a radical move away from Adam Smith-style specialism and the silo mentality of functional disciplines in companies to a value added, integrated approach that is customer oriented and essentially about processes rather than specialisms and products.

Most vitally, under the heading 'What to avoid', the authors stress that the practitioner should not 'Fail to differentiate re-engineering from other business improvement programmes'. In essence BPR involves rethinking the way a company does business – or any part of its business – from the beginning, cutting out unnecessary stages and using information technology where appropriate to improve efficiency.

Since I believe the competition for the hearts and minds of Western executives falls broadly within the systems outlined within this chapter I have attempted to contrast and compare this in Tables 6.3–6.5.

What follows is a summary of:

- Typical re-engineering outcomes drawn from *Re-engineering the Corporation.*
- Typical changes expected from implementing re-engineering
- The enabling role of IT

At first sight, TQC, Lean Production and re-engineering all seem to be aiming to solve similar problems for corporations in the 1990s.

Table 6.3 *Business improvement programmes compared*

Conditions for growth	TQC	Lean Production	Re-engineering
'Creative' crisis	Satisfy customers	Halve human effort Halve manufacturing space Halve investment Halve engineering hours for development Halve the inventory few defects greater variety	customer focus
	Economic production		Cost reduction
			Process related
Process orientation	Improves managerial performance		
Renewal instinct	Innovation	Combination of both required e.g. Diechanging Re-engineering	Radical and innovative
'Group-think' Teamwork Gradualism	Incremental improvement		
Business needs to accelerate development and cut costs	Integrates design/ sales/production	Reduction in engineering hours by simultaneous or concurrent engineering > variety of products	Also encourages integration and simultaneous working
Need to reduce inventory and improve quality	Supplier integration	Just in Time philosophy	Supplier integration JIT can be an outcome

Table 6.4 *Business improvement programmes compared*

Conditions for growth	TQC	Lean Production	Re-engineering
Need to cut rework training	Customer concept in process	Fundamental building blocks for Lean Production to succeed	Not a system for improving quality *per se* or for employee involvement
Eliminate inspection QC tools	Build quality into process		
Involvement and communication visible management	QC Circles		
Need to consult and communicate vision	Policy deployment	Implicit	Top down vision vital to create movement
Confidence in shop floor control over quality	Poka-yoke	Pull cord for each station	Delegation to this level only by use of IT
Top down Conformance Culture	Zero defects	Similar target	Slogans only no system for producing results
Need for optimal design – for customer satisfaction and economical production	Taguchi	Implicit	Does not address

Table 6.5 Business improvement programmes – compared

Conditions for growth	TQC	Lean Production	Re-engineering
Self-discipline Housekeeping	5 'S' system	5 'S' system	No delegation or discretion given at this level
Need for deep investigation to resolve and avoid a 'fix'	5 'W' + 1 'H'	The 5 WHYS	
Need to radically reduce costs		Focus on added value	Focus on added value Overhead reduction a priority
IT breakthroughs needing to be applied to reduce costs			IT as major enabler of change

WHAT DO THEY HAVE IN COMMON?

All would agree on these priorities:

- Customer focus
- Cost reduction
- Integration of functions inside organisations
- Supplier integration
- Focus on added value

All these are process related.

Here the similarity of re-engineering with the first two ends. TQC and Lean Production are in essence complementary, with Lean Production using TQC for an unashamedly commercial result, particularly applied to automotive manufacture. Both TQC and Lean Production may start with a top down initiative, however their internal momentum essentially is, and must continue to be 'bottom up'.[9]

Typical Re-engineering Outcomes

Several jobs combined into one	–	Multi-skilling
Workers make decisions	–	Degree of empowerment (via IT)
Processes have multiple versions	–	Pragmatism
Work performed where it makes most sense	–	Lowest achievable level
Check-up and controls reduced	–	Quality principle (via IT)
Reconciliation minimised	–	JIT principles (via IT)
Case manager simple point of contact	–	Empowerment (via IT)
Hybrid centralised/ decentralised	–	Product of IT systems

Implementing Re-engineering

Typical changes expected:

FROM	TO
Functional Departments	Teams
Job Changes Simple Tasks	Multidimensional
Role Changes Controlled	Empowered

Job preparation
    Specific
    Training
	Continuing
	Education

Focus of Performance Activity	Group results
Advancement Criteria Performance	Ability (promotion not as reward but as recognition of ability)

Values change
    Protective
    (boss focus)
	Productive
	(customer focus)
	Strong interpersonal skills
	Pride in achievement of others

Organisational Structures Hierarchical	Flat
Executives Score keepers	Leaders
Role of IT Fringe	Enablers of Change

Enabling Role   *in Re-engineering*
of IT

Before Re-engineering After Re-engineering

Old rule	Disruptive technology	Anticipation
Deductive thinking Problem definition and solution	Inductive Recognise powerful solutions	find problems it can solve
Sequential and costly	Integrated and Value Added	(i.e. JIT systems for supply)
Info in one place at one time	Shared databases	Info appearing simultaneously
Only experts perform expert work	Expert systems	Generalist can do 'expert' work
Choose between Centralisation/ Decentralisation	Telecoms networks	Businesses can be both
Managers make all decisions	Decision support tools (database access)	Decision-making part of everyone's job
Field personnel need offices for receiving, storing, transmitting	Data communication portable computers	Field personnel can send and receive wherever
You have to find out where things are	Auto identification and tracking technology	Things tell you where they are
Plans get revised periodically	High-performance computing	Plans revised instantaneously

Re-engineering is not just 'top down', but 'bottom up' modes are actively discouraged on the grounds that lower echelons will resist change due to vested interests and will not have a wide enough vision or remit to initiate re-engineering solutions.

Similarly, re-engineering excludes incremental improvement (or Kaizen) as not radical enough or helpful in rethinking processes. Although the authors talk of 'empowerment' and decision-making by lower management, it is only in the context of initial brainstorming and then, participation in integrated information systems to give instantaneous control throughout an organisation.

What re-engineering does offer as a specialism is an integrated development of IT as an enabler of process change (see p. 165).

Creating synergy

With care, organisations should be able to use elements of all three vehicles of change. However, it is important to recognise the origins, development and limitations of the three before wholesale implementation.

TQC originated as a method of enhancing quality and reducing cost in a manufacturing shop floor setting. Its unshakeable belief lies in the premise that shop floor workers can take responsibility and use brain power to improve processes. It is therefore in essence 'bottom up'.

From early beginnings it has been developed into complete philosophies for companies (see the Komatsu example in this Chapter and Chapter 4) and can be applied top down in policy terms as well as bottom up for ongoing momentum, i.e.:

- Annual, mid-term and long-term TQC plans integrated with specific departmental and shop floor targets
- Integration of functions in a TQC manner to accelerate product development – for example, with the customer as arbiter
- Integrated relationships with suppliers on a JIT principle to reduce inventory and improve quality
- TQC design approaches, i.e. Taguchi methodology
- Delegation to workers via
    Building quality into the process
    QC circles   ▮   5'S' system
    Poka-Yoke   ▮   5'W' and 1'H'

Lean Production is a recent label for a package of measures, many coming from the TQC stable, that has gained the status of conventional wisdom for automotive manufacturers worldwide. Quality is not in this setting seen as an issue: it is taken for granted that zero defects is the aim. The measure and thrust is on getting dramatically more for less and relies on top down initiatives rather more than TQC to give the essential focus in relation to the competition. In this sense, Lean Production is a sharper commercial development of TQC, although companies that thoroughly integrate TQC with strategic commercial policy would argue otherwise.

Re-engineering has a totally different starting point, 'top down', and does not depend on 'bottom up' for ongoing momentum. For Western corporations, it can be attractive from a number of viewpoints:

- It does not require the major shift in culture that full-blooded TQC or Lean Production requires
- It does not challenge the status quo in that it is wholly 'top down'
- It promises to assist in 'flattening' existing hierarchies
- It is not necessarily 'manufacturing' related
- It is potentially applicable to bureaucracies in the Service and public sectors, where TQC and Lean Production methodologies need some adaptation
- It promises to be radical and innovative, which coincides with Western 'Step Change' aspirations rather than the incremental Japanese approach
- It focuses on 'processes' – consistent wisdom that it shares with TQC and Lean Production.
- Lastly, it gives a *raison d'être* for IT applications in process change where Western corporations have in the past expended huge investment for often little gain.

However, managers beware – these systems are not mutually exclusive. Process Re-engineering cannot deliver all the benefits of TQC and Lean Production – executives will still need systems to deliver quality, cost and delivery after re-engineering. Also re-engineering can sap employee motivation and diminish loyalty to the organisation as been found in a recent study of City Institutions post re-engineering.[10] Professor Rajan concludes that, too often, re-engineering has not included the necessary culture change to give 'a management style that is consistent with successful empowerment'. Staff morale has suffered: 'staff morale and customer satisfaction are inextricably linked. To win one is to win the other.'

It is one thing to radically re-engineer companies: it is another to motivate and retain those staff that remain.

Creating innovation

Post-TQC, Lean Production and Re-engineering World Class companies will be in a better position to manage innovation. In fact a new term of Total Innovation Management, or TIM, has been coined by Mark Brown of Innovation Centre Europe who emphasises that 'total innovation, like total quality, is fundamentally about attitudes. Do people focus on customer needs? Do they find real meaning in their work? TIM depends for success on the mobilisation of people's combined intelligence and the translation of their new thinking into action. That rests on empowering people (or rather getting out of their way) so they can take initiatives within a disciplined framework.'[11]

NOTES

1. T. Peters, *'Liberation' Management*, Macmillan, 1992.
2. W. E. Deming.
3. Masaaki Imai, *Kaizen*, McGraw-Hill, 1986.
4. Ibid.
5. J. Womack, D. Jones and D. Roos, *The Machine that Changed the World*, Rawson Assoc., 1990.
6. Ibid., p. 53.
7. Ibid., p. 99.
8. M. Hammer and J. Champy, *Re-engineering the Corporation*, Nicholas Brealey, 1993.
9. Ibid., pp. 207–8.
10. Prof. A. Rajan, *Winning People*, CILNTEC and London Human Resource Group, CREATE, 1994, pp. 6–7.
11. R. Heller reporting in *The Observer*, ' "Tiny TIM's" big idea', 26 June 1994.

7 What Now for Japan?

'Japanese style management and US and European style management are moving closer together' (Takeshi Murakami, Nomura Research Institute).

THE JAPANESE MULTINATIONAL

Up to the 1980s it was relatively simple for the Japanese. Having built a solid base at home in terms of economic production at good quality levels and a substantial home market share, the key to growth was to follow the Yoshida doctrine[1] and export abroad, initially using the trading companies (Sogoshosha descendants of pre-war Zaibatsu). Once an overseas market had been established, the tentacles of sales companies were extended into overseas countries.

As Ford found some sixty years earlier, trade and tariff barriers influence manufacturing strategies, and for the Japanese the opportunity was often presented by host governments of LDCs (Less Developed Countries) to establish manufacturing bases outside Japan. So it was with Komatsu in Brazil, Mexico and Indonesia. The TQC system adapted to meet the challenge of the Caterpillar Joint Venture with Mitsubishi (Komatsu's trading house links have been with Marubeni, Sumitomo and Nissho Iwai) was neatly developed to cope with increased internationalisation. The TQC system was transferrable in manufacturing terms easily from country to country, especially where local content was low and critical operations were under the control of expatriate Japanese managers schooled in TQC.

As we have seen in Chapter 6, TQC was developed to go beyond improving manufacturing quality to encouraging cross-functional links, simultaneous engineering, and linking overall corporate policy to localised plans, targets and measurement.

The weak links inevitably were where this intensive detailed system was not watertight. Unfortunately, this was the point closest to the customer – the distributor network.

Like most capital goods manufacturers, Komatsu had to enlist local indigenous distributors who often had allegiance to other competitors, and who might be very impressed by TQC – but would not necessarily participate or wish to regard themselves as extensions of Komatsu.

Dealerships were often granted when Komatsu was small in world terms and of no consequence locally. The growth of Komatsu to number one has meant these situations have had to be looked at afresh. Sometimes, uncomfortably, earlier relationships have had to be unscrambled and more appropriate distributorships established. The clock has often turned full circle and new distributor share participation arrangements have been made with the original global trading partners – the Sogoshosha Marubeni for the UK and France and Sumitomo for Spain – for perhaps at least they understand TQC.

These arrangements look strange in the West, since often these trading companies share the same name as competitors of manufacturers for whom they distribute, *i.e.* Sumitomo in Spain distributing for Komatsu, when a significant competitor for Komatsu in Europe is Sumitomo, who has formed a joint venture with JCB of the UK. To Japanese companies this is not a problem. The Sogoshosha are seen as neutral.

The Japanese implants in the West

The 1980s saw a considerable number of Japanese companies investing in the USA and Europe. This was all to do with the next phase – increasing market share where trade friction was anticipated or already existed. Such trade friction could be purely tariffs or technical barriers or administrative barriers. It could also be customer barriers, *hence* the TQC logic 'let's design and build closer to the customer'.

Japanese inward investment in the USA and Europe happened in parallel, but differed. The main difference concerned local content for the 'transplants'. In the USA it has been a minimum requirement of 25 per cent or even less: in Europe, a standard of 60 per cent minimum has been established, often rising by individual member country requirements to 80 per cent or more.

Here the analysis by Womack, Jones and Roos[2] of the potential end effect of the US policy is interesting:

Many in Europe have congratulated themselves on their aggressive stance towards Japanese investment. They view the US approach . . . as extremely naive (cars made at US transplants, that is, don't count against the quota on Japanese finished-unit imports. And this holds true even if the assembler does nothing but screw together Japanese parts). This approach yields only 'screwdriver' plants they argue, with very little manufacturing value added. The heart of the industry, they maintain, will remain in Japan.'
Womack, Jones and Roos argue that the logic of lean production will take over. The system is based fundamentally on doing as much manufacturing as possible at the point of final assembly, 'The logic of the system tends powerfully to bring the complete complement of production activities including product development along as well.'[3]

Womack, Jones and Roos may be right in the long term: however, the EC policy has had two particular short-term effects – pressure on local suppliers to match Japanese cost and quality levels and an acceleration of design and development as has been seen at Komatsu UK with the introduction of the first model designed, produced and manufactured outside Japan.

Effect on suppliers

> 'I ask when they will deliver the parts . . . I ask them which day and what time. They reply that they cannot say. . . . So I ask them why not change and do it better – but they say they cannot change!'
>
> BBC TV Documentary 1987

The immediate requirement in 1986 to achieve a 60 per cent minimum local content for the first models at Komatsu UK caused some panic among Japanese purchasing specialists.

The Trevor and Christie study for the PSI[4] in 1988 under the heading 'Our most serious problem', quoted a BBC TV documentary concerning the difficulty Komatsu UK was encountering in obtaining correct parts punctually delivered:

The Japanese purchasing director expressed his amazement and frustration at local attitudes towards the customer. 'I ask when they will deliver the parts and they say during a certain week, but I ask them which day and what time. They reply that they cannot say. But I ask them why not? They answer because it is their way. So I ask them why not change and do it better – but they say they cannot change!'

The PSI study went on to explain in some detail the logic of the Komatsu approach:[5]

In the Komatsu case, one local supplier dropped out after six months of negotiations. On the Japanese side there were tight demands on the three crucial issues; price, quality and delivery. On the supplier's side there were doubts whether the contract would be profitable enough and doubts about what revealed itself as a fundamentally different way of conducting relations between a customer and its suppliers.

Komatsu, like other Japanese companies, was used to close relations with its suppliers at home and to having frequent meetings with them, including visits to their plants. For the first time, British suppliers had to try to accustom themselves to visits by the customer's engineers as often as three or four times a week and to discussing their plant layouts, production systems and costings with them in detail.

In Japan this is normal procedure when starting business with a new and untried supplier, after which visits will not be so frequent, although they will continue as a means of sharing technology and information. It is an important aspect of the way in which Japanese companies sharpen their competitive edge.

But in Britain such close relationships between customer and suppliers are exceptional. The company that dropped out of negotiations with Komatsu was evidently one of those that felt that the change from the distance, not to say indifference, of British customers was too great. They appeared to be a firm that preferred the usual way of agreeing a price, signing a contract and then doing the work in their own way – and in their own time. They implicitly rejected the possibility of technical or managerial transfer from the customer company.

The BBC TV programme pointed out that the Japanese were 'slightly contemptuous' of the apparent local assumption that you could agree a business deal by 'instinct' or whether you felt you could 'trust' the negotiating partner. They saw this as 'sloppy'. Their method was first to analyse production systems, costings and requirements in detail; after which, provided performance was delivered, a relationship of long-term trust could develop. In Japan it is not unusual for a new sub-contractor to have to supply the company history and a chart showing the production system to the customer company at the beginning of the relationship.

They then point to the contrast between Japan and the UK in terms of competition:

The frequently repeated phrase, 'the customer is king' is largely a fact, and not just rhetoric. With lower levels of competition than in Japan, British customers are expected to be grateful for whatever they can get. The British customer, whether an industrial firm or an individual, is rarely king.

The expectations of customers in Japan to have their demands taken seriously explain Komatsu's assumptions, which it showed in its visits to local suppliers and in its approach to negotiating with them.

They end with a vindication for Komatsu's thorough approach:

. . . it would appear that Komatsu's criticisms of some local suppliers had a sound basis. . . . It seems to have gone into greater detail and to have offered the possibility of closer relations, with technological and managerial transfer, than is normal with British firms. Its professional, fact-seeking approach contrasts with the tendency of managers in some local firms to proceed according to their 'instinct', without adequate forethought, or to 'fly by the seat of their pants', as the popular phrase vividly expresses it.

Komatsu's implied criticisms of local supplier practices may have been expressed for the first time in the popular British media but they and the whole attitude of shocked amazement at the sloppy local management were by no means new.

Having studied the early Japanese experiences with British suppliers, mainly in the electronics industry, Trevor and Christie highlight a major difference in approach between the UK and Japan. UK industry has in the past seen merit in directly manufacturing as much of the product as possible, usually because of perceived control over quality and delivery, even when the demonstrated cost has been cheaper by subcontracting. UK manufacturing sub-contractors have been managed at a distance with little security of tenure. However, Japanese manufacturers entering the UK have arrived with totally different expectations.

Technova Inc., Japanese consultants commissioned by the DTI in 1980,[6] placed great emphasis on the importance of suppliers for the success of the manufacturing process as an integrated whole: 'The competitiveness of Japanese industries is supported largely by the work provided by the sub-contractors. To be able to maintain that competitiveness, Japanese firms abroad must have the services of local sub-contractors. This is a major concern of Japanese firms seeking advancement in the EEC.' Technova went on to point out that EC local content regulations 'demanded the expansion of sub-contract industries to serve Japanese firms producing in the UK'.

'In most UK industry, the relationship between contractor and supplier remains distant – and in some cases is more adversarial that cooperative.'

Another parallel study confirms the contrast between: 'the close bond between customer and supplier is a fundamental part of production strategy in Japan' and 'In most UK industry, the relationship between contractor and supplier remains distant – and in some cases is more adversarial than cooperative'.[7] This confirms the findings of Chapter 5 that the Japanese seek high-dependency relationships with suppliers.

There seemed to be little in the way of reinforcement of the infrastructure of subcontractors and suppliers prior to the introduction of Komatsu and Nissan in the North East in the mid-1980s: perhaps it was difficult to anticipate requirements, but in my view a major opportunity was lost in not helping indigenous suppliers to accelerate to a competitive level.

At a *Financial Times* manufacturing conference, Ian Gibson, then Purchasing Director of Nissan MUK, described the productivity improvement figures of British supply companies as 'abysmal' and urged British suppliers to adopt the Japanese suppliers' approach of making cost deductions through improved productivity and competitiveness.

'You run a business through people, not machines. . . . You cannot convince people [about TQC] unless senior management are convinced. Unless you have that commitment at the top you cannot expect it at the bottom'[8] (reported by Nick Garnett, *Financial Times*).

Drift to the Continent

The UK government is rightly proud that it has attracted over one-third of all Japanese inward investment in Europe into the UK. However, if subcontract, supplier, high-tech and business centre workload drifts to Continental Europe, the gains are significantly diminished: furthermore, the UK will not have taken advantage of the opportunity to improve the industrial infrastructure.

In reality, this profound disappointment with UK suppliers' performance by Japanese inward investors who were encouraged to choose the UK for their manufacturing plants has led in my view to a drift towards continental suppliers, despite the problems and cost of travel and freight, together with often unfavourable exchange rates and language complications. The EC insistence on high local content, and the failure of the UK government to deal with the problem (despite its own commissioned reports that predicted the issue), has exacerbated the situation. Local DTI officials have certainly done what they can in terms of liaison, support and sympathy, but the infrastructure of subcontractors and suppliers was completely unprepared to fill the requirements of the incoming Japanese. Even today, the capability of SMEs (small and medium-sized enterprises) is insufficient to underpin regional development.

Technical and high-level business support outside manufacturing plants has also been absent. It is significant in my view that the majority of high value-added inward investment into Europe has concentrated around Dusseldorf in Germany because of the high-tech infrastructure it offers. The latest Japanese External Trade Organisation (JETRO) survey of research, design and development (RD&D) centre location in Europe shows Germany continuing to obtain the majority of new investment (Christopher Lorenz, *Financial Times*, 28 March 1994).

It was also a great disappointment to witness Komatsu establish its European coordination HQ in Brussels in 1989, and not the UK – partly due to perceived inadequate business and communication links for such a centre in the North East of England.

The UK government is rightly proud that it has attracted over one-third of all Japanese inward investment in Europe into the UK. However, if subcontract, supplier, high-tech and business centre workload drifts to Continental Europe, the gains are significantly diminished: furthermore, the UK will not have taken advantage of the opportunity to improve the industrial infrastructure.

TQC and suppliers

The picture is not totally negative, however. Komatsu has persevered with many UK suppliers willing to form mutual partnerships who have, as mentioned in Chapter 3, travelled to Japan and vastly improved quality and performance levels. Komatsu UK has introduced a Supplier Development Team which has systematically aimed at improving supplier performance and introducing TQC approaches within suppliers. It is significant that Sumitomo in their joint venture with JCB since 1992 have discovered that Komatsu has beaten a path to almost all the potential major UK component suppliers who have been, in many cases, influenced by Komatsu supplier development teams – understanding and implementing TQC.

This experience serves to illustrate that with inward investment into Europe in the 1980s companies like Komatsu were entering a vastly more complex stage of international development and one that they could not easily control. The desire to be 'insiders' in the face of opposition via anti-dumping measures and earlier accusations of Japanese inward investment being 'screwdriver' plants has helped the trend towards higher value added outputs. Witness the development of the Primera and Micra models at Nissan MUK. With increasing degrees of UK-based design and development to produce European versions, similar to the development of the wheeled excavator range at Komatsu UK, state of the art IT has revolutionised this approach with satellite-linked CAD between the North East of England and Japan, enabling UK engineers to share the same design information simultaneously with their Japanese colleagues.

To indigenise or not to indigenise?

The Japanese in the 1980s faced the same dilemma as Henry Ford in the 1920s. What degree of indigenisation was sensible? Up to then it was simple, the outposts like Komatsu Europe, the sales and marketing subsidiary in Brussels, had been staffed on an 'oil and water' basis: Japanese managers on three-year secondments from Japan with Belgian administrator and sales and service personnel as support. No Belgian had penetrated into the decision-making area. It worked, despite early misgivings by expatriate Japanese who felt themselves sidelined from advancement in Japan. It gave career development and international exposure to a number of Japanese managers who brought the experience to bear elsewhere in the world. To the Belgians it gave job security and stability at reasonable wages. The pattern was repeated successfully elsewhere, notably in the USA and Australia up until the late 1980s when indigenous managers were appointed.

Both the UK and US manufacturing plants, however, promised to be different. Komatsu Japan knew that local managers had to be found who could both establish appropriate links with the community and also be the champions of TQC with a local labour force. In common with other Japanese they could not understand the predilection of Westerners for 'job hopping' between employers. As we saw in Chapter 2, there has been until very recent times no job market for 'salarymen' in Japan, and changing jobs has been unthinkable. This has led some Japanese to regard the attitudes of Europeans in this area as inferior and lacking in loyalty and trustworthiness.

Despite these perceived difficulties, visionaries in Komatsu Tokyo such as Tetsuya Katada persisted, insisting that the policy should be for British managers eventually to assume the top positions at the Birtley Plant.

Sony were the first to appoint a British Managing Director, Bill Fulton, in 1978. Nissan led the way in the North East, with the appointment in 1989 of Ian Gibson CBE as the first British Chief Executive of Nissan MUK. Toshiba had also appointed Des Thompson and Epson UK Don Pinchbeck, Chief Executives respectively in the late 1980s. However, these examples were rare. The perception of Western managers is often of a two-tier society in Japanese implants.

Womack, Jones and Roos quote a General Motors manager, 'I can hope to get to the top at General Motors, but I can never hope to rise above the middle level of one of the Japanese foreign subsidiaries, no matter how superior my performance.'[9] Sir Peter Parker, Chairman of Mitsubishi Electric UK, agrees that 'the big problem for a British executive in a Japanese company is the career structure, which is primarily geared around lifetime employment'.[10]

Dick Wilson says 'Working for a Japanese firm is, they say, like joining the Navy: you know you'll never make Admiral.'[11] For many it is a game of patience, but the British manager who is willing to play a long-term game may find patience rewarded. Others conclude that in their situation it will never happen, e.g. Ian Paterson, ex Marubeni-Komatsu (Komatsu distributorship in the UK), interviewed by Stephanie Jones.

> Although it is possible for a British executive to reach a high position in a Japanese company, to a certain extent there is a limit to how far a senior British executive can go . . . I left Marubeni-Komatsu because I felt I was banging my head on the ceiling.[12]

Is the key learning Japanese?

Opinions among British managers are divided on this important issue and the Japanese are schizophrenic over language. Generally, the Japanese do not encourage indigenous managers to learn their language – this is a product of recognising how difficult it is, an opposite aspiration for Japanese to learn English, and an inherent defence against foreigners penetrating 'Japaneseness'. On the other hand, they are flattered when you do make the effort to understand.

Sir Peter Parker takes a positive view, having recognized that British managers are only an appendage to the Japanese company career structure: 'As one of the few British executives with a Japanese company who speaks Japanese, he realizes the added understanding and insight which this gives. It is a major undertaking to learn Japanese, but it signals true commitment unlike anything else.'[13] James Shaff, formerly Vice-Chairman of YKK, reinforces the point: 'I realise now that if I had learned Japanese and made a total commitment to the company right from the outset, I could have become Chairman of YKK's operations in Britain.'

However, Ian Gibson, Chief Executive of Nissan MUK, and Keith Tipping, Managing Director of Komatsu UK, would both be at pains to point out that their knowledge of the Japanese language is not extensive. Further, Kazahiro Aoyagi, President of Komatsu Europe International, would maintain it is not essential for progress.

Local managers became a fashionable trend

The Japanese are as susceptible to fashions and trends as anyone else and it now appears *de rigeur* to appoint local directors and managers to run European operations – even the financial sector has succumbed, as Stephanie Jones reports with the appointment of John Howland Jackson as Deputy President of Nomura.

Not all observers think the trend is good for the enterprise. Womack, Jones and Roos recall the Ford experience after 1915: 'The wholesale substitution by domestic managers . . . to deal with investment friction quickly degraded the performance of Ford's production system toward the existing English level.'[14] Further, they point out that from their survey of assembly plants in North America and Europe they found strong evidence that those plants that perform best are those with a very strong Japanese management presence in the early years of operations. However, they point out that it is not the 'Japaneseness' of management that is the issue. Rather, it is how well transplant managers understand Lean Production and how deeply they are committed to making it work.[15]

Nick Oliver, in his Cambridge University report,[16] suggests that there is a cultural barrier between managers of Japanese organisations and the British workforce, leading to a decline in the effectiveness of 'Japanese management practices' in implants by 1991. This could be due to the increasing use of indigenous managers, and perhaps in turn due to their feelings of insecurity at often not being perceived as part of the career development system. It is certainly exacerbated by any lack of ownership of the 'new culture' by middle managers.

The need for dialogue

In Chapter 2 we saw the difficulties in misunderstandings that easily arise because of the Japanese 'sixth sense' among themselves where explanations are not thought necessary or because of the Western need for opinions and thoughts to be spelt out in words of two syllables.

There is no area that is more in need of dialogue than that of performance and potential promotion of Western managers. The Japanese are uncomfortable about conducting performance appraisals for Western managers – often because of the language problem and the inevitable barriers that have to come down to make it effective: 'Tatemae' to 'Honne' – 'the face' to 'the truth'.

This art will have to be mastered for Japanese multinationals to attract, retain and motivate the best indigenous staff, even though it goes against the grain for Japanese executives to make themselves vulnerable in this way. The new role for middle managers, described in Chapter 5, is just as valid in Japanese implants as in Western enterprises that are trying to emulate world-class systems.

Many Japanese multinationals are making huge efforts to create an 'international' workforce. The ownership of ICL by Fujitsu has enabled imaginative exchanges between Japanese and European personnel, as reported by Lucy Kellway in the *Financial Times*.[17] This is a pure learning experience on both sides. One Japanese personnel officer was 'amazed at the care with which ICL graduates were picked. . . . In ICL', he noted, 'personnel objectives are clearly defined and that improves motivation. In Japan people are forced into uncomfortable objectives.'

Heidi Hunter, the first woman to be sent to Fujitsu, reported: 'The biggest shock was on the morning of the first day to hear the company song on the PA, followed by exercises.' As a female engineer she was regarded as a freak. 'For the first six weeks the Japanese didn't know where to pigeonhole me. To survive, you have to have a lot of confidence. You've got to get up and do it. All have now acclimatised and have adapted to differing cultures.'

This is directly parallel to the policy Komatsu adopted for a number of years from 1988 onwards, where I successfully recruited graduates in the UK for three years' training in Japan. They often found it daunting but came back fluent in Japanese and with a unique knowledge of Japan, its culture and an intimate understanding of the company. The test will be over Komatsu's ability to use and retain this talent.

The multi-regional enterprise

By 1989, Komatsu in Japan had concluded that the phase of establishing wholly owned plants in the industrialised nations was over. Komatsu America Manufacturing Corporation (Chattanooga Plant) and Komatsu UK at Birtley would complete this stage of development. Despite the boom time for construction of equipment in Europe and USA, it was clear that there was major production overcapacity in both key markets and Komatsu needed to speed up market penetration.

The next phase would be link-ups with existing manufacturers. In the USA in 1988, Komatsu formed a 50:50 joint venture with Dresser, which would potentially give a market share of 20 per cent in North America. In Europe in 1989, Komatsu took a controlling interest in Hanomag, a famous West German construction equipment manufacturer, with a turnover of $200m p.a. and with a history of manufacture stretching back over 100 years.

These two moves added to the earlier tie-up with the Italian manufacturer of mini-excavators, FAI, for joint production and sales. The focus shifted from weaning new wholly owned factories such as Komatsu UK to major problems of co-ordination.

Komatsu set up Komatsu Europe International SA in Belgium as a co-ordination company for Europe, but not as a *control* or reporting centre. The main focus was to unravel the Byzantine and overlapping dealer networks throughout Europe and establish sensible policies on production and supply co-ordination.

Torio Komiya, who had moved from Birtley to be KEISA's first President, needed all his diplomatic skills. The Hanomag management at the time, now since departed, saw no need to change the status quo, felt they had little to learn from the Japanese, and a proud tradition. Moreover, the two-tier West German Board Structure was extraordinarily difficult to penetrate, even when Komatsu Ltd had a controlling interest.

Here the Japanese found themselves at a disadvantage. Their instinct to quietly encourage and to show by example to produce change was fazed in the face of the bombastic and self-confident style of German management.

Tetsuya Katada, now President, the original architect of Komatsu UK and expansion into Europe, patiently supported from Tokyo 'in the manner of a family doctor'.[18] His policy as reported in the *Financial Times* was one of 'harmonious global operations and fully localising production and product development activities to put our global operations on to a stronger footing.' In the same article he talked of the other 'basic pillar of management strategy' in diversifying away from construction equipment manufacture further into robotics, electronics and plastics. Komatsu was becoming truly global and multi-regional, with all the problems and ambitions that US and European multinationals had themselves experienced.

Patience has been rewarded however, with a new indigenous Hanomag President, Herr Seidel there has been much improvement. In contrast to the early days Tetsuya Katada found much to praise on his visit in April 1994:

> Hanomag has made a remarkable change in production technology. I believe that Hanomag will achieve cost and quality targets for their new model line due to be launched through our newly integrated distributors this year.

The three 'G's

Tetsuya Katada will be seen as the third great architect of Komatsu growth. Yoshinari Kawai and his son Ryoichi Kawai can rightly claim successful introduction, embedding and growth of TQC and its translation into a philosophy affecting all the elements of the business. Tetsuya Katada has been the visionary of the 1980s and 1990s. He saw the need for successful indigenised plants in Europe and the USA; the need for integrated sales and production in Europe; and developed the philosophy of the three 'G's:

- Globalisation
- Growth
- Groupwide

The phases of this policy are now clear:

1985–8   Establishment of wholly owned plants in the Europe and USA

1988–93   Indigenisation of implants

1988–93   Joint venture and strategic alliances in Europe and the USA

1993–94   Progressive shifting of production from Japan to overseas to combat the ever-rising value of the yen – 'Endaka' or 'Yendaka'

1994
onwards   Globalisation in raising Hardware, Software, 'Humanware' performance throughout Komatsu operations world wide (see Fig. 7.1) by integration

e.g. 'Integrate the globalised Komatsu Group organisation and Systems in order to make the most of corporate resources.'

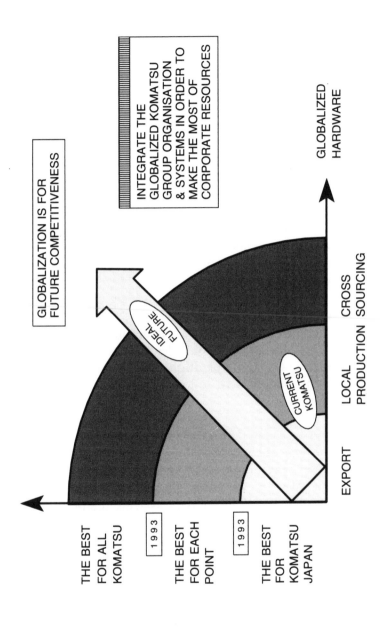

Fig. 7.1 *Komatsu globalisation concept*

Kazahiro Aoyagi, President of Komatsu Europe International, explains in relation to Fig. 7.1.

'Komatsu's philosophy in the next stage of development.

The horizontal line shows the evolution of types of business. The vertical line shows progress of software, or the mind of company staff involved.

We have to acknowledge that we are currently in the lower end of the diagram, it means a high level of integrated software is not present in each business unit, because we have been concentrating on production with target cost and quality, in order to catch up to Japanese production models and to supply the competitive products into each territory.

Now we have almost reached to the level of Japanese produced models in cost, and quality we are aiming to promote cross sourcing, such as exporting Komatsu UK products into USA or the Japanese market or elsewhere.

Then we will face another phase of problem arising from non integrated management.

Hence we are now concentrating on achieving the same management level of production control, sales administration, procurement, development, parts operation and so on, regardless of location and type of company, so long as it is within the Komatsu group.'

Which pattern are the Japanese to follow?

Ever since the Meiji restoration, the thrust for Japan has been to catch up with the West. As we saw in Chapter 2, they have been the world's best shoppers – carefully studying systems and products from the developed world and then improving on them in their own factories and business approaches.

Dick Wilson in *The Sun at Noon*, points out that the Japanese were strangely prepared for competition even in the period of isolationism:

Under the Shoguns of the eighteenth and early nineteenth centuries, Japan was already goal-oriented, and the economy was open to competitive individual enterprise with little government intervention, benefiting from the diversity of feudal divisions as well as from a surprisingly good banking system. Economically, Japan at the time of Napoleon resembled Europe more than China or India. She had only to cast off the superficial garb of feudalism, to 'change her costume, not her soul', as John Randolph put it, and she was ready for modernity. Even the living standards of 1800 may have been higher than Europe's or America's. Japan owed nothing substantial to the West.[19]

However, with virtually every major blue chip company in Japan talking of 'globalism' and 'internationalism', I wonder whether they have an example to follow or a strategy formulated (perhaps Komatsu is an exception).

The clear control principles of TQC that dovetailed into Komatsu worldwide expansion of the 1960s, 1970s and 1980s are not easy to apply when central management does not have complete control over joint ventures and part ownerships. The key has to be to persuade inherited local management by example and benchmarking in a similar fashion to the pattern followed for local suppliers.

Which example from previous international experience should the Japanese follow? The American multinational with country-to-country presence, clear centralised control by the US HQ, and top jobs reserved for US citizens? Or the European 'federal', rather more democratic, but perhaps uncontrollable, model?

Have the Japanese a clear idea of the best way of managing such an enterprise or are they subject to policy 'drift' as in so many areas of their national life?

Which way for the Japanese multinational?

- Centralised decision making with plans run by indigenous management
- or 'Federal' model with delegated powers?
- or policy 'drift'

'Pursuer' to 'Pioneer'?

Dick Wilson, in *The Sun at Noon*, in talking about a potential world role for Japan says:

Most Japanese have no idea what they would like to do in the world with their economic achievement, and the usual advice by politicians is, in one Prime Minister's phrase, to be 'a porcupine and not a roaring lion'. Japan sways with the tides like a sea-anemone, skilled at day-to-day survival but without a direction or strategy.[20]

However, things are changing; Ian Gow has analysed that MITI encouragement of business growth in biotechnology and new materials is part of an overall strategy to change Japan's strategy from 'pursuer' to 'pioneer'.[21]

Womack, Jones and Roos[22] offer some advice for setting up the multi-regional enterprise. The concept, they say, is simple:

> Devise a form of enterprise that functions smoothly on a Multi-regional basis and gaining the advantage of close contact with local markets and the presence as an insider in each of the major regions. At the same time it must benefit from access to systems for global production supply, product development, technology acquisition, finance and distribution.
>
> The central problem is people – how to reward and motivate thousands of individuals from many countries and cultures so that they work in harmony.

Womack, Jones and Roos go on to reject the three known forms as inadequate to meet this specification:

(a) Centralisation of decision-making at HQ, invariably located in the home country and staffed by nationals of the home country. This was Ford's approach from 1908 to the 1960s. Centralisation produces bad decision-making and resentment in outlying regions.

(b) Extreme decentralisation into regional subsidiaries, each developing own products, systems, career ladders in isolation. Ford of Europe of the 1970s and General Motors Europe today fit into this category. This 'sealed' division results in narrow focus, ignores cross-regional advantages and produces insular hierarchies.

(c) Strategic alliances with independent partner firms from each region as a variant of (b) as the last approach. The example Womack, Jones and Roos give is of Mitsubishi with Chrysler and General Motors with Isuzu and Suzuki. The weakness is the issue of central coordination and overall management. These 'federal' arrangements have proved inherently unstable and importantly undynamic.

Womack, Jones and Roos propose a new form called Post-National Multi-regional enterprise. Key features would be:

- An integrated global personnel system that promotes personnel from any country in the company as if nationality did not exist. (In 1988 I started recruiting UK engineering graduates to train in Japan for three years as a potential stock of international managers for Komatsu Ltd – see p. 180).

- A set of mechanisms for continuous horizontal information flow among manufacturing, supply systems, product development, technology acquisition and distribution. (Similar to existing approaches, with Japanese companies using TQC principles or simultaneous/concurrent engineering. Such international teams are widely used in Komatsu.) (See Fig. 7.1.)

- A mechanism for co-ordinating the development of new products in each region and facilitating their sale as niche products in other regions – without producing lowest common denominator products. (Now overseas production arms of Nissan and Komatsu are selling into other world markets, e.g. US-produced earth graders to Europe and UK-produced excavators to the USA.)

Such a feature presupposes that products will move region to region in roughly equal volumes in order to ignore currency shifts. Developing products locally to suit the region is conceivable: finding markets for those products in other regions may not be.

Womack, Jones and Roos lay down one other environmental condition – internationalised finance and equity. Against such criteria emerging, Japanese multinationals could often demonstrate concurrent thinking. However, the first key feature would probably be the most difficult to mimic.

I am pleased to say that in Europe Komatsu has recently made important steps forward in this area. Komatsu UK now has its first British Managing Director, Keith Tipping, who joined as Production Manager in 1986. Similarly, with Hanomag, Komatsu Europe and Komatsu Baumaschinen (German Sales company) – all have Europeans as Chief Officers. Many other examples exist. In Japan, both Sony and Itochu Corporation now have Westerners on their main boards. Perhaps this is the start of a new international phase.

However, the focus for Japan in recent times shifted from problems overseas to the crisis at home. Many commentators are predicting collapse in Japan due to the increasingly unstable political scene, internal corruption, a distorted taxation system, and massive industrial over-capacity. The balance of economic growth has for the first time in a decade shifted from Japan to the USA.

America's computer and electronic industries feel that they have not only survived but are positively thriving . . . the extent to which layers of (overhead) staff have been removed has given business across the Atlantic the comfortable sense that it has swallowed a pill which over cosseted Europe and overstaffed Japan have yet to do.[23]

NOTES

1. *Financial Times*, 25 January 1993.
2. Womack, Jones and Roos, *The Machine that Changed the World*, pp. 254–5, Rawson Assoc., 1988.
3. Ibid., p. 255.
4. Malcolm Trevor and Ian Christie, 'Manufacturers and Suppliers', in *Britain and Japan*, p. 1, Policy Studies Institute, 1988.
5. Ibid., pp. 3 and 4.
6. Technova Inc., *Japanese Direct Investment in the UK. Its Possibilities and Problems*, Toyko 1980.
7. J. H. Dunning, *Japanese Participation in British Industry* p. 111, Croom Helm, 1986.
8. Trevor and Christie, op. cit. p. 115.
9. Womack, Jones and Roos, op. cit., p. 273.
10. S. Jones, *Working for the Japanese*, p. 93, Macmillan, 1991.
11. D. Wilson, *The Sun at Noon* p. 167, Hamish Hamilton, 1986.
12. S. Jones, op. cit., p. 202.
13. Ibid., p. 282.
14. Womack, Jones and Roos, p. 273.
15. Ibid., p. 274.
16. N. Oliver, Judge Institute of Management, University of Cambridge, 'Making it in Britain', 1993.
17. *Financial Times*, 28 September 1993.
18. *Financial Times*, Nick Garnett, 15 November 1989.
19. Wilson, op. cit., p. 201.
20. Ibid., p. 18.
21. I. Gow, 'Japanese Technological Advance: Problems of Evaluation', *European Management Journal*, vol. 16, no. 2, pp. 127–33.
22. Womack, Jones and Roos, op. cit., p. 234.
23. A. Hamilton, *The Observer*, 2 January 1994.

8 Should We Be Concerned about Manufacturing in the West?

> 'Progress is impossible without change, and those who cannot change their minds cannot change anything' (G.B. Shaw 1856–1950).

Has manufacturing passed us by in the West? Can we survive economically on the service and financial sectors? Or have the Japanese bitten off more than they can chew? Lastly, what can we do?

JAPAN IN CRISIS

There is a view that the shifts in focus for Japanese multi-regional enterprises as they have moved away from exporting finished products to exporting productive capacity to the West will cause significant problems for Japanese management. 'Endaka' has meant increases in overseas production and retrenchment at home – including factory closures.

Offshore plants, while achieving impressive quality and productivity gains using TQC and Lean Production techniques, have imposed a burden on Japanese management because of the spread and complexity of their international organisation.[1] Recession has finally hit Japan in a serious way.

Consequently, these difficulties for the Japanese may appear to give welcome relief to Western competitors. This view is the voice of optimism over experience since the early years for the embryonic Japanese international enterprise with plants in LDCs were a good training ground. Until the latest phase of international development, using joint ventures and acquisitions, only one local plant was seen as sufficient for Komatsu in Europe and the US markets.

In the last twenty years Japanese companies have also shown a remarkable ability to turn adversity to their advantage. History has shown that it never pays to underestimate the Japanese when they feel isolated and in a corner. Witness the events of dollar shock 1971, 'oil shock' in 1973, 'endaka' (rapid rise of value of the yen – between June 1985 and September 1988 the Japanese yen appreciated by a phenomenal 85 per cent against the dollar), growth of protectionism in the 1980s. All this has given a shift to more entrepreneurial and international styles of management.[2]

Barrie James, in *Trojan Horse*,[3] believes it is naïve to assume that the ten to fifteen-year lead that American and European companies are claimed to have in understanding how to operate on a multinational basis over Japanese firms will translate into a competitive advantage. His pessimism is increased by the overwhelming evidence of Western multinationals being outflanked by their Japanese rivals and the innate short-termism displayed by Western companies even when they do have the advantage.

'Endaka' or the deliberate rise in value of the Japanese yen, was a market intervention measure agreed upon by the group of five (G.5.) industrial nations in 1985 in order to address the soaring trade imbalance between the West and Japan. The contrasting strategic reaction to this situation by Japanese and US companies is an object lesson. Most Japanese companies decided to absorb much of the yen appreciation to preserve market share and, consequently, reduced margins. US companies tended to adopt a policy of maintaining offshore prices by increasing export prices to both Japan and Europe, even though the dollar had lost value against both the yen and EC currencies. Also, US domestic producers seized the opportunity, and rapidly followed any price increases of Japanese products in the USA to improve their margins. Hence the behaviour of US companies when given a competitive advantage was short-term profit making rather than building market share with lower prices.[4]

Western manufacturers have no room to feel complacent. In the context of 'endaka', the regime of 'easy money', and the bubble economy in Japan in the late 1980s (partly caused by the appreciating yen increasing the cash reserves in real terms), Japan switched the focus of overseas investment away from supplier countries (raw materials and labour) to consuming markets in North America and the EC, doubling manufacturing investment between 1974 and 1986 in these markets.[5]

In the latest period of 'endaka', Japan's new investment in the USA and Europe has slowed and the focus has switched to the Pacific rim.

The enthusiasm for the Pacific rim is shared by the USA. Mr Winston Lord, US Assistant Secretary of State for Asia in the Clinton administration, has said, 'Europe is still very important but, in relative terms we believe Asia has become more important for America – and not just for economic reasons.'[6]

Inside Japan, a revolution is underway at both macro and micro economic levels. Despite the fragility of previous Prime Minister Hosokawa's coalition, the government put in place a massive cut in income tax and an increase in public works spending to stimulate the economy. The yen started to recede in 1994, and US officials recognised that a strong yen is not in the interest of the US or international economies. Also, economists expected a further decline in Japanese interest rates.[7]

At the micro level, industries have drastically reduced domestic production and increased production overseas (Komatsu announced a major restructuring programme in August 1993, increasing component imports). As a result, the trade surplus has already begun to shrink in both volume and yen terms. 'In addition the Hosokawa coalition was the first Japanese government to advocate voluntarily the deregulation of the economy, something that the US has long sought in the hope of reducing the current account surplus.'[8]

Lastly, experience in this recession in Japan has differed from the past. Previously, lifetime employment was adhered to universally, which ensured people had jobs, even if they had no meaningful work to do. This time, companies are cutting staff, albeit in small numbers and as a last resort, to reduce costs and improve profitability. 'Early retirement' is now common parlance in Japan. According to William Dawkins,[9] 'companies are now employing between 1m and 2m people more than they need – perhaps the same number again as the 1.75m officially unemployed'.

White-collar Japan, traditionally very inefficient, is now catching up with Western enthusiasm for re-engineering. However, Frank Petro writing in Vol. 6 No. 1 of *Insights CSC Index* comments: 'Rather than cutting staff, Japanese re-engineering efforts will look to create new value added opportunities for employees'.

Petro adds that Japanese corporations have a number of advantages which will help them gain the most from re-engineering:

- The labour force – employees are already accustomed to teamwork, job rotation, process orientation with on going training and education.
- Absence of front-office automation. Japanese corporations are

not generally saddled with out of date inflexible mainframe computer systems.

- Long-term perspective. The Japanese have always taken a longer perspective in business strategy. They have the patience to perfect new process designs.
- Continuous improvement. Kaizen experience gives an appreciation for process – which is lacking in the West.

All of which indicates that, firstly, Japan has a potential route out of recession because, yet again, both macro and micro level policies can be complementary and, secondly, as in so many other ways, Japan is learning the business methods of the West. The question is whether these changes of policy, such as the dent in the façade of lifetime employment, will shatter the customary loyalty of the Japanese to their companies. William Dawkins, discussing this in the *Financial Times*,[10] quotes the views of Tatsuro Toyoda, President of Toyota, 'Maybe it is a good idea to have two types of employees, a "stock" type (lifetime employment) and a "flow" type (temporary).' Putting this philosophy into practice will, however, be very slow. The Japanese education system does not favour the type of person who wishes to map out his own career.

> 'I've gone through a few recessions, but everyone is saying this one is different. Besides, we're all growing old. We don't have the energy to fight any more' (Japanese subcontractor).

Economic changes within Japan are likely to hit hardest at subcontractor or supplier level. According to Tokyo Shoko Research, bankruptcies in small and medium-sized businesses were up 30 per cent in 1993 over 1992, compared with about 4 per cent in large companies.[11] In addition to the effects of recession, Japan's subcontractors, which make up 56 per cent of the country's small businesses, have been hit by the manufacturers' changes in production policy. In line with Lean Production techniques, there are fewer model changes, longer production cycles, shorter model development times, and fewer subcontractors, due to single-sourcing policies. Components are increasingly shared between models, and often big companies are starting to produce many parts and components themselves. Client companies are encouraging their suppliers to become *less* dependent and to diversify – again, the opposite to the trend in the West where Lean Production and single sourcing are being belatedly discovered.

Commentators believe that MITI, which used to wield great power and influence, has lost control as corporate Japan has become increasingly international and powerful.[12] One subcontractor said, 'I've gone through a few recessions, but everyone is saying this one is different. Besides, we're all growing old. We don't have the energy to fight any more.'

If there are victims of this recession in Japan they are more likely to be further down the pyramid where bankruptcies and unemployment will be more prevalent – again providing a pattern not unlike the West. However, the similarity ends when we study the extent of manufacturing decline in the West. In Japan it is a case of redistributing the workload rather than a savage reduction in capacity coupled with indifference. Both Japanese and Germans were staggered at the nonchalant reaction in Britain over the sale of Britain's last independent car maker to BMW in February 1994. Could this be another sign of the lack of perceived dependence of the economy on manufacturing?

'The money game is fine, but industry is the only way for a country to survive, and I wonder how the British expect to make a living in the future'.

> Nobuhiko Kawamoto
> President of Honda Motor Company
> commenting on the sale of Rover to BMW
> (Guardian, 22 February 1994).

WHAT HAS BEEN HAPPENING IN THE USA AND EUROPE?

Western management has an inbred fear of change. This had led to a flight from risk taking and often adopting the line of least resistance. Soft options were taken in the face of determined Japanese competition, and typically many moved up market to more secure, but smaller volume, higher-value niches. As we have seen, such elements of Lean Production that have been adopted by Western companies tend to concentrate on lower wage costs, not customer-driven product development, longer-term thinking and culture change:

Many Western firms failed to recognize that it does not follow that you will become more competitive if you just lower your costs and increase your quality.

Competitive advantage is a more complex issue and is built on managing converging competences in production, finance, quality, design, technology and service [my italics]. Japanese strategies are designed to produce strong future competitive positions for global brands with the potential for cross-market subsidisation.[13]

The economic problems of the USA and Europe have been broadly the same, just different in degree. Both economies have been unable to expand real incomes despite major shifts in competitiveness. European economies such as the UK started to improve from a very low base in the 1980s. Much of Europe suffers from intractable unemployment, often double the level of the USA. It has failed to create sufficient new employment while maintaining protection for a vast range of uncompetitive industries. Productivity gains have been low; major pockets of poverty exist, and they are growing. Europe's technology base is eroding relative to that of the USA and, increasingly, Japan, reducing value-added contributions to its economies.[14] Few of its manufacturing companies have the critical mass necessary to compete on equal terms with their US and Japanese rivals.

Even more devastating is the fact that the leading NICs, Brazil, Hong Kong, Korea, Singapore and Taiwan, have acquired cash and technology and have developed human resource skills that come within striking distance of closing the comparative advantage gap with the West in selective areas of high value-added manufacturing.

A ROLE FOR THE SERVICE SECTOR?

'The Western response to the steady decline in its comparative advantage in manufacturing was a steady drift . . . to services. Of the 11 million jobs created in the US since 1981/82, 80% have been in services – retailing, restaurants, financial and business services, transportation, health and education – estimates suggest 9 out of 10 new jobs up to 1995 will be in services.'

'The effectiveness of the service sector is linked to the ability to support manufacturing. As manufacturing employment declines, demands for services increase. General Motors' major supplier is not a steel, tyre or electronics firm, but a health insurance company.'[15]

'The move out of manufacturing has had depressing effects on Western competitiveness. Service jobs generally pay 10–20 per cent less than the manufacturing jobs they replace and generate low levels of productivity.'[16]

Lastly, few service industries offer significant export opportunities. It is well known that manufacturing, in general terms, has the potential to export 80 per cent of what it makes, whereas services are limited to around 20 per cent. Also, since services up to now have not been regulated by GATT, most countries have operated trade barriers that control service industries thereby restricting foreign competition. The move from manufacturing to service has compounded, rather than solved, our problems with competitiveness.

Simon Caulkin, writing in *Management Today*, concludes:

> Far from being an innately superior kind of business activity service companies had to be taught to excel by humble manufacturers. The message is clear: a country which has not absorbed the lessons of manufacturing is unlikely to be any good at services either, in the long run.[17]

WHAT IS THE CHALLENGE FOR MANUFACTURING IN THE UK?

'European Industry must either get smarter or it will get poorer' (Tony Jackson, 'Can Europe Compete?', *Financial Times*, 25 February 1994).

'A country which has not absorbed the lessons of manufacturing is unlikely to be any good at services either, in the long run' (Simon Caulkin, *Management Today*).

Place in the UK economy

Fig. 8.1 shows that in terms of spending on manufactured goods, consumers spend over 55 per cent of total spent on manufactured

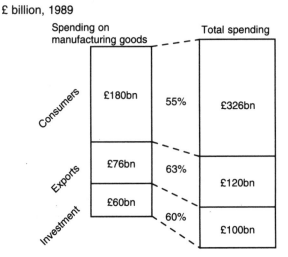

Note: UK manufacturing value-added in 1989 was £101bn.
Source: CBI calculations based on UK National Accounts.

Fig. 8.1   *UK expenditure on manufacturing goods*

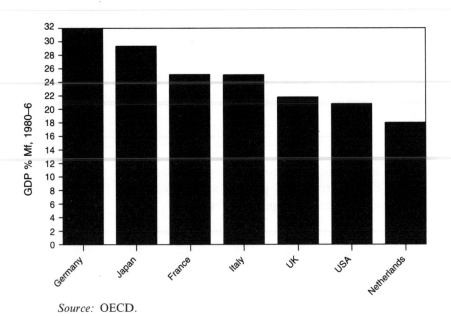

Source: OECD.

Fig. 8.2   *Share of manufacturing in GDP (average, 1980–6)*

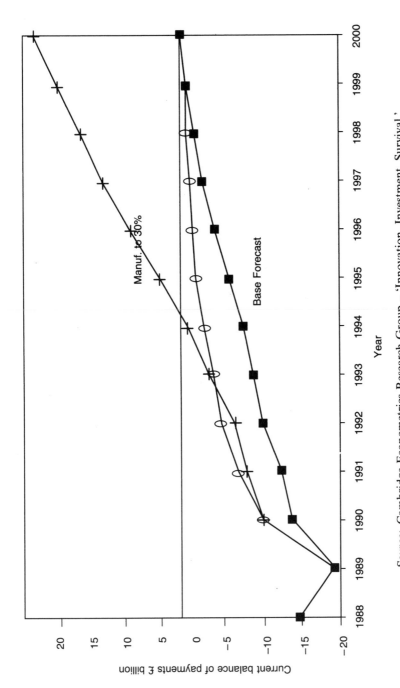

Source: Cambridge Econometrics Research Group – 'Innovation, Investment, Survival.'

Fig. 8.3 *Returning manufacturing to 30% GDP: balance of payments scenarios*

goods. More importantly, manufacturing employs just under one-fifth of the workforce, 4 million people, and it is a major generator of employment in the rest of the economy. Research at St Peter's College, Oxford, has shown that manufacturing is a more important creator of employment than the service industries, and also manufacturing purchases more from the rest of the economy than do the service industries. In addition, manufacturing creates a further 5 million jobs in service and other support industries.

The share of manufacturing in gross domestic product is also important. Fig. 8.2 shows that the UK share of manufacturing in GDP was in fact little more than 20 per cent, whereas in West Germany it was 32 per cent, and in Japan nearly 30 per cent. Fig. 8.3 which originates from the Cambridge Econometrics Research Group,[18] shows that if the UK could mimic Germany or Japan and return manufacturing to producing 30 per cent of GDP, then the UK balance of payments would be in the black rather than the habitual red, but this would be to reverse dramatically a thirty-year decline, as Fig. 8.4 shows, with the manufacturing percentage of GDP slipping from 37 per cent in 1960 down to our current level of 20 per cent, to 22 per cent at the end of the 1990s. Simon Caulkin

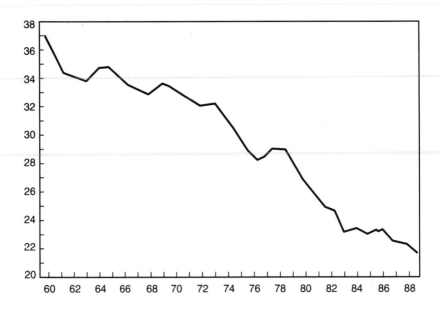

Fig. 8.4 *Manufacturing in GDP, 1960–89 (percentage)*

points out that 'not only does manufacturing matter, but that UK capacity is approaching the danger point where it becomes impossible to regenerate itself, let alone the economy as a whole'.[19]

Since 1991, the Cambridge Econometrics Research Group, working with the Royal Society of Arts, has produced a scenario in which a package of tax incentives, increased spending on training and education and greater effort put into selling into the EC, could lead to a 10 per cent improvement in the British innovation effort in the years 1993 to 2000. The results are startling: sustainable economic growth of 4 per cent a year from 1995, a balance of payments moving into surplus, unemployment falling to under 1 million – and a manufacturing sector that grows to 27 per cent of GDP.

The cost of the package is put at £3.5–£5.5 billion a year – not all of which would come from government. In addition a lower PSBR would, in their calculations, outweigh the cost of tax concessions for innovation over a five-year period.

What has happened in recent years?

The Confederation of British Industry survey published in 1991, called *Competing with the World's Best*, shows some dramatic changes in the last decade. Table 8.1, manufacturing output growth between 1975 and 1990, indicates a major swing from negative figures in the 1970s through to an annual percentage increase in real added value of 3.5 per cent in the last five years. However, this is at the average of competitor countries. In terms of manufacturing productivity growth, Table 8.2, demonstrates that in the last decade a real change has come about where the annual percentage change for the UK moved from less than 1 per cent increase to 4 per cent average in the last decade, above the average among the competitors listed in Table 8.2. However, it is important to look at the relative manufacturing productivity – in other words, the base from which the UK started. Fig. 8.5 shows that despite this good news in increase in productivity growth, the UK starting point was so low in relation to competitors that such growth is a little academic:

Despite the productivity gains made in the early 1980s, British manufacturing productivity is low, as are British wages, when compared with the international competition. A report made in 1987 by the National Institute (*Economic Review*, no. 20, summarized in *Financial Times*, 28th May 1987) stated that Britain's recent 'moderately favourable' productivity performance still left a 'formidable' gap between it and its rivals. Measured in terms of output per hour, American productivity was two-and-a-half times greater, and that of Japan, West Germany and France around 80 per cent higher. In contrast, Britain came a clear second-from-bottom (to Ireland) in a league table of 12 industrial nations covering unit hourly labour costs, when taking employers' social charges into account. America's costs were 61 per cent higher and Japan's 29 per cent. The report's conclusion was that the British competitive advantage of very cheap labour was 'more than offset' by its very low level of productivity'.[20]

Table 8.1 Manufacturing output growth, 1975–90

| | Annual % increase in real value-added | | |
	1975–80	*1980–5*	*1985–90*
Japan	7.6	7.3	4.7
US	4.1	3.4	3.7
West Germany	3.2	0.6	3.5
UK	−0.1	0.7	3.5
Italy	5.6	−0.8	3.2
France	2.9	−0.4	2.8
Average	3.7	1.8	3.6

Note: Figures for 1985–90 and for Italy are based on the change in manufacturing production.

Source: OECD National Accounts and *Main Economic Indicators.*

Table 8.2 Manufacturing productivity growth, 1975–90

| | Annual % increase in real value-added per person employed | | |
	1975–80	*1980–5*	*1985–90*
UK	0.9	5.4	4.0
Japan	7.3	6.0	3.9
US	1.7	4.4	3.6
Italy	5.7	1.8	3.3
France	4.0	2.1	3.2
West Germany	3.6	2.6	2.0
Average	3.8	3.8	3.3

Source: OECD National Accounts and *Main Economic Indicators, CSO.*

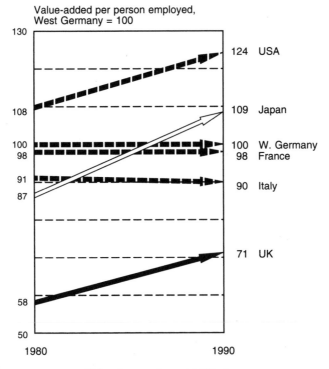

Value-added per person employed,
West Germany = 100

130

124   USA

108

109   Japan

100   100   W. Germany
98   98   France

91
87   90   Italy

71   UK

58

50

1980   1990

Source: CBI estimates from OECD data.

Fig. 8.5   *Relative manufacturing productivity*

If we look deeper by analysing what has happened industry by industry, this overall pattern becomes quite dispersed. Fig. 8.6 shows that the varying industries have grown at wildly different rates and the average 4 per cent growth hides the extremes of between 9 per cent and zero.

Inward Investment

Because of the distance that the UK has to make up on its competitors, much faith has been put in the short- and long-term rewards of inward investment into the UK. Fig. 8.7 shows that there is a distinct difference between the performance in terms of value added between foreign-owned companies and UK-owned companies within the UK. Also, it is interesting to note that investment levels in

Annual output growth, 1985–90 (%)

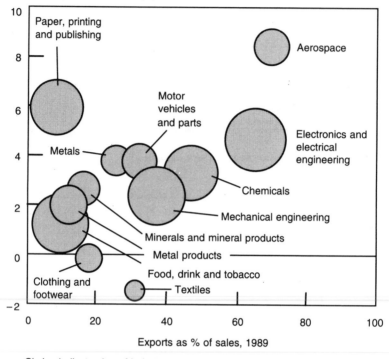

Circles indicate size of industry

Source: CSO.

Fig. 8.6 *Growth and competitiveness in manufacturing industry*

foreign-owned companies exceed their comparative companies in the UK. There is little doubt that inward investment has assisted in reducing unemployment.

Fig. 8.8 shows that the North of England between 1980 and 1989 was above average for the UK as a whole, with 1 per cent of the total workforce numbers being created through inward investment. This impact of inward investment has affected the region in other ways, such as general buoyancy and increase in income, and also by osmosis of ideas between companies. Research at the University of Northumbria for the Department of Employment has shown indigenous companies have been following very much the same path as the inward investors often seen to be innovators. This is now reflected across British industry in that management is focusing on change to produce greater competitiveness.

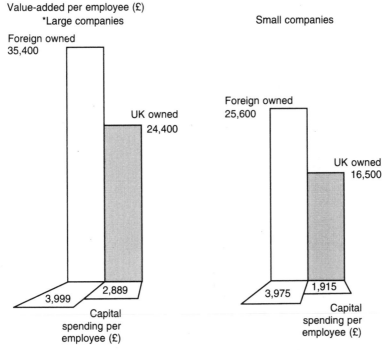

*Net output in excess of £200m.

Source: 1988 Census of production, Business Statistics Office.

Fig. 8.7   *Relative productivity of UK manufacturing, 1988*

Table 8.3   Main priorities for management

	Very important	Quite important	Not important
Importance of factors for company profitability and market share in the year ahead			
Weighted % of manufacturing companies responding			
Cost reduction	66	34	–
Improve customer service quality	64	30	4
Improve product quality	54	39	3
Introducing new products	45	42	9
Rationalisation/restructuring	30	31	33
Increasing investment	25	53	11
Diversification	6	14	61
Making new acquisitions	5	38	37

Source: CBI/AT Kearney Survey of Business Prospects, June 1991.

Jobs created, 1980–9, as a percentage of workforce in 1989

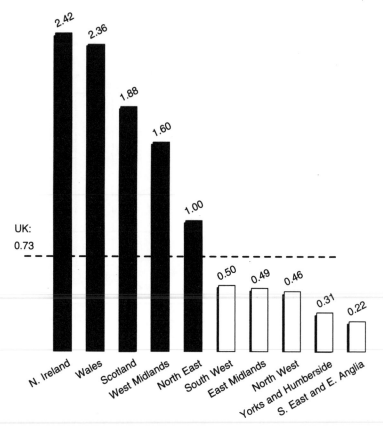

Source: DTI Invest in Britain Bureau and CSO.

Fig. 8.8 *Impact of inward investment on regional unemployment rate*

Lean Production

Table 8.3 (on page 203), from a survey conducted by CBI and AT Kearney, illustrates the main priorities for management today are all about cost reduction, improving quality, and introducing new products, when ten years ago the same management would have put creating profit at the top of that agenda – instead of today now recognising that competitive advantage comes from good performance in a range of areas.

£billion, 1989 prices

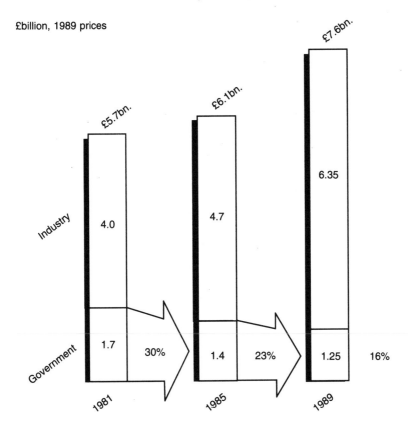

Source: Department of Trade and Industry.

Fig. 8.9 *UK research and development expenditure in business*

Research and development

Much of the UK's long-term future competitiveness depends on research and development. Fig. 8.9 shows healthy increases in overall R&D expenditure between 1981 and 1989. However, Table 8.4 shows that the UK was the only country in the early 1980s to register a decrease in industrial output growth, hence the real growth in the UK is seen to be a factor of five or ten times behind the annual growth of our competitors. However, the good news is that some big blue chip companies in the UK are maintaining their competitive advantage by massive increases in R&D expenditure every year (Table 8.5).

Economists who analyse technical progress are unanimous in their findings that about 40 per cent of the growth of GDP in the UK is attributable to technical progress. With manufacturing responsible for about 85 per cent of R&D investment, it is therefore the essential driving force of growth in the economy. *For this reason alone, manufacturing is the major determinant of the health of the whole economy.*

Table 8.4 Growth rates of industrial R&D, 1967–83 (annual percentage changes)

	R&D	R&D/Output
USA	4.1	1.7
Japan	10.7	5.3
West Germany	5.6	3.5
France	5.8	2.7
United Kingdom	1.1	–0.6
Italy	5.1	2.4
Sweden	6.6	5.3

Source: OECD.

Table 8.5 R&D expenditure, 1990

	Expenditure £m	% change On 1989
ICI	591	+6
Shell	473	+5
Unilever	408	+3
Glaxo	399	+24
Smithkline Beecham	393	+1
GEC	390	+32
BP	329	+1
STC (inc. ICL)	271	+28
Rolls Royce	237	+47
BT	228	+10
Total	3719	+14

Source: R&D Scoreboard, prepared by Company Reporting Limited for the Department of Trade and Industry.

CBI CONCLUSIONS

Having commissioned a major study in 1991, the Manufacturing Advisory Group of the CBI concluded that for manufacturing to increase its contribution to the economy:

1 The best world practice must be applied.
2 Government must play its full part in supporting long-term investment in manufacturing.
3 Relationships must be built between industry and the financial community.
4 Industry must dispel the outdated image of manufacturing among young people and opinion formers. Also, they point out that the dispersion between the best and worst in British industry is far too wide. The average productivity at the top 25 per cent of top UK manufacturers is *over five times* the average of the bottom 25 per cent.

If value added per employee in the major economies continues to increase at the rate achieved in the 1980s, UK manufacturing productivity will overtake Italy and nearly catch up with France and West Germany by the turn of the century, but the gap with the USA will have closed only slightly and that with Japan will have widened yet further.

By 1993 progress was encouraging in the UK, for in the first half of 1993 alone:

- Manufacturing output rose by 2 per cent
- Productivity rose by 7.3 per cent
- Unit labour costs fell by 2 per cent
- Exports rose by 2 per cent, but the trade deficit was 7 billion (£1 billion worse than 1992)
- Capital investment was flat

WHO HAS REACHED WORLD CLASS?

However, the CBI feel that more needs to be done to improve the balance of trade and manufacturing investment. Whereas there are clearly UK companies that are world class, they are small in number and tend to be concentrated at the larger end of the business spectrum, whereas growth will be required in SMEs to achieve world class in order to stimulate recovery.

Simon Caulkin writing in *Management Today*, has said, 'While the good British firms are a match for anyone, there simply are not enough of them, particularly small ones.'[21] Dr Michael Cross of MBS[22] has compiled an analysis of 'world-class' manufacturing operations based on the Malcolm Baldridge National Quality Award criteria. The survey covered 12,000 companies, of which 1,039 scored over 900 on the Baldridge Scale. Of the 1,039 in total, 675 were Japanese-owned, 221 North American, 71 West German, 40 British and 32 French. However, when the number of operations were split by location a different pattern emerges. Of the Japanese-owned operations, 510 are in Japan, for North American-owned operations 113 are in North America, Germany 67, France 29, yet for the British operations, 34 are located outside the UK, leaving just 6 British owned world class operators on British soil, according to this survey. Michael Cross concludes, 'I think we have a long way to go if UK manufacturing is to become world class.'

In a parallel survey in 1993, Phil Hanson of IBM and Professor Chris Voss of the London Business School produced the following results:

IBM/LONDON BUSINESS SCHOOL
SURVEY OF UK COMPANIES 1993.   'Who is World Class?'

2% World Class
                                      } The Leaders
42% Aspire to World Class

56% ?   The Laggers?

Biggest inhibitor – ability to implement change quickly enough.
No quick fixes – leading companies better than laggers because they have adopted better practices and improved their performance at *every level.*

Phil Hanson, IBM
Professor Chris Voss, LBS

The need for critical mass was also recognised by the President of the Board of Trade, the Rt. Hon Michael Heseltine, at the CBI Conference in November 1993:

Mr Heseltine warned that a handful of world class companies could not transform the performance of an economy. Although there were examples of British excellence he was concerned with averages and those at the bottom of the performance scale. 'As a nation, as individuals, at every level of authority and appointment', he said, 'we must seek improvement'.[23]

To widen the horizons of companies, particularly smaller companies, the CBI set out an agenda for aspiring companies in the future:

- Establish a clear sense of strategic direction ensuring this is communicated, understood and implemented throughout the business and its shareholders
- Benchmark against the best performers in areas like productivity, time to market and stockturn
- Develop greater customer focus in every facet of the business
- Recognise that innovation will differentiate winners and losers
- Recognise that people are the crucial factor in the business and invest in them
- Encourage partnership sourcing between customers and suppliers

Simon Caulkin notes 'that countries like the US and UK where de-industrialisation has proceeded fastest, have experienced much slower growth than the two most successful economies; Germany and Japan'.

The challenge for UK manufacturers has been laid down clearly by the CBI. UK manufacturing productivity is still some 30 per cent lower than West Germany overall, 35 per cent below Japan, and around 45 per cent below the USA. Closing the productivity gap with West Germany by the year 2000 will require UK productivity growth to exceed German performance by 3.5 per cent each year and a doubling of investment. However, UK competitors are not standing still, and this therefore implies an annual productivity growth of at least 5 per cent to 6 per cent – no mean task.

Recent experience has shown that with Britain's flexible low labour-cost economy, it continues to be the most attractive country in Europe for inward investment – a major factor in BMW's decision to purchase Rover in February 1994. The critical issue is whether low-cost labour can lead to higher productivity and high value-added content.

Can we achieve a mutual dependency between manufacturing and financial institutions?

Manufacturers continue to be dependent on 'the City', a situation that Ackroyd et al. (1988) argue has existed throughout this century, but the City continues to be reluctant to commit itself to manufacturing, at least to British manufacturing. . . . The problem for UK manufacturers is that their dependency on the City is not reciprocal, and, in the absence of measures by the government, reciprocal dependency seems unlikely to emerge.[24]

'The problem for UK manufacturers is that their dependency on the City is not reciprocal' (Oliver and Wilkinson).

WHAT LESSONS CAN WE DRAW FROM THIS STUDY?

Place of manufacturing and R&D in the economy

- A world-class competitive manufacturing sector is essential for the future of Western economies.
- Manufacturing rather than services creates wealth, and funds social aspirations of economies.
- Service-sector performance is just as important, not least in the role of supporting manufacturing with high quality and low cost. Therefore TQC and Lean Production must apply here too.
- R&D growth is vital for competitive growth and is inextricably linked to growth in manufacturing.
- Productivity growth for the UK and other European economies has to be the number one priority.

Has Japan peaked? Is the sun setting? Can Western business relax?

- Continuing Japanese trade surpluses would indicate not.
- Certainly, Japanese industry is now finding 'globalisation' and 'Internationalisation' a new challenge, and is in danger of 'drift'-led policies rather than strategic approaches. In addition, recession has hit business confidence hard in Japan. However, recent experience shows that adversity is treated as a challenge by Japanese industry.
- Western business cannot afford to be complacent – its instinct is short term rather than long term.

- Not many observers subscribe to the doomsday scenario painted by Brian Reading in *Japan the Coming Collapse* of a Japan bent on self-destruction from within.

What lessons for Japanese management?

- They need to find the effective formula for 'Internationalisation' – the multi-regional enterprise.

  Aims: – To function smoothly on a multi-regional basis
  - Close contact with local markets
  - 'Insider' in each region
  - Access to global production
    supply
    product development
    technology acquisition
    finance
    distribution
  - Solve problem of rewarding and motivating all those employed directly and indirectly from the range of countries and cultures involved, so that they work in harmony

This implies:
  - An effective global personnel system incorporating all nationalities
  - Horizontal information flows and co-operation between functions worldwide
  - Co-ordination of product development and globalisation of sales

What lessons are there for Western management?

- To apply best world practice
  - TQC
  - Lean Production
  - Re-engineering processes
  - At the same time increase mutual dependency, viz:

- Change internal cultures from:
  - Product to process oriented
  - Command and control to commitment
  - 'Status'-driven hierarchy to 'support for those for whom I am responsible'
  - Managerial privilege to teamworking, 'short termism' to 'long termism'

- Change relationship with trade unions from:
  - Adversarial to enterprise
  - Arm's length to involvement
  - Opposition to ambassadorial

- Change relationship with suppliers from:
  - Adversarial to integrated
  - Chinese walls to 'open book' policies
  - 'Catch as catch can' to mutual development

Similar changes also apply to the local community.

What can government do?

● If industry is being urged to drop adversarial approaches, surely it is time for government to show a lead in the same area?

Sir Peter Parker, in his Dimbleby lecture, said many years ago: 'We [in the UK] are the world's original, originating industrial power: We are the world's oldest parliamentary democracy. And we have failed to make the right connections between them. That, alas, is our glorious heritage.'[25] It is true then that the mutual dependency between industry, the City and government has probably *never* been recognised in the UK, and that it is worth taking a look at the Japanese corporate system in order to learn further lessons.

Should we adopt elements of the Japanese corporate system, halfway between communism and capitalism? If we take what has been until recently the two opposing world philosophies of capitalism and communism (state socialism), we find the former depends for its life blood on the success of the individual and the latter depends on the success of the state. We all know of the limits to success of both systems. Almost by chance, without design and evolution, the Japanese have hit on the formula that combines the elements of corporate identity and self – the group with shared mutual interests in society.

The group provides both protection and challenge to the individual. It allows competition to flourish, but it can help to avoid the 'political' in-fighting of individuals trying to protect themselves against others. Thus the consensus approach in Japan, with shared visions and responsibilities between government, industry and labour, has demonstrated success when compared to the sustained adversarial approach of the West that leads to lowered competitiveness: 'The West's economies are a reflection of partisan politics and pressures by interest groups, rather than a planned manipulation of natural comparative advantages to develop a more productive and effective industrial sector to improve national competitiveness.'[26]

In the West, government industrial policy is not generally coupled with fiscal and monetary policies – in contrast with Japan. Fiscal policy in Japan has been used as the main instrument to improve the infrastructure (Keynesian?) and to develop the industrial base, capital accumulation and exports. Similarly, monetary policy has funded industrial development by channelling funds to specific industries.[27]

The 'management challenge' goes on to conclude:

Japan's industrial policy has succeeded not because it is highly planned but because it is a disciplined approach to achieving consensus between government, industry and labour. Government's role in Japan is a facilitator, using administrative guidance to allocate resources using market forces. In Japan industrial policies link *the virtues of planning with the virtues of the market* and do not use one to thwart the other as in the West.

Thus government, if it is minded, can:

- Provide a long-term vision
- Concentrate on cause (increased productivity and competitiveness)[28] rather than on effect (social needs)
- Focus on future opportunities (rather than protect and subsidise old industries)
- Provide proper linkage with fiscal and monetary policies that increase production rather than promote consumerism

- Provide encouragement for industry (in its widest sense) and labour to share futures, values and responsibilities
- Provide recognition that the crucial *links between capital, education and technology give a powerful multiplier effect on industrial competitiveness*
- In short, create a culture of mutual dependency by demonstrating the vital importance of manufacturing growth to the economy

Simon Caulkin concludes in his thorough review of manufacturing in the economy:

'As for intervention – if the lesson of the 1980s is anything, it is that the remains of the British industrial base cannot afford another 14 year of absentee landlordism at the DTI and indifference at the Treasury. It needs macroeconomic encouragement to speed up the good work of the 1980s and begin the task of recreating the manufacturing capacity that has been lost. For the first time it can be stated without special pleading that industry is playing its part: the buck now stops in Downing Street and Victoria Street'.[29]

Capital
- Incentives to encourage investment and capital formation will be an essential plank of such an integrated policy (i.e. not aimed simply at reducing corporation tax) – Japan has consistently pursued a policy of direct tax incentives with investment tax credits, accelerated depreciation and special depreciation allowances. As a result it has been able to channel a large percentage of its GNP into industrial investment.[30]

  Western industry should note that this also calls for a response in changing from short term to long term by investing in new equipment to generate productivity using relatively expensive capital, rather than being beguiled by short-term depreciated marginal cost and costly labour.

Education
- The higher the quality of education, the better a nation is able to exploit its stock of capital, technological and natural resources to maximise its wealth. As we saw in Chapter 2, Japan has outstripped the West in terms of educational attainment, both in quantity and quality. 'By grafting a high level of education onto a disciplined, cooperative, but individually competitive population

accustomed to hard work, Japan forged a competitive advantage.'[31]

Technology

- The vital nature of R&D expenditure was the focus earlier in this chapter. The responsibility has to be via joint cooperation between industry, government and academia – just as in the area of capital investment government's responsibility has to be one of catalyst and enabler, but with overall responsibility for performance since the long-term advantage for the economy has to be achieved through new technology. In summary, for government, we must return to the starting point – vision. When you do not know where you want to go, it is impossible to plan effectively to get there.

THE CASE FOR MUTUALITY

Mutuality or shared responsibility in the community is gaining momentum in UK circles. The Royal Society of Arts Inquiry into *Tomorrow's Company* published its interim report in February 1994. The authors concluded: 'In order to be internationally competitive the company requires a supportive operating environment. The responsibility for maintaining this is shared between business, government and other partners who therefore need to develop a shared vision and common agenda.'

The Engineering Employers Federation (EEF) produced a report for the DTI entitled *Action for Growth and Competitiveness* in Spring 1994. It said: 'UK industry is increasingly aware of intense global competition and of the need to become "World Class". Government and industry are recognising the importance of technology, skill and education. But greater awareness does not yet amount to a national strategy.'

The Government White Paper on *Competitiveness* published in May 1994 is wide-ranging and shares the analysis in this chapter and many of its conclusions. Mutuality is also expressed. In the introduction by the Prime Minister he says: 'Our aim is commercial and industrial success and the rewards it will bring for all of us. To achieve this we seek a new partnership between Government and industry – a partnership for prosperity in a competitive world.'

Amitai Etzioni, Professor of Sociology at George Washington University, has influenced thinking on mutuality on both sides of the Atlantic – in the Clinton administration and now in the UK Labour Party under Tony Blair. Etzioni argues that due to over-emphasis on rights of the individual state solutions have failed and the market has failed. His aim is a society based on mutual obligations.

In New Zealand in the late 1980s the Labour administration developed a partnership strategy for wealth creation which put industrial and export growth at the top of the political agenda. In the early 1990s New Zealand has been consistently outstripping its large neighbour Australia in growth terms year on year.

GOVERNMENT SUPPORT FOR INDUSTRY

Aerospace is a case in point. The US defence industry is not only heavily subsidised but has more than doubled exports from $6bn in 1989 to $15bn in 1993, while Europe's defence exports have halved to around $5bn during the period of 'peace dividend'. General Electric (GE) which boasts the largest market value in the USA has strategically avoided areas where Japan is strong and focused instead on European competition such as power generation and aero engines (*Financial Times*, 25 February 1994): 'The DTI has a role in the UK in providing direct R&D grants and launch aid. The figures are not encouraging as the latest DTI annual report shows. Aerospace research funding is set to fall from £26.3m in 1992–3 to £22.7m in 1996–7. Industry pleas to quadruple this budget have been refused. This is an industry crying out for a strategy,' (*Guardian*, 19 March 1994). These companies will be forced without such support to trade leading edge technology for short-term survival in alliances, further undermining the UK's competitive edge.

Rather than government aid being increased, the UK Treasury has challenged whether there should be any support at all, which led in August 1994 to exposure of a full-scale row between Ministers highlighting the conflict over the question of intervention.

ENCOURAGING INVESTMENT

The CBI believes that corporate tax reform is necessary to encourage industrial investment in the shape of reduced rates of corporation tax or increased capital allowances, allowing the cost of equity raising against tax, and reducing capital gains tax rate (which is seen to hinder direct equity investment). Howard Davies, Director-General of the CBI, suggests that the Chancellor should taper the rate on realised gains in line with the length of time the amount was held. Hence rewarding long-termism. It is a measure also favoured by the Labour Party (*Financial Times*, 15 June 1994). It is now clear that recovery in the UK after recession is liable to peter out due not to feared inflation but to expensive finance and high returns expected by UK investors – in short due to a lack of mutuality between City, Government and Industry.

POSTSCRIPT

I can think of no better way of finishing this book than quoting the summary of the lessons from *Japanese Style Management* by Keitaro Hasegawa (p. 156):[32]

> *Think quality*. Never be satisfied. Strive constantly to improve your product. Inspire everyone from chairman to newest employee to seek ways to do everything better. Cut the product rejection rate. Be proud of what you help to make and of how it will benefit people.
>
> *Be competitive*. Match or exceed every improvement made by competitors. Keep prices in line. Give 100 per cent service. Think not of protectionism but of ways to outperform competitors. Aim to make your product, your packaging, your promotion, the best in the business.
>
> And a corollary: *Treasure your employees*. Of course, these goals call for an efficient, dedicated workforce. So treat workers fairly. Give all employees equal consideration. As nearly as possible, provide lifetime employment, or at least, fire no one before exhausting every other possibility. Let everyone share in the company's good times with regular bonuses. In a word, treat all employees like the conscientious, loyal, intelligent, and hardworking people you want them to be. And that's what they will surely be.

NOTES

1. *Financial Times*, 24 November 1987.
2. *International Management*, March 1987.
3. B. G. James, *Trojan Horse*, Mercury Paperback, 1990.
4. Ibid., p. 45.
5. Ibid., p. 105.
6. Alexander Nichol reporting in the *Financial Times*, 15 November 1993.
7. Yoshio Suzuki, Nomura Research Institute.
8. Ibid.
9. *Financial Times*, 12 January 1994.
10. *Financial Times*, 1 December 1993.
11. Emiko Terazono, reporting in *Financial Times*, 23 November 1993.
12. Ibid.
13. G. Hannel and C. K. Prakalad, 'Do You Really Have a Global Strategy?', *Harvard Business Review*, August 1985.
14. James, op. cit., p. 156.
15. *Business Week*, 3 March 1986.
16. *Business Week*, 27 April 1987 .
17. *Management Today*, May 1993.
18. Promoted by Ivan Yates, ex-Deputy Chief Executive of British Aerospace.
19. *Management Today*, May 1993.
20. N. Oliver and B. Wilkinson, *The Japanization of British Industry*, Blackwell, 1992, pp. 335–6.
21. *Management Today*, May 1993.
22. Letter to *Financial Times*, 14 December 1993.
23. *CBI News*, January 1994, p. 11.
24. Oliver and Wilkinson, op. cit., pp. 336–7.
25. Introduction, p. xi to *The Art of Japanese Management*, R. T. Pascale and A. G. Athos, Penguin Business, 1987. The Ackroyd et al. (1988) reference is S. Ackroyd, G. Burrell and M. Hughes, 'The Japanisation of British Industry', *Industrial Relations Journal*, vol. 19.
26. R. P. Nielsen, 'Industrial policy. The case for national strategies for world markets', *Long Range Planning*, vol. 17, no. 5, October 1984.
27. L. C. Thurus, *The Management Challenge: Japanese Views*, MIT Press, Cambridge, Mass., 1985.
28. There are positive signs. The DTI 1994 White Paper on Industrial Policy focuses on 'Competitiveness'.
29. *Management Today*, May 1993.
30. *America v. Japan*, T. K. McGraw, (ed.) Harvard Business School Press, Bolton, 1986.
31. *The Japanese School: Lessons for Industrial America*, B. Duke, Praeger, New York, 1985.
32. K. Hasegawa, *Japanese Style Management*, Kodahsha International, Tokyo 1986.

Appendices

Contents

APPENDIX I: KOMATSU UK EMPLOYEE PERSONNEL HANDBOOK – EXTRACTS

(i) Your Influence on Komatsu UK

Involvement and communication

Teamwork is vital. Teams do not work unless there is good communication . . . but people are very busy. In Komatsu UK we are trying to get effective communication throughout the Company. This means two-way communication for messages in all directions between departments and sections. However, despite training, policy and encouragement, things are rarely perfect. We shall all need patience, understanding and determination to succeed. **If you think communication can be improved, speak to your boss first and your Advisory Council representative**.

The Success Of Komatsu products depends on QCD:-

QUALITY
COST
DELIVERY

Success will depend on your involvement. The policy of Total Quality Control focuses on the part played by each individual. Improvements in all three areas will not happen unless individuals or teams face problems and come up with ideas which have been properly considered and are passed on for development.

Quality Circles

Total Quality Control
A mainstay of Komatsu's growth has been our Company-wide quality control programme, referred to as Total Quality Control (TQC). The pervasiveness of TQC at Komatsu stems from the complete commitment made by management to the programme when it was introduced in 1961. Applied to every level of our organisation, TQC at Komatsu is more than a technique to control product quality. It is an integrated management philosophy. Today, as in the past, TQC remains an essential element supporting the continued growth and prosperity of Komatsu.

Also, Komatsu believes that complete customer satisfaction is the foundation of Company growth. To meet the full range of user needs, we are expanding our construction equipment lines, strengthening our sales and service network, improving our products through the application of advanced technology and developing new products in areas outside of the construction equipment field.

A fundamental aspect of quality control and improvement is the operation of the Quality Circle. This can be involvement of the most productive and exciting kind, bringing benefits to employee and Company alike.

If you are interested in Quality Circles you should enquire about forming one yourself or join an existing circle.

Don't worry! In accordance with our policies of staff development and education, training will be provided.

The 5 'S' System

The 5 'S' system involves all employees in awareness of and activity in the appearance and safety of the whole Company. Again, get involved.

System

In order to run an efficient plant it is essential to have systems. Systems are there to provide uniformity of action so that any person knows the way in which something is to be handled. Systems are there to be followed and strict discipline must be observed. Short-cuts will lead to confusion and will ultimately adversely affect some other item.

Scrutiny

Look carefully about you. Evaluate each item. Ask yourself, is it necessary? Is it effective? Could it be done better? Do not accept anything because it has always been that way. Be on the look-out all the time for improvement.

Spotless

Neatness and cleanliness are needed to make us feel better and to promote an image of high quality to employees and customers. We should take as much pride in our work places as we do in our own homes or our cars. A clean work place or machine will highlight even minor defects much faster than a dirty one.

Shipshape

In an efficient environment everything we need has its place and is in its place. Time spent looking for something is wasted time. When everything is in its place, it becomes easy to identify excesses or shortages.

Safeguard

Safeguards are put in place to protect against incorrect procedure, or accidental misuse, by even the most experienced employee. This not only applies to machinery, but to procedures and systems throughout the organisation.

Remember it applies to all areas – office as well as shop floor.

Every employee a salesman

Komatsu UK is confident that you will not only take a pride in your work, but also in the product. People you meet outside work will take an interest in the Company and its products and it is important that you have the information to hand to speak authoritatively about the product, the company policies and non-confidential plans. The way we deal with the world outside Komatsu is important as well, especially visitors and telephone callers. Politeness and a helpful attitude can often tip the balance in our favour when dealing with potential customers, suppliers or others who have influence.

As Komatsu UK policy includes training staff at all levels, you may find yourself on a 'contact skills' course at some point in time. Remember the important little things, like not keeping a caller waiting on the phone; give the messages you take to the recipient before you forget them (write it down!) and always be polite.

You are an ambassador

You are an ambassador for the Company and you should remember this when you deal with visitors, suppliers, customers etc.– and within the Company itself.

Be courteous; you represent the Company at all times. Your attitude can result in whether work is done faster or slower, whether a company's quotation is high or acceptable (in other words, whether outsiders want to do business with us), and whether customers want to buy from us.

Use a pleasant tone of voice; often it's not what you say, but the way you say it which counts.

If you cannot deliver work on time, let the person know immediately and give them a choice about waiting. Give as much information as possible.

Training and development policies

Congratulations
You have succeeded in coming through one of the most rigourous selection procedures that is operated within the UK. Komatsu UK is determined to gain the best staff available and naturally the interest does not stop there.

The Company's policy is to match individual development with that of the Company. Through the joint operation of a career development and performance review scheme, described later, you will have regular opportunities for face to face discussions with your boss over performance and career development. This helps to fulfil our policy to help staff develop their own careers by identifying training needs in order to help the Company grow.

Growth comes from extending job knowledge and breadth of skills. Being exposed to a new environment as we have in Komatsu, it is probable you will need to attend courses, and for the fortunate few, to visit Japan. Naturally the needs of each individual have to be evaluated and training costs money. However the Company will want to consider your suggestions for your own training and development and the performance and appraisal programme is geared to this.

Take the opportunity to learn new things – for instance, the simple techniques and systems of:-

TQC   Total Quality Control
PDCA   Plan, Do, Check, Action
The 4 'M's Man, Method, Material, Machine

The skills you learn at the various courses will eventually be reflected in the performance and appraisal reviews which take place on a regular basis.

Sports and Social Club

This was originally established to aid communication between Japanese and British staff – it is just as important, of course, to have good social relations within the British community. The Sports and Social Club will always need ideas, support and enthusiasm – get involved!

Various members of staff are on the committee and organise sporting events, if you are interested in a particular sport, contact the relevant committee member, or give the Secretary any ideas you have for additional items.

For full details of current officers and members of the Social Club committee see noticeboards or ask the Administration Section.

Trade union membership

The Company has concluded an agreement with the AEU which gives that Union sole bargaining rights and the sole right to independently represent employees.

The Company and Union view this agreement as an expression of partnership, assisting us to ensure the success and prosperity of the Company and the long-term security and well-being of employees. It is partly to achieve this end that the agreement establishes the Advisory Council.

Appendix I (iii) contains the Trade Union Agreement which forms part of your terms and conditions of employment. However, to illustrate how much importance the Company and Union place on the ongoing relationship, we quote below the essential Aims of the Agreement:-

1. To encourage the growth and profitability of the Company and the prosperity of employees;
2. To develop mutual trust between the Company, its employees and the Union;
3. To resolve issues affecting these relationships in an efficient manner;
4. To help involve employees at all levels in the ongoing success of the business.

In order to achieve these aims, both parties agree:-

1. To develop a production unit based on the highest levels of quality, productivity, and work task flexibility employing the best of modern technology, with the aim of producing profitability in a highly competitive environment;

2. To respond rapidly to changes in the market and in technology to take advantage of these for the benefit of Company and employees;
3. To involve employees in plans, progress and policies to further their contribution to these aims;
4. To avoid disruption of any sort.

The Company encourages membership of the Trade Union, which is open for representation purposes to the majority of employees.

Advisory Council

In Appendix I (iv) you will find the constitution of the Advisory Council. It may seem a bit heavy going but the aims of the Advisory Council are worthwhile and as the primary aim of the Council is to represent your views, you should be familiar with the Council constitution and activities. You are encouraged to read the sections covering the Advisory Council thoroughly.

You are represented on the Council no matter what job you do in Komatsu UK; whether or not you are in the scope of the trade union; whether or not you are a member of the trade union.

The Advisory Council is not a 'talking shop' without muscle, neither is it a traditional 'Works Council' where managers and employee representatives sit and glare at each other from entrenched positions. It exists to share information, pool ideas, represent staff and company interests and come to agreed conclusions. It cannot dictate to Komatsu UK what policy will be, but it can and will influence the Company's future direction in the mutual interest of Komatsu UK and Komatsu UK employees.

The biggest enemy and brake on progress is apathy. If we all lose interest in supporting the Advisory Council and its members then the Company may stagnate and rot can set in – be active and participate.

(ii) Performance and Appraisal Scheme

The Company's policy is to encourage the growth of individual staff in the belief that this ensures growth for the Company.

Development is very much a personal thing and requires both ambition and nurturing, hence we expect you to contribute to self development and your Manager or Supervisor to encourage and provide the right conditions for growth. Each six months during the first two years of employment, and annually thereafter, you will have a face to face review with your boss with two different, but related objectives:-

Performance Review (Looking at performance so far) and Career Development

Not everyone can be Managing Director, but everyone can improve the scope and knowledge of their own jobs and their own performance. Also, things change rapidly in these days of high technology and intense competition, so we often need to re-evaluate how we define particular tasks and encourage greater flexibility. Regular reviews help in focusing on the job you do, how it fits in the organisation and how things can develop.

Careers Development

The attached form A aims to help you to identify how your future performance could be improved and how you would like your career to develop.

Performance Review

In order to give you some idea of the factors the Company believe are important, we are attaching form B which is used by the reviewer and his boss to assess your performance at each half-yearly face to face review.

STAFF DEVELOPMENT   FORM A

SELF ASSESSMENT

A. Employee Details

Surname:

Department:

Qualifications:

Courses attended since last review:

Date of Review:

B. Explanatory Note:

The aim of this is to help to identify how your future performance could be improved, based on an assessment of how you currently do your job.

The value of completing the form is that it helps you to prepare for the appraisal interview so that you and your appraisor can obtain maximum benefit from a two-way discussion.

NOTHING IN THIS FORM AFFECTS THE MONETARY OUTCOME OF YOUR PERFORMANCE APPRAISAL

Instead, the outcome should be an assessment of your job progress to date, and of your future training and development needs.

C. QUESTIONS	Appraisee Comment	Reviewer's Comment
1. Thinking about how you do your job now can you outline: a) The specific area where you feel most confident. b) What new skills/ knowledge you have acquired in recent months.		
2. In order to improve your future performance please identify areas where you need: a) More job knowledge or experience. b) Greater or lesser responsibility. c) Training or development.		
3. Which aspects of your work do you find particularly interesting and would like to develop?		

	Appraisee Comment	Reviewer's Comment
4. Which aspects interest you least?		
5. How would you like to see your career develop?		
6. What interest do you have outside work which may help you at work? (for example, do you play an active role on any committees?) In addition, please mention any courses of education you are undertaking.		

Thank you for your responses.
Please hand the completed form to your Appraisor, but keep a copy for your own reference in preparing for the interview.

D. TRAINING PROPOSAL:

This section is to be completed during the interview.

Training required:	To be discussed with/ arranged by:-

Signatures of: Appraisee ....

                 Appraisor ....

Date ....

Review Date.........................

PERFORMANCE APPRAISAL

STRICTLY CONFIDENTIAL

NAME..................................... SALARY NUMBER ....

POSITION .... DATE OF PRESENT

APPOINTMENT ....
DEPARTMENT............................

FIRST REVIEWER TO CONDUCT REVIEW

POSITION ....

SECOND REVIEWER TO CONFIRM REVIEW

POSITION ....

THIS FORM TO BE COMPLETED IN MANUSCRIPT AND RETURNED TO THE
PERSONNEL MANAGER

BY ....

FORM B   PERFORMANCE FACTORS STAFF ASSESSMENT
JOB KNOWLEDGE

1. Complete job knowledge Seeks to extend and improve.	Acceptable job knowledge and Progressing.	Below required knowledge and improving steadily.	Below required knowledge and not progressing well.
☐	☐	☐	☐

FLEXIBLE WORKING (not core skill)

2. Performs tasks outside of core skill/ area of responsibilty well.	Performs some tasks outside of core skill/ area of responsibilty with attempts to improve.	Performs no tasks outside of core skill but demonstrates eagerness and willingness to do so.	Performs no tasks outside of core skill/ responsibilty and demonstrates reluctance to do so.
☐	☐	☐	☐

QUALITY OF WORK (relates to core skills)

3. Quality is unacceptable.	Of varying quality and efforts to improve are not consistent.	Nearly always good quality produced and demonstrates efforts to improve quality.	Absolutely correct at all times.
☐	☐	☐	☐

WORK SPEED/RESPONSIVENESS

4. A Always achieves and often exceeds standard time.	Nearly always achieves and occasionally exceeds standard time.	Only sometimes achieves standard time	Mostly fails to achieve standard time
☐	☐	☐	☐
B Always responsive to demands and requirements of job.	Generally recognises priorities but sometimes fails to respond.	Fails to recognise priorities and responds poorly.	Unresponsive.
☐	☐	☐	☐

RELIABILITY

5.

Can be relied upon implicity.	Can be relied upon but requires additional prompting.	Needs to be closely managed most of the time.	Generally considered unreliable
☐	☐	☐	☐

ADAPTABILITY TO CHANGE

6.

Accepts planned changes enthusiastically.	Sometimes finds it difficult to cope with change but is willing.	Appears to dislike changes planned or otherwise.	Activity resists change.
☐	☐	☐	☐

PERFORMANCE AGAINST SET OBJECTIVES

7.

Does not take seriously.	Under achieves.	Mostly achieves.	Almost always achieves.
☐	☐	☐	☐

5 'S' SYSTEM

8.

Meets all the standards set.	Meets most of standards.	Meets only some of the standards.	Rarely meets all the standards.
☐	☐	☐	☐

PROBLEM SOLVING/COPING WITH DIFFICULTIES

9.

Faces up to and overcomes problems and difficulties on all occasions.	Faces up to most problems and overcomes the majority.	Dislikes problems and prefers others to solve them. Sometimes solves on own.	Will not deal with a problem or difficulty on arising in own work even though should be able to do so.
☐	☐	☐	☐

DETERMINATION

10.

Always persists with and concentrates on work.	Nearly always persists with and concentrates on work.	Is fairly easily distracted or gives up.	Is often distracted and rarely persists in the face of difficulty.
☐	☐	☐	☐

ORGANISATION

11. A **Self**

Well organised mainly controls events.	Influences events by setting priorities.	Tends to be driven by events.	Chaotic – does not set priorities or controls events.
☐	☐	☐	☐

B **Subordinates**

Ineffective control of team.	Team frequently disorganised.	Occasional confusion.	Delegates and controls well.
☐	☐	☐	☐

PLANNING OF WORK

12.

Effective planning.	Occasional lapses.	Sporadic planning.	Does not look ahead.
☐	☐	☐	☐

TEAMWORK

13.

Always seeks to involve others.	Works well as team member.	Occasionally causes friction in the team.	Does not integrate with other team members.
☐	☐	☐	☐

GROUP COMMUNICATIONS

14.

Communication is markedly poor and infrequent giving rise to real or potential problems.	Causes misunderstanding or fails to communicate on fairly frequent occasions.	An effective but inconsistent communicator. Some occasional problems.	An effective and consistent communicator. No problems.
☐	☐	☐	☐

PERSONAL CONTACT SKILLS

15.

Sensitive – establishes warm relationships.	Usually gains cooperation of others.	Occasionally upsets people.	Creates antagonism in contacts.
☐	☐	☐	☐

DEVELOPMENT OF SELF/STAFF

16. Devises and implements development plans.

Makes attempts to develop.

Develops only when instructed.

Shows little interest.

☐   ☐   ☐   ☐

TIMEKEEPING/ATTENDANCE

17. Never absent or late.

Is only absent or late where this is beyond control and the incidence is very infrequent.

Could make more effort to achieve better attendance and timekeeping.

Has been warned informally that must improve.

☐   ☐   ☐   ☐

BEYOND THE CONTRACT

18. Participates in a wide range of activities beneficial to the business.

Shows interest in voluntary activities and participates to some degree.

Attends only when pressure is applied.

Rigidly adheres to terms of contract.

☐   ☐   ☐   ☐

GENERAL COMMENTS

....

....

....

....

....

....

....

....

....

OVERALL PERFORMANCE RATING

OUTSTANDING – Leaves little to be desired, consistently exceeds objectives and makes significant contributions.

COMMENDABLE – Regularly but not always, exceeds objectives. Will display some 'Outstanding' characteristics but not consistently.

PROFICIENT – Acceptable performance. Normal objectives met and assignments properly handled.

IMPROVABLE – Performance does not fully meet requirements of position. Some objectives and assignments met but not consistently. Above normal supervision required.

Signed .... Position .... Date ....

COMMENTS DURING COUNSELLING

Signed .... Position .... Date ....

COMMENTS OF EMPLOYEE

Signed .... Position .... Date ....

COMMENTS OF SECOND REVIEWER

Signed .... Position .... Date ....

(iii) Agreement on Terms and Conditions of Employment between Komatsu UK Ltd and Amalgamated Engineering Union

Throughout this Agreement Komatsu UK Ltd will be referred to as the 'Company' and the Amalgamated Engineering Union as the 'Union'.

This Agreement applies to all full time employees, male and female, of the Company, up to and including Supervisor and equivalent levels.

1. Aims of this Agreement

   (a) The aim of this Agreement is
      (i) to encourage the growth and profitability of the Company and the prosperity of employees;
      (ii) to develop mutual trust between the Company, its employees and the Union;
      (iii) to resolve issues affecting these relationships in an efficient manner;
      (iv) to help involve employees at all levels in the ongoing success of the business.
   (b) In order to achieve these aims, both parties agree
      (i) to develop a production unit based on the highest levels of quality, productivity, and work task flexibility employing the best of modern technology, with the aim of producing profitability in a highly competitive environment;
      (ii) to respond rapidly to changes in the market and in technology to take advantage of these for the benefit of Company and employees;
      (iii) to involve employees in plans, progress and policies to further their contribution to these aims;
      (iv) to avoid disruption to production of any sort.

2. Recognition of Rights

   (a) The Company recognises the rights of its employees to belong to the Union and of the Union to represent its members, and encourages all employees within representational scope to join the Union.
   (b) The Union recognises and encourages the right of the Company to manage and decide on the ongoing plans and the operation of the Company.
   (c) 'The Company and the Union recognise their joint responsibility to ensure this Agreement is effective, and in the event of any ambiguity the spirit and intention of the aims above should be paramount.

3. Scope of this Agreement

   (a) The Amalgamated Engineering Union is recognised as having sole representational rights for all personnel up to and including Supervisor level and equivalent positions employed by the Company at the Birtley plant;
   (b) The Company will encourage employees within representational scope to join and actively participate in Union Activities;
   (c) However, any employee who chooses not to join the Union will not suffer discrimination at the hands of the Company or the Union;
   (d) The Company will establish and maintain a system of Union membership subscription deductions from individual monthly salaries.

4. Advisory Council

    (a)   The Advisory Council exists to provide a forum for the active involvement of employees and the Union in regular discussions on the ongoing progress of the Company. The Company and the Trade Union support the Advisory Council as the single representative body on all matters affecting groups of employees.

    (b)   The detailed role and constitution are separately defined. (See Appendix I(iv))

      (i) Representation
           The Advisory Council is to be a forum comprising elected representatives covering all employees appointed by the Company, together with the Union Divisional Organiser as an ex-officio member of the Council;

      (ii) Scope
- All matters of collective interest. Issues of individual interest will not be discussed by the Advisory Council;
- Review of the operation of this agreement;
- Company investment policy and business plans;
- Company trading performance, sales and market share;
- Company manpower plans;
- Company productivity, operating efficiency and quality achievements;
- Work rules;
- Terms and conditions of employment including pay and benefits, conditions of service;
- Work environment and conditions.

5. Employee Representation

    (a)   The Company and the Union shall agree areas of representation of constituencies to cover all employees within the scope of this Agreement. The constituencies shall be the same as those of the Advisory Council;

    (b)   One representative shall be elected for each agreed constituency and will normally be a member of the Union; election will take place annually in accordance with this Agreement (Appointment and Conduct of Employee Representatives). No employee shall be eligible to act as a representative unless employed in the agreed constituency.

6. Resolution of Issues

The Company and the Union recognise that issues affecting employees should be resolved speedily and effectively without recourse to industrial action of any sort.

    (a)   Internal procedure
           The Union and the Company are determined to resolve matters 'in-house' and hence the following procedure will apply:-

      (i) Issues affecting individuals

The Disciplinary and Grievance procedures have been designed for issues to be resolved informally between the employee and his immediate supervisor. This may not always be possible, therefore the formal procedure for the resolution of issues is agree – Stages I, II and III;

(ii) Collective Issues

Matters affecting groups of employees may be raised at Stages II and III of the procedure above. When the issue affects the Company as a whole, or concerns unresolved interpretation of an existing Agreement or Company policy, the issue can, by prior arrangement, be referred to the Advisory Council for discussion. Periodic annual reviews of salaries and conditions of employment will be conducted in the Advisory Council at the beginning of the year prior to the contract date of 1st March. The Union Divisional Organiser and the Managing Director will be required to ratify all recommendations reached at Stage IV of the procedure;

(b) External procedure

The Company and the Union are totally committed to resolving negotiations as above within domestic procedure. However, exceptionally, in the case of non-resolution by domestic procedure, both parties agree to refer the matter for conciliation to the Advisory Conciliation and Arbitration Service.

If the matter is still unresolved, both parties may agree to refer to an independent arbitrator who will determine positively in favour of one side or the other. The arbitrator will take into account the common ground achieved between the parties. Both parties agree to accept the decision of the arbitrator.

There will be no industrial action of any kind while an issue is in procedure or the subject of conciliation and arbitration. In the unlikely event of total exhaustion of the above procedure without resolution, no industrial action will be taken without a full, secret, audited ballot of all affected employees.

7. Use of Manpower

In reaching this Agreement, the Union recognises and supports the complete flexibility and mobility of the work force between jobs and duties within the Company and departments.

For its part, the Company recognises and accepts the need for training and re-training in the broadening of skills and dealing with new technology developments to improve efficiency and profitability.

Hence the following working practices are agreed:-

- Complete flexibility and mobility of employees;
- Changes in processes and practices will be introduced to increase competitiveness and that these will improve productivity and affect manning levels;
- To achieve such change employees will work as required by the Company and participate in training of themselves or other employees as required;
- Manning levels will be determined by the Company using appropriate industrial engineering and manpower planning techniques.

Detailed Terms and Conditions under this Agreement are attached as an indivisible part of this Agreement.

Signed
On behalf of the Company

T. KOMIYA
Managing Director

C. N. Morton
Personnel & Administration Director

Signed
On behalf of the Trade Union

G. ARNOLD
Executive Council Member AEU

J. Cellini
Union Divisional Organiser

(iv) Role and Constitution of the Advisory Council

1. Objectives
   (a) The meetings of the Advisory Council will provide the opportunity for the meaningful and active participation by the members of the Council in regular discussions on the activities and plans of the Company. The members of the Council will give advice to the Company on those activities and plans.
   (b) The Company and Union emphasise that the Advisory Council system is to complement and not replace other channels of direct consultation between the Company and Company employees.
   (c) The Council will be the central forum for the resolution of all collective issues between the Company and Company employees.
   (d) The Council will promote the joint interest of the Company and employees and the commercial success of the Company with the mutual support of the Company employees and the Union.
2. Role and Constitution
   (a) Consultation
      (i) The Council will be given full necessary and appropriate information to enable it to discuss the items below, to make recommendations to the Company concerning these items and to allow meaningful discussions to take place in the interests of commercial success.
      (ii) Topics discussed will include:

Company investment policy and business plans
Company trading performance, sales and market share
Company manpower, training and development plans
Company productivity, operating efficiency and quality achievements
Work rules
Work environment and conditions

      (iii) This list is not exhaustive and the Council may discuss any matter of collective interest with the intention of furthering the success of the

Company and the welfare of the employees. Issues of individual interest will not fall within the gambit of the monthly Council meetings.

(b) Collective issue resolution

The Advisory Council exists to provide a forum for the active involvement of employees and the Union in regular discussions on the progress of the Company. In this respect the Advisory Council recognises and respects the partnership the Company seeks to achieve with the Trade Union.

Under the grievance procedure issues of a collective nature may be discussed at a meeting of the Council which will make recommendations to the Company and the Union. Such discussions may include review of the operation of this agreement and periodic reviews of salaries and conditions of employment.

NOTE   Matters of collective interest are defined to be those affecting groups of individuals where such issues are one of principle or could give precedents for other groups. Often matters affecting more than one individual are not collective in the sense above and every effort should be made to resolve such problems without reference to the Advisory Council.

3. Advisory Council Representatives

(a) Eligibility

All employees will be eligible subject to satisfying the requirements below for nomination for election to the Council on the basis of the constituencies proposed by the Advisory Council and jointly agreed to by the Company and Union.
An employee:-
(i)   must be a permanent full time employee of the Company with at least one year's continuous service with the Company at the date of the election;
(ii) must be employed within the relevant constituency. Where a member moves from one constituency as a consequence of a temporary job change, he/she will not be required to give up membership of the Council;
(iii) must be proposed and seconded by two members of the relevant constituency;
(iv) must have no formal written warnings on his/her employment record;
(v)   will normally be the accredited employee representative for the constituency in question and will preferably be a member of the Trade Union;
(vi) must not serve more than three consecutive terms as an Advisory Council Member.

(b) Deputies

(i) In each constituency a deputy Advisory Council Member may be elected.
(ii) The role of the deputy will be to:-
(a) Assist the Advisory Council Member in communicating with constituents;

    (b) Deputise for the Advisory Council Member at meetings in the event of any unavoidable absence of that member.

    (iii) The deputy does not have any right to a seat upon the Advisory Council but may act as above (ii b) and as an accredited Employee Representative in the absence of the Advisory Council Member from his constituency.

(c) Constituency areas and representation

    (i) Whilst the Company is in the process of building up towards full strength, suitable interim arrangements regarding constituencies and representation will need to be implemented. These arrangements will be subject to change from time to time in order to accommodate new developments;

    (ii) Reviews of the constituencies will be carried out at least annually to ensure that job changes do not cause a cumulative distortion of representation. Any necessary re-organisation will be considered by the Advisory Council. Normally such adjustments will be synchronised with the annual election.

(d) Council composition

    (i) The Council will consist of elected members corresponding to the agreed constituencies together with nominated management representatives. The council will elect one of its members as Chairman and there will be a President who will normally be the Managing Director of the Company. The chairman will be elected for a one year term of office;

    (ii) Because of the administrative duties of the secretary he/she will be appointed by management and will be a member of management;

    (iii) One elected representative will be nominated by the elected representatives to act as co-ordinator for a minimum period of one year;

    (iv) The Union Divisional Organiser will be invited to attend as he/she sees fit in the capacity of an ex-officio member;

    (v) Other specialist personnel may also be invited to attend to advise as agreed between the Secretary and the Co-ordinator.

(e) Elections

    (i) Elections will be organised by the Company and will be co-ordinated with those for the employee representatives;

    (ii) An election sub-committee of the Advisory Council will be appointed and this committee will publish a notice of elections and invite nominations. The election will be by secret ballot with the person gaining the most votes within each constituency to be elected the council member for the constituency;

    (iii) The term of office will be two years so that members retire by rotation. It is not permitted for any member to serve more than three terms of office consecutively.

4. Council Procedure

(a) Council meetings will be held monthly in Company hours with a maximum of three hours per meeting;

(b) The Council expects to convene meetings which include all members. In a genuine emergency situation an attendance of 60% of members plus Secretary and President will be accepted as a quorum for the conduct of business;

(c) Council members who are on shifts, at the time of a meeting of the Council should make the necessary arrangements with their supervisor to ensure they are able to attend for the full meeting;

(d) Items for the agenda must be submitted to the secretary a minimum of 10 working days before the council meets. The Secretary and Co-ordinator are asked to agree the agenda and issue it to all members 5 days before the meeting day;

(e) In exceptional circumstances emergency items may be raised for inclusion on the agenda outside this timetable and may be added at the discretion of the Chairman;

(f) Full minutes will be prepared by the Secretary, agreed with a nominated Council Member and displayed and circulated within 7 working days of the meeting;

(g) All Council members agree to, and will respect, the confidentiality of certain information identified by the President or the Chairman.

5. Mandates and Recommendations

(a) It is the clear role and responsibility of each elected Council member to actively seek the views of all his constituents on all relevant issues and to accurately present those views at the Council meetings. The Council will examine all issues openly with every member endeavouring to achieve the best recommendations for the commercial success of the Company and welfare of employees;

(b) Recommendations made should reflect a consensus achieved by the Council members as a consequence of such free and open discussions. In the event of consensus not being available it is recognised, and it is the duty of every Council member, to re-examine all the facts and to continue with dialogue in an earnest attempt to obtain unanimity;

(c) The Council through its members has a responsibility to ensure that it is an effective organ of representation and that constituents are fully aware of Advisory Council activities and of the ways in which they should use the Council to express their views and wishes.

6. Working Parties

(a) Working parties may be formed on terms of reference determined by the Council to examine issues in depth and make recommendations to the Council.

(b) Representation on such working parties should be determined taking account of:-

(i) The ability of members to make a contribution to the subject under discussion

(ii) The availability of members to participate fully and effectively.

APPENDIX II   THE IMPORTANCE OF CULTURE

- Influences the behaviour of all individuals and groups

- It is the basis on which people value themselves and others

- It shapes the image the 'public' has of your product or service

- It ultimately determines the service you provide

Culture is central to effective performance

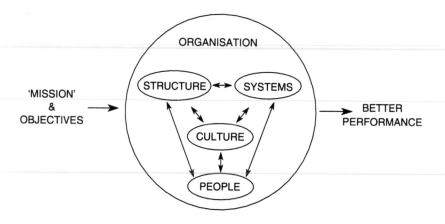

Diagnosing current culture . . .

Four core dimensions

- How do people treat one another?
- What values do they live by?
- How are they motivated to perform well?
- How do they use power?

'Pleasing the boss' (power)

- People are best motivated by external rewards or punishments

- Hierarchy and inequality are accepted as legitimate and a source of power

- Therefore politics and power struggles are frequently engaged in

- Paternalism and a strong sense of vision and justice may bring balance

☐ Rule by fear and possible abuse of power

☐ High suspicion may occur

☐ Lack of co-operation may also occur

'Doing things right' (role)

- Efficiency and order are valued

- Predictability and correctness are important therefore people need to be monitored

- Authority is tied up with the job and status

- Systems and procedures enforce rules

- The contract is key

☐ Initiative can be stifled

☐ Inflexibility may occur

☐ A lack of trust is implicit

☐ Limited delegation

'Getting things done through passion and commitment' (achievement)

- Emphasis on results (team and individual)

- Authority is tied up with ability

- Communication is open (in all directions)

- People are motivated by liking their work and in line with a clear sense of purpose

- People will control themselves

- ☐ Stress can build up quickly

- ☐ Elitism of special teams may arise

- ☐ May be under-organized

Social harmony (support)

- Employees valued as people

- Harmony is most important

- No blame

- People have warm relationships and feel cared for

- A sense of belonging is fostered and this motivates people

- ☐ Issues may remain unresolved and tough decisions may be avoided

- ☐ Lack of focus on outputs may mean poor results

- ☐ Differences in skill and ability ignored

Index